Alcuin

Alcuin

His Life and Legacy

Douglas Dales

James Clarke & Co.

James Clarke and Co
P.O. Box 60
Cambridge
CB1 2NT

www.jamesclarke.co
publishing@jamesclarke.co

ISBN: 978 0 227 17346 6

British Library Cataloguing in Publication Data
A record is available from the British Library

For Christopher, Gwendoline, & Basil

with affection and gratitude

Optima et Pulcherrima vitae suppellex amicitia

Cicero, *De Amicitia*

'Those ancient and far distant ages . . . we may, we ought to leave far behind in
what we hope to achieve. But in our eagerness for improvement, it concerns
us to be on our guard against the temptation of thinking that we can have the
fruit or the flower, and yet destroy the root; that we may retain the high view
of human nature which has grown with the growth of Christian nations, and
discard that revelation of Divine love and human destiny of which that view
forms a part or a consequence; that we may retain the moral energy, and yet
make light of the faith that produced it. It concerns us that we do not despise
our birthright, and cast away our heritage of gifts and powers, which we may
lose, but not recover.'

Dean Church, *Gifts of Civilization*

Sis memor Albini per tempora longa magistri.

In Christo sit unitas, sine quo nulla perfecta est caritas.

Contents

Illustrations

These images have been generously provided by the British Museum archive of artefacts and have been chosen to illustrate the cultural context in which Alcuin lived and worked.

Preface

This book is part of a comprehensive study of Alcuin that is completed in *Alcuin: Theology and Thought*. The whole study owes a great deal to my pupils and colleagues at Marlborough College, as well as to my wife, Geraldine, for their steady interest, encouragement and patience during a ten-year project. Particular thanks must be given to Colin Fraser, Julian Lloyd, Niall Hamilton and Philip Dukes, who each read parts of the text; also to our children, Christopher, Gwendoline and Basil. Thanks must go to the Master of the College for his steady encouragement, and to the Council of Marlborough College for granting me sabbatical leave in the summer term of 2009, when much of the extensive and detailed research for this book was accomplished in the Bodleian Library in Oxford, whose staff have given unstinting and courteous assistance at every stage. I am most grateful also to my publisher, Adrian Brink, for his encouragement, advice and help in preparing this book for publication.

I am most grateful also to the Archbishop of Canterbury, Dr Rowan Williams, for his constant friendship, interest and encouragement, and also to my friends Father John Blacker, Sister Benedicta Ward, Professor Peregrine Horden, The Rt Revd John Kirkham, The Rt Revd John Bickersteth, Dr Charles Miller, Sir Andrew Moylan, Gareth Playfair and Dr Derek Craig. I have appreciated very much the interest, prayers and friendship of Father Innocenzo Gargano at San Gregorio in Rome, and of my monastic friends at Vatopedi and Simonospetra monasteries on the Holy Mountain of Athos. Finally, thanks must go also to Reuben, who has proved to be a faithful scholar's cat, always at hand, and ever alert in his loyalty and attention!

Tribute must also be paid to the many scholars from the Continent and the English-speaking world whose work underpins this enterprise, and from whom I have learnt so much with great enjoyment and interest. Pre-eminent among these must be M-H. Jullien, & F. Perelman, the editors of the *Clavis Scriptorum Latinorum Medii Aevi – Auctores Galliae 735-987: tomus II – ALCUINUS* (Brepols/Turnhout, 1999), without whose meticulous work it would have been impossible to compose this book outside the university in the midst of my multifarious duties as Chaplain of Marlborough College. Equally indispensable has been the masterly and comprehensive annual bibliography, *Medioevo Latino*, published in Florence by SISMEL – Edizione del Galluzzo, which is one of the many valuable and wise legacies of the late Claudio Leonardi.

Any work on Alcuin owes much to the pioneering labours of the late Donald Bullough, whose tenth anniversary of death falls in 2012. His posthumous volume, *Alcuin – achievement & reputation* (Brill-Leiden & Boston, 2004) is now the indispensable starting point for any study of Alcuin up to 796. Moreover in 2004, there were two notable symposia in France and Switzerland to mark the 1200th anniversary of Alcuin's death, whose papers are published in Depreux, P. & Judic, B., (eds.) *Alcuin de York a Tours: écriture, pouvoir et réseaux dans l'Europe du haut moyen âge* (Rennes, 2005), & Tremp, E., & Schmuki, K., (eds.) *Alkuin von York und die geistige Grundlegung Europas* (St Gallen, 2010). In England there was a fine exhibition at York in 2001, commemorated in Garrison, M., et al., *Alcuin & Charlemagne – the Golden Age of York* (York, 2001). This book is intended to complement these and to give a complete overview of the wealth of scholarship that relates to Alcuin. It is intended for the general reader as well as for those studying, teaching or researching this period of early medieval history and theology in schools and universities.

As I composed this work in the Bodley I was often mindful of the debt that I owe personally to the late Dr Henry Chadwick who, as Dean of Christ Church, showed me every kindness when I was a student, and who introduced me to the study of patristics and ecclesiastical history. My earlier studies of St Dunstan and the tenth century reformation in England, and of the period of Christian mission in and around the British Isles in the period leading up to the death of St Boniface, provided the framework and motivation for this study of Alcuin and they complement it.

At a time when there is widespread concern across Europe about secular amnesia and ignorance of its Christian foundations, and continued ambivalence in England towards entanglement with continental affairs, it is worth recording the words of Jacob Burckhardt that were quoted in the conclusion to the seminal work on this period by Wilhelm Levison, *England and the Continent in the eighth century*: 'A truly rich nation becomes rich by accepting much from others and developing it.' This certainly happened on both sides of the Channel in the early middle ages. Levison fled from Germany to Durham in 1939 to find refuge from political tyranny and intended his great book to be a bridge across troubled waters. This book is written in the same hope, challenging a secular miasma of perception, while bridging the gap that can sometimes appear between continental and English-speaking scholarship, and between the several academic specialisms that have to be considered together, if the full picture of the achievement of Alcuin and his collaborators is to be appreciated and understood: for no society or church can flourish unless it is true to its own foundations, and understands them accurately.

Alcuin and those who worked with him applied Christian theology, deeply rooted in the Bible and the teachings of the Fathers, to the pressing needs of their society as they perceived them to be; and the foundations that they laid survived the Viking onslaughts to become the basis for subsequent Christian medieval civilisation in Europe. Alcuin was truly a hidden saint of the Church, of the same stature and significance as his predecessor Bede. To work closely with his writings for so long and on so many varied topics, and especially with his letters, prayers and poetry, is to come close to a remarkable Christian thinker and educator, who was also a person of deep spirituality, insight, determination and love.

Douglas Dales
Feast of St Dunstan & Memorial of Alcuin:
19th May, 2012 – at Marlborough College.

Abbreviations

AGG   Tremp, E., & Schmuki, K., (eds.) *Alkuin von York und die geistige Grundlegung Europas* (St Gallen, 2010)

AL   Archiv fur Liturgiewissenschaft

ALC   Jullien, M-H., & Perelman, F., (ed.) *Clavis Scriptorum Latinorum Medii Aevi – Auctores Galliae 735-987: tomus II – ALCUINUS* (Brepols/Turnhout, 1999)

ASE   Anglo-Saxon England (Cambridge)

AY   Depreux, P. & Judic, B., (eds.) *Alcuin de York à Tours: écriture, pouvoir et réseaux dans l'Europe du haut moyen âge* (Rennes) 2005

CBA   Council for British Archaeology

DA   Deutsches Archive

DAB   Bullough, D. A., *Alcuin – achievement & reputation* (Leiden & Boston) 2004

EETS Early English Text Society

EHD   Whitelock, D., (ed.) *English Historical Documents vol.1* (London) 1979

EHR   English Historical Review

EME   Early Medieval Europe

EL   Ephemerides Liturgicae

FK   Berndt, R., (ed.) *Das Frankfurter Konzil von 794: Kristallisationspunkt karolingischer Kultur* (Mainz) 1997

GL   Houwen L. & Mac Donald, A., (eds.) *Alcuin of York: scholar at the Carolingian court* - proceedings of the third Germania Latina conference held at the University of Groningen, Germania Latina 3, (Groningen) 1998

H&S   Haddan, A., & Stubbs, W., (eds.) *Councils & Ecclesiastical Documents,* vol. 3 (Oxford) 1869

HBS   Henry Bradshaw Society (London)

HE   Colgrave, B. & Mynors, R. A. B., (trs.) *Bede's Ecclesiastical History of the English people, (Oxford) 1969*

HTR   Harvard Theological Review

JEH   Journal of Ecclesiastical History

JML   Journal of Medieval Latin

JMH   Journal of Medieval History

JTS   Journal of Theological Studies

MGH Monumenta Germaniae Historica

MLR   Modern Language Review

PL   Patrologia Latina

PMR   Proceedings of the Patristic, Medieval & Renaissance Conferences

RB   Revue Benedictine

SSCI   Settimane di Studio del Centro Italiano di studi sull'alto medioevo (Spoleto)

TRHS Transactions of the Royal Historical Society

VG   Vulgate

Introduction

This book examines the life and career of Alcuin in England and on the continent; it also considers his legacy as a churchman and a leading political figure. His intellectual legacy as a theologian, teacher and poet is considered in detail elsewhere in *Alcuin – Theology and Thought*, but it has to be borne in mind if his historical significance is to be fully appreciated. The first thing to establish therefore is the context in which he grew up and his Christian cultural inheritance.

Alcuin was a conscious heir to the rich traditions of the English Church, which had been created among the Anglo-Saxons in the century and half before his birth in around 740. The father of this church was Pope Gregory I, known as Gregory the Great, the 'apostle of the English'; and all that Alcuin set out to accomplish was consistent with the pastoral and evangelistic approach as outlined by Bede which had governed the pope's mission, led by Augustine of Canterbury and Paulinus of York, to the Anglo-Saxons in the seventh century. As a Northumbrian, born probably near York and certainly educated there, Alcuin modelled his learning and teaching upon the memory of Bede, who had died in 735 just around the time that he was born. Bede's study of the Bible, and his *Ecclesiastical History of the English People* which explains how the early Anglo-Saxon church had been created, provided the framework for much of Alcuin's own thinking. Bede and Alcuin were both disciples of Gregory and their own work in expounding the Bible and Christian theology flowed from his example and legacy and complemented it.

From Gregory's teaching there also sprang the sustained partnership between evangelism and education that was the hall-mark of the early Anglo-Saxon church, and of its missionary activities on the Continent. The Pope's own approach to the rulers of his day, recorded in his many letters, guided the way in which Alcuin addressed the political and ecclesiastical leaders with whom he had regular contact at the height of his powers. The memory of the missionary initiative of the Roman Church kindled a deep devotion to the See of St Peter in Alcuin's mind, as it had done in Bede's, and this is particularly apparent in some of his letters. At the same time, like Bede, he was interested in scientific matters, notably the calculation of sacred time; and also in Latin language and poetry, of which he was a great master. Both men were committed teachers and showed a deep devotion to their pupils that was reciprocated. Like Gregory, Alcuin is best approached through his many letters: for both were masters of the epistolary art; and in each case their letters were carefully recorded for the benefit of contemporaries and later generations. This means that Alcuin is one of the most accessible of early medieval Christians; and like Anselm of Canterbury later, one of the most attractive and interesting of people.

Although Alcuin remained a Northumbrian Christian at heart, the part of his life about which most is known was spent on the Continent, when he was attached for some time to the peripatetic court of Charlemagne, then at Aachen, and finally, towards the end of his life, as Abbot of the monastery of St Martin at Tours, where he died in 804. Here he produced most of the written work that now remains, distilling long years of experience as a teacher and scholar. He never lost contact with his homeland, however, nor with the church of his education at York, and many of his letters were directed to friends and contacts in England and Ireland. But his most significant and lasting work was evidently accomplished on the Continent and his influence on the early medieval Western Church was an abiding one.

In this work he followed in the footsteps of his kinsman Willibrord, whose *Life* he composed in prose and in verse; and also of Boniface, the great missionary to the Germans and the Frisians, who died a martyr's death in 754. English disciples of these two pioneers remained active in both Francia and Germany throughout the period of Alcuin's formation at York and during his own time on the Continent. The nature and work of these English missionaries is vital background to what Alcuin was able to achieve when he was invited by Charlemagne to join the growing circle of scholars which the King was attracting by his patronage and prestige. So it was that Alcuin became associated with what has come to be described as 'the Carolingian renaissance'. With the King's support he was enabled to play a crucial and very distinctive role along with others in the revival of Christian learning and education within Charlemagne's domain. Alcuin saw this as his personal vocation as a Christian, a voluntary though not always contented exile from his homeland.

Alcuin's letters and many of his poems reveal a person hungry for friendship and human affection: for Alcuin was a born communicator, reaching out continually to those whom he valued, though not always sure whether they reciprocated his affection. The difficulties of communication at that time emerge frequently throughout his letters, aggravating his feelings of isolation and anxiety on some occasions. He retained the loyalty and affection of many of his pupils throughout his life and after his death. Yet despite this galaxy of contacts and associates, Alcuin emerges from his letters as someone very sensitive and in some ways insecure. For him, friendship was one of the distinctive hallmarks of Christianity, a preparation and foretaste of life in heaven, where none of the vicissitudes of this present life would obscure the communion of friends in Christ. It is this deep affection, swayed sometimes by vulnerability, which makes Alcuin so interesting and unusual. Occasionally he bent the established forms of letter-writing, and Latin itself, to communicate something of his own inner feelings, hopes and fears. It is sad that no letters remain from his friends in response to his.

Alcuin was a person of deep Christian faith, tenacious in his loyalty to orthodox Catholic theology, being rooted in the Bible and steeped in the liturgy of the Church. It is his skill as a poet of prayer as well as an educator that marks Alcuin out as a seminal influence upon his own generation and those that came after him. The fact that it is sometimes difficult to disentangle what was in fact his own writing from those of others moulded by his teaching and example, who wrote in the ninth century after his death, reflects his deep and creative influence. His love of God and his grasp of Christian theology were rendered original in their creative impact by his gifts as a teacher and poet. In his hands, the very traditional theology that he inherited, and to which he felt bound, took new wings. But always there is the tremulous under-current of compunction and uncertainty as to his personal worthiness. This reaches out even now to the sympathetic and attentive reader, cloaked as it is in mellifluous Latin.

His originality therefore lay more in how he said things than in what he said, for he was ever the studious servant of tradition as well as a subtle mediator and communicator of the theology of Augustine. Yet like Anselm, there is a gleam of creative genius running through his desire to communicate the richness of Christian theology, clearly and with fervour, more often than not with particular persons in mind whom he valued as his friends. To read his letters and his eloquent poetry is to be included within a loving heart and addressed by a keen mind. The abundance and quality of his writing, and the clarity of his Latin, indicate the scope and richness of the material attributed to him, or associated with him, as well as the remarkable range of his own reading. For Alcuin must rank with Bede, Boniface, and Dunstan as one of the most notable and influential of Anglo-Saxon Christians, uniting English and continental Christianity in a unique manner, which left a lasting legacy within the Catholic Church of Western Europe.

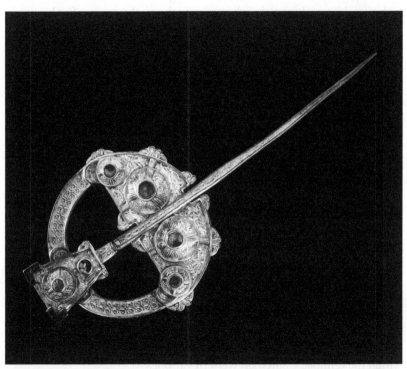

The Londesborough penanular brooch of Irish origin from the eighth or early ninth century, crafted and inlaid out of tin, silver, gold, glass and amber.

Part One
England

Chapter 1
York

Alcuin was probably born around the year 740,[1] in or very near to York in the Anglo-Saxon Kingdom of Northumbria. From a young age he was entrusted to the *familia* of clergy that served the cathedral in the city, perhaps because of the early death of his parents: this became his home and it left an indelible impression. Like Bede and Willibrord before him, he was truly a child of the Church. Throughout his whole life he regarded York as his spiritual home; more than half his adult life was spent there, and he looked back to it with nostalgia and gratitude to the end of his days. He never lost his close connections with the church in York, retaining and fostering many friendships there, which he kept alive in his later years while abroad by his letters. He always hoped to return there to die and to be buried within the precincts of the church that he loved. But it was not to be: he died in Tours in 804. He was probably one of the first Anglo-Saxon Christians to grow up wholly within the confines of a fast growing city and emporium, and this coloured his attitude at times to the peasant society which the Church largely served.[2] His own upbringing brought him into close contact with the aristocracy of Northumbria: the King and the Archbishop of his youth were brothers. For him the Church in York was at the heart of this urban renewal – indeed it was the true *urbs*.[3] In its development he was to play a significant role, intellectually and physically, during the first part of his life as a deacon and teacher.

Family and childhood

In a letter, written probably in 794 from Francia to friends at York, Alcuin spoke warmly of his nurture there.[4] He addressed them as 'beloved and venerable brethren'. Their care of him during the fragility of his childhood was maternal, being patient with his adolescent waywardness, guiding him by learning and discipline. They remained always at the heart of his prayers during his 'exile' and journeying abroad.[5] They might be his sons in terms of their age, but he regarded them as his fathers in their holiness. He implored their prayers, privately and in church, 'for their son Alcuin': 'O most beloved fathers and brethren, remember me: I will be yours, whether in life or in death!'[6] He expressed the desire to be buried by them and with them, sensing however that this was unlikely. Then he made an interesting reference to the memory of a common friend, long dead: 'I firmly believe that the souls of our fraternity will be reunited in heaven, as our boy *Seneca* once glimpsed and testified'. This almost certainly refers to the episode with which Alcuin closed his poem on the history of the church of York, which he probably composed somewhat earlier, perhaps in response to a return visit from the continent to his home city in either 786 or 790-3.[7]

Right at the end of the lengthy and eloquent encomium in this famous poem for his former teacher Aelberht, who was like a father to him, Alcuin inserted a more personal and evidently shared reminiscence about this friend of his youth, Seneca, a person 'simple of spirit but energetic in act, who deeply influenced my boyhood with his counsel.'[8] This boy had a vision, while praying in the chapel of 'the Mother of Christ', of an angel, who showed him an open book, with the promise that 'now you know this you will witness even greater things'. Shortly afterwards he fell ill and almost died in Alcuin's arms, but surfaced to recount a vision of heaven. In due time he succumbed, during an epidemic of the plague, and one of the community saw him received into glory. This memory, thus recalled, was included as Alcuin's closing tribute to the place, the 'port of York, which had reared me as its foster-son.'[9] The way Alcuin portrayed this common memory, which had clearly stayed with him as a guiding light for many years, was perhaps modelled on a similar experience recounted in Bede's *History*.[10] In a later poem, *De Abbatibus*, composed by Aethelwulf early in the ninth century in an unknown Northumbrian monastery, the influence of Alcuin's description can clearly be seen in the language describing a similar vision with which that poem ends.[11] The significance of Alcuin's story, however, lies in its distinctive details and corroboration in his letter, and in the light that it sheds on the close atmosphere of friendship and spiritual formation which Alcuin experienced in his childhood and youth as part of the *familia* of the church of York.

It corroborates also some of the stories in the *Life of Alcuin*, written between 821 and 829 at the request of Aldric, Abbot of Ferrières, which drew upon the long memory of Alcuin's close friend and disciple, Sigwulf, who had recently been abbot there since the year of Alcuin's death in 804, as well as of other disciples at Tours.[12] It is heavily weighted with information about his time in York, and in its style and historical preoccupation it stands in a distinct tradition of exemplary hagiography emanating from Northumbria, evident in the earlier *Lives* of Wilfrid and Ceolfrith.[13] One distinctive feature of the *Life of Alcuin* comprises Alcuin's visionary dreams: 'the reminiscences and reports of intensely personal experiences in Alcuin's early life must have come ultimately from his own lips', presumably via Sigwulf.[14]

The earliest of these occurred when he was still quite young, about the age of ten. Sharing a cubicle with a frightened peasant boy who feared the dark,

Alcuin had a nightmare in which he was reproached for enjoying Virgil more than the psalms! The other youngster slept past the time of divine office and Alcuin had to ward off the devil by chanting psalms and making the sign of the Cross.[15] There is a sharp contrast drawn here between the reaction of the noble boy, Alcuin, and his peasant companion, who almost collapsed. It is a strange tale, but a witness perhaps to Alcuin's early precocity in Latin. It demonstrates also how fundamental to education at that time was the learning of psalms in Latin by chanting them in church. It reflects also the tussle within Alcuin throughout his life between the Latin of the Bible and the Fathers, and the charms of the classical authors, especially the poets. Despite his occasional protests, Virgil was never far from his thoughts and writing.[16]

The *Life of Alcuin* asserts that Alcuin was of noble birth, dedicated to the service of the Church from his childhood. His nobility is not certain, however, and the only evidence about his family circumstances is found in his *Life of Willibrord*, who was a kinsman.[17] This *Life* was a two-fold composition, an *opus geminatum* following the example of Bede's *Life of Cuthbert*, written by Alcuin before the year 797, in prose and verse, with a homily attached. In its opening chapter, and also in the prologue dedicating the work to Beornrad, Abbot of Willibrord's monastery at Echternach and later bishop of Sens, who had commissioned it, Alcuin revealed that he was the heir and trustee of a small monastery founded by Willibrord's father, Wilgils.[18] He is described as a *paterfamilias*, a successful landowning *ceorl*, who attracted the generosity of the local aristocracy and of the king in order to create a small monastic cell of St Andrew at the mouth of the river Humber.[19] This would seem to place Alcuin's kin in the southern part of Northumbria called Deira, now Yorkshire. Alcuin's *Life* of his kinsman Willibrord appears to be primarily a personal act of familial piety; but it also addressed the question of how missionary work should be tackled and the due patronage of a king towards it, and so it also had a more topical relevance.[20] It is impossible to know whether Alcuin had any siblings, however: a passing mention in a letter to his friend, Adalhard Abbot of Corbie, written from England in 790, may hint at this possibility; but it is unclear if this is simply a rhetorical device.[21] It seems therefore that Alcuin came 'from a modest landowning family.'[22] If there were any wider kin they are not evident in his letters. The church of York became his *familia* from an early age.

The rebirth of a city

Alcuin's reference at the end of his poem about York to the city as a 'port' was not just a rhetorical metaphor, the longing for home of someone away on a long and uncertain voyage of exile.[23] It precisely alluded to the importance of York as a major centre of trade, whose wealth was vital for the prosperity of the church there and for the rebirth of the city. 'To York from various peoples and realms far away they still come, seeking profit and

wealth from this rich land.'[24] The ninth century *Life of Liudger* by Altrid tells
how this disciple of Alcuin's, who came from Frisia and later became the
first bishop of Munster in Germany, had to flee England when the Frisian
colony in York was obliged to depart temporarily from the city in order to
avoid revenge for the killing of a nobleman by a Frisian merchant.[25] Trade
from York to Dorestad and the Rhine trade-route became the city's life-
blood in the eighth century, accompanied by missionary activity, in which
the church of York played a leading role from the time of Wilfrid.[26] In
another poem, written around the year 794 for his *familia* in York, Alcuin
bade the young men privileged to live within the noble walls of the city 'to
fill the ships of the Frisians with their sacred songs.'[27] As the place where
Paulinus had baptised King Edwin in 627[28] and where Gregory the Great
had intended that a second primatial see should be established,[29] York
grew in importance as a church centre as the city grew as an emporium.
In 735, its Bishop Egbert was finally granted the *pallium* by Pope Gregory
III[30] and York was affirmed as a metropolitan church, whose authority
stretched throughout Northumbria and the regions under its political
sway.[31] Alcuin knew that the city had been founded by the Romans and
that in its day it had rivalled London as 'an emporium by land and sea'.[32]
The pattern of its recent gradual revival as a trading centre also mirrored
that of London somewhat earlier. But for Alcuin what mattered was that
Pope Gregory I's 'immediate command was this city should be the head
of its churches, possessing the pinnacle of honour; and that its bishops
should be invested with the *pallium* and consecrated there.'[33]

Recent archaeology has gradually confirmed the development of the
city at this time. It would appear, like London, to have had several poles
of economic and political activity, hardly constituting a continuous city
within enclosed walls of the ancient or medieval kind. Some limited
settlement occurred within the Roman walls and the ruins of the old
basilica, some parts of which were still standing and usable. This was the
site of the first church, dedicated to St Peter,[34] created by Paulinus out of
wood and later rebuilt as the cathedral by Wilfrid. On the west bank of
the river Ouse lay the site of the old Roman *colonia*, resettled in part by the
Anglo-Saxons, with perhaps a British enclave nearby as well. Excavations
at the Fishergate have revealed a trading zone that was systematically
developed in the eighth century and quite distinct from the later Viking
port of Jorvik at the Coppergate. It contained evidence of trade with the
Rhineland and further afield, and in size it corresponded to contemporary
developments at Hamwic (near Southampton), Aldwych in London and at
Dorestad itself in Holland.[35] Coins circulated throughout Deira (southern
Northumbria) from around the year 740, the time of Alcuin's birth, some
inscribed with the figure of Archbishop Egbert.[36] The growth of trade
was promoted by royal attention and residence, and in the eighth century
York became the virtual capital of Northumbria, with its 'high walls and

lofty towers'[37] of Roman origin but in places augmented by the Anglo-Saxon rulers.[38] It became a place of burial for kings and nobility, whose disposable wealth must have been derived from the profits of trade as well as extensive land-holding. Some of this surplus wealth was used to enrich and develop the church and its resources, including its books and works of art. Alcuin's poem about York indicates in its title that kings as well as bishops and saints were being celebrated. It is therefore a self-conscious and patriotic monument to a sustained urban and economic development of which Alcuin was a direct beneficiary.

Hagia Sophia

It seems that the enrichment of the church at York started in earnest under Wilfrid, its controversial Bishop, but his impact upon Northumbrian politics and the wider life of the English Church may well have contributed to the delay in granting the *pallium* to the bishops of York. It may also account for the tenacity with which the church at Lindisfarne defended its privileges and promoted the cult of St Cuthbert.[39] It is strange that Alcuin makes no mention of this aspect of Wilfrid's episcopate in York, portraying him rather as an active missionary abroad; for his work on the cathedral was significant, restoring its stone structure and leaking roof as well as glazing its windows around the year 669. He whitewashed its interior, showered it with liturgical gifts and endowed it with lands, though whether these benefactions survived his several exiles is unclear. Unfortunately his building, along with much else in York, was consumed by fire in 741, according to the Anglo-Saxon Chronicle.[40] This catastrophe probably provoked an energetic re-building programme, utilising the growing wealth of the city and its surrounding region, and perhaps exacerbating the inherent tension, economic and political, between the two Northumbrian provinces of Bernicia in the north and Deira in the south. The assertion of York as the centre of the Northumbrian church may lie behind signs of tension, leading to the siege of Lindisfarne in the annals for 750 as recorded by Simeon of Durham in the early twelfth century, who incorporated Northumbrian records now lost. Likewise Roger of Wendover, writing in the early thirteenth century and using other unknown northern annals, recounts how 'Egbert, archbishop of York, laudably recovered the *pallium*, which had been neglected by eight bishops since the time of Paulinus, the first archbishop of York'.[41] The account of the obtaining of the *pallium* for Eanbald, placed in the year 783, strikes the similarly assertive note that the king sent to Rome for it and then gave it to his bishop. All this may explain to some extent the way in which Alcuin selects from Bede's *History* and slants his poem about York, extolling the version of its recent ecclesiastical history with which he had grown up.[42] For example, his treatment of Cuthbert of Lindisfarne is of a saint of the whole Northumbrian church and the role of the Irish and of Lindisfarne itself is played down, despite his own personal friendship with that community.

When Alcuin wrote about the York bishops after Wilfrid, he was on surer ground in terms of the ideal that he was seeking to commend. He described Bosa as a 'good and sincere person', a true spiritual father who endowed the church of York, and began to create a distinctive clerical *familia* that was separated from the life of the city. He insisted on a life of unceasing prayer within the community, alternating holy reading with holy prayer; all property was to be shared.[43] Bishop John of Beverley similarly merited high praise: 'an outstanding bishop in the mould of the Fathers, from whose pure heart flowed rivers of learning'[44] He was a true pastor, working miracles of compassion according to Bede, to whose authority Alcuin deferred, and who retired to a monastery at the end of his days. Likewise, his successor Wilfrid II is portrayed as the ideal bishop of a fast growing city and its churches, a generous benefactor who could command the lavish patronage of wealthy people. Alcuin describes vessels of precious metals, altars covered with silver and gilded crosses.[45] He describes also the Bishop's generosity to the poor and his retreat into contemplative life.[46] As Bishop John's auxiliary he was also 'abbot of York' though of which monastery is unclear.

All this was a sign of the emerging role of the bishop as the protector not only of the cathedral *familia*, but also of some kind of monastic institution within the city and its emerging school. Ecclesiastically, York was developing along lines already well established in the south at Canterbury.[47] With the accession of Egbert, the brother of the king of Northumbria, the Archbishop became patron of the renewed *civitas* and capital of the Kingdom. Concerning Egbert, the Archbishop of his youth, and his beloved successor, Aelberht, Alcuin had much to say. But central to it all was the assertion that these were happy years for the Northumbrians and their church, ruled by a harmonious partnership between king and archbishop, which he had witnessed at close quarters and which contrasted sharply with the tensions there that troubled Alcuin's later years. This harmony remained his ideal for the rest of his life and it explains much of his work and teaching, and the vision that underlay it, both in England and in Francia.[48] His experience of relative political stability and economic prosperity was matched by his experience under Charlemagne. His was an unusual formation and experience, therefore, but it gave scope for the development of a theology that would underpin his whole Christian political ideology. For Egbert ruled the church of York as Bishop for 34 years and his brother, Eadberht, was King for 21 years: it was upon this political stability, as well as upon the growing wealth of a trading city, that developments within the church of York were built.

In his description of the episcopacy of his mentor, Archbishop Aelberht, whom he described as committed by temperament to the *via media* as a bishop, Alcuin gave a vivid description of the decoration of the cathedral church of St Peter,[49] with its great altar over the site of Edwin's baptism, covered in gold, silver and jewels and dedicated to St Paul, above which hung an elaborate chandelier. On the high altar the Archbishop raised a large cross of solid silver, and elsewhere he created an ornate altar to the martyrs of the Church. The altar cruet was of solid gold and of great weight. All this reflected the pride and wealth of the city, its traders and aristocracy – the hallowing of their profits and the products of their journeys. There remain in Charlemagne's chapel at Aachen today examples of such glittering liturgical provision from a later age. England was rich in mineral wealth and Anglo-Saxons were renowned metal-workers, at home and abroad, with an unquenchable appetite for such lavish creations.[50]

Most significant, however, is Alcuin's description of the basilica of *Hagia Sophia* that he helped to build in collaboration with Aelberht's other distinguished pupil, Alcuin's friend Eanbald, who in due time became Archbishop of York.[51] No remains of this church have ever been found but it is described as lofty, supported by many columns and arches, with inlaid ceilings and glazed windows, surrounded by chapels and galleries and thirty altars in all, some of which were probably in the galleries. It was dedicated by Aelberht to Holy Wisdom – *Hagia Sophia* – on the eve of All Saints' Day in 780, nine days before his own death. It may have been round in its shape like the royal chapel in Aachen was to be, modelled perhaps on the rotunda of San Vitale in Ravenna, but this is not certain. With so many altars, it presupposes proximity to a significant clerical community, probably the community and school within which Alcuin worked.[52] The circumstances of its dedication appear to be recorded in a calendar from Prum in Germany: this has many English commemorations, with the unique commemoration of the *titulus Agiae Sophiae* in close proximity to a commemoration of the death of Archbishop Aelberht on 8 November 780.[53] Whether the origin of this unique dedication in England was derived from the cult of St Sophia in Rome, newly affirmed by Pope Paul I, or from reports of Hagia Sophia in Constantinople is unclear: the latter may be more likely as this was in Greek *he polis* – 'the city' par excellence.[54] Its location may have been close to the cathedral itself or in some other part of the city, perhaps across the river Ouse at Bishopshill, alongside an existing religious community for whose existence at this time there is some evidence.[55] A close association with the school is most likely, however, for in Alcuin's mind the basilica and the library that he goes on to describe were the twin benefactions of Aelberht, and fitting monuments to his wisdom and generosity. There is no doubt also that Holy Wisdom as a particular way of envisaging Christ lay at the heart of much of Alcuin's own theology and writing.[56] Indeed the creation of a church specifically to embody a particular vision of Christian theology and learning remains a distinct possibility, emulated later perhaps by Alcuin's friend Angilbert in his recreation of St Riquier in Francia at the end of the eighth century,[57] and possibly by Charlemagne himself in the creation of his royal chapel at Aachen.[58]

Northumbrian kingship

How was Alcuin able to address Charlemagne and the rulers of the English Kingdoms, even the Pope himself, with such clarity and confidence as he set before them their duties as Christian rulers? In his many letters, and elsewhere in his writings from the second part of his life in Francia, he articulated a dynamic political ideology which had deep roots, not only in the thought of the later Latin Fathers, but also in the traditions surrounding Christian monarchy that had grown up in England during the century before he was born. These found their most eloquent expression in Bede's *History,* which has been aptly described as 'a mirror of princes of unexampled power.'[59] Like Bede, Alcuin grew up in a relatively stable environment; but unlike Bede he was closer to the seat of power and had an appetite for participation in it. He lived in an *urbs* within an *urbs*: the Church at the heart of the royal city of York. In his poem about this environment, his *patria,* he looked back to the time when the King and Archbishop were brothers as a model period in the recent history of Northumbria, as well as an example of partnership to be emulated and if need be restored.

   Anglo-Saxon kingship was the key to the story of the conversion to Christianity in the seventh century; and in the process kingship itself was metamorphosed.[60] The king retained his position as the father of his people, the guarantor of their prosperity in peace and of victory in war. His person was sacred, enhanced by his role as law-giver. He was also a mediator with God, His deputy among His people. In this task he was guided by his bishops as well as the nobility, and to some extent the Christian aspects of his office became construed in the light of episcopacy. This is one of the most consistent themes of Anglo-Saxon history throughout more than four hundred years. By the time of Alcuin, its implications had been spelled out in written law-codes to which he alluded, although none from Northumbria at his time now remain.[61] Behind this process lay a rich theological tradition with its roots in the genius of Isidore of Seville (died 636), who brought the thought of Augustine of Hippo in his *De Civitate Dei* to bear upon the Visigothic monarchy.[62] The cardinal principles of a Christian ruler were *iustitia* and *pietas:* if these were cultivated, a king's rule over his kingdom would be effective, and he would serve as the protector of the Church. Isidore injected a powerful moral direction into both aspects of ruling, and his thinking became normative for all subsequent development of Christian political thought in the Western Europe in the early Middle ages.

   Another strand within the tradition in which Alcuin was formed, and to which he gave voice, was derived from Ireland. Irish influence during the conversion of Northumbria in particular had been profound. Irish Christian kingship in the sixth and seventh centuries was tribal and traditional in its form. One of its most potent written expressions was created at the same time as Isidore was writing: it is called *De duodecim abusivis saeculi*, which among other things described the *rex iniquus* and the dire consequences of his misrule.[63] This tract had a long influence, as did the writings of the British priest, Gildas, whom both Bede and Alcuin cite as an awful warning of how a Christian people could betray themselves by apostasy and infidelity.[64] Behind this minatory approach lay the Old Testament, the exemplar by which the politics of the day was continually interpreted by Christian theologians and bishops.

Well before Alcuin ever met Charlemagne, the Franks had come to regard themselves, at the prompting of various churchmen including the pope, as the new Israel, re-enacting the history enshrined in the Bible, their success being a sign of God's favour. In this sentiment, Bede through Boniface had partly led the way by his perception of the Anglo-Saxons as the chosen conquerors of Britain, with a manifest destiny and a single religious and racial identity. The hapless Britons, even though they were Christians, were to be swept aside as unworthy, like the Canaanites of old.[65] Alcuin inherited this racial prejudice, considering that 'God in His goodness had deemed that this corrupt people should forfeit the kingdoms of its ancestors on account of its crimes, and that a more blessed people should occupy their cities' – including York itself.[66] Part of this lack of sympathy and Christian charity may have its root in suppressed insecurity and anxiety, perhaps even guilt too: for Northumbria, especially its northern part Bernicia was by virtue of its geography seldom free from serious British raids and reprisals during the lifetime of Bede and probably during Alcuin's childhood too. In 793 it was the first to bear the brunt of Viking attacks from the sea with the sack of Lindisfarne, an event which clearly shook Alcuin. In writing about Frankish affairs, Alcuin transferred this rationale of justified Christian supremacy to those whom Charlemagne and his forebears conquered. Thus his poem about the kings and saints of the church of York was partly a justification for a received tradition of Northumbrian history that was acceptable, like the great and probably contemporary poem *Beowulf*, to the aristocratic elite, royal, lay and clerical, whom he was addressing.

In his advocacy of the partnership between king and holy men Alcuin was preceded by other early English hagiographies, notably the anonymous *Life of St Cuthbert* and Felix's *Life of Guthlac*.[67] In his poem about the church of York, Alcuin followed Bede's theological lead closely, even if his own selection of material revealed a specifically pan-Northumbrian 'patriotic' bias.[68] Bede's approach to kingship was heavily influenced by Gregory's *Pastoral Rule*, which although written for bishops and abbots, quickly became applicable to Christian kings as well.[69] The moral duty of a ruler was paramount and for this he had to be prepared by the wisdom of the Church and particularly the teaching of the Bible. So the qualities of a king were the cardinal virtues of prudence, courage, justice and temperance: he was called to embody them and to disseminate them among his people. Saul, David, Solomon and Josiah became role-models, but also cautionary tales. For over all human kingship stood the kingship and judgement of Christ: in this faith and fear lay the unity and identity of a Christian people; and the king with the Church was the focus of that unity and identity. Bede's *History* was of course a theological interpretation of the process of conversion and its necessary political support, a chapter of 'salvation history' closely modelled on the history books of the Bible; it probably served the interests of the Kentish as well as the Northumbrian church at that time to appropriate and articulate its own history in this way.[70] Alcuin's poem about York was a similarly motivated encomium. For him Bede's *History* and Gregory's *Pastoral Rule* were fundamental texts for his own thought, and were to be commended to others far and wide, including bishops and kings.

Alcuin extolled three Northumbrian kings in particular in his poem about the kings and saints of York. As in the anonymous *Life of St Gregory*,[71] his initial focus was upon Edwin, the first Northumbrian King to accept Christianity at the hand of Paulinus, the first Roman bishop of York. Alcuin portrayed him as a model king: 'he sought the best interests of his people, being generous to all, not wielding the sceptre fiercely but kind in his piety; he became the love of his people, the father of his *patria* and the adornment of his court. He was triumphant over the strongholds of his enemies, adding many people to his 'imperial' rule. . . . Having first established peace he ruled as a strong-armed judge.'[72] His laws were 'ordered in justice and equity' and he encouraged conversion to Christianity both by gifts and threats, building the first cathedral in York near the site of his baptism.[73] To Alcuin's mind, no subsequent king had wielded such effective power. Oswald, the next King in his encomium, was portrayed as a Christian warrior – 'a man of military prowess, the guardian and lover of his *patria*' who followed the example of Christ in his care of the poor, his kindness and his piety, in which connection Aidan is briefly mentioned. Oswald too was a benefactor and builder of churches, who died as a martyr in battle against 'the pagans.' His sanctity was marked by miracles and by his subsequent fame in Ireland and in Germany.[74] Alcuin then gave a rather edited version of the reign of Oswy, whose victory over the Mercians led to their conversion to Christianity.[75] He was 'a paragon of justice, issuing equitable laws, being invincible in battle and faithful in peace, generous to those in need, even-handed to all and pious.'[76] His description of the dual rule of King Eadberht and his brother Archbishop Egbert was irenic: 'one was brave, the other devout; one was energetic; the other was kind.'[77] Writing against the background of deterioration in Northumbrian political affairs, which Alcuin traced back to the reign of Aelfwald who died in 788,[78] Alcuin was subtly challenging his fellow-country men, in his poem and also in his letters, to new efforts to reform their affairs.

Whoever reads the Holy Scriptures and considers ancient histories and the fortunes of the world will find that for their sins kings of old lost their kingdoms and peoples their country: the strong and the unjust seized the possessions of others and they justly lost their own.'[79]

From the time that King Eadberht retired from office to enter a monastery in 758 until 792, the eve of the sack of Lindisfarne, there were six kings of Northumbria and much bloodshed along the way.[80] It appears that it was the turbulence at home after the murder of King Ethelred in 796 that deterred Alcuin from ever returning there towards the end of his life.

One king receives a brief but potent mention by Alcuin in his poem about the church of York: after Ecgfrith's disastrous defeat in 685 by the Picts at the battle of Nechtanesmere, he was succeeded by an illegitimate brother called Aldfrith who died in 704. Following the judgement of Bede, who described him in his *History* as *vir in scripturis doctissimus*,[81] Alcuin extolled him as someone who from his youth had been nurtured in 'the love of holy learning, endowed as a scholar with great eloquence and a sharp mind: a king who was also a teacher.'[82] He gave great support to the Northumbrian church and it was during his relatively peaceful reign that the first *Life of St Cuthbert* was written. He was a friend of Aldhelm of Malmesbury with whom he had studied as a youth under Irish teachers and to whom later Aldhelm wrote a famous letter about learning.[83] Aldfrith circulated copies of a book about the Holy Land composed by Adamnan, Abbot of Iona, and he was an active patron of Bede's monastery of Monkwearmouth-Jarrow.[84] From them he acquired a magnificent copy of the *Cosmographers* which the Abbot Benedict Biscop had brought back from a visit to Rome. Bede himself was a beneficiary of Aldfrith's sympathy for Christian learning and for its Irish practitioners in particular.[85] The link between Iona and Monkwearmouth-Jarrow was strong: Adamnan and Abbot Ceolfrith were friends, as Bede reported.[86] Stenton observed that Aldfrith 'is the most interesting member of the remarkable dynasty to which he belonged, and he stands beside Alfred of Wessex among the few Old English kings who combined skill in warfare with desire for knowledge.'[87] The fact that a Christian king could be both learned and politically effective was axiomatic to Alcuin's political theology. This conviction appealed directly to Charlemagne, who aspired to be both, as it did later to King Alfred the Great. The reality of its possibility had been established in Northumbria, amidst all the political vicissitudes of the period, in the older generation that nurtured Alcuin within the church of York.

An early ninth century Anglo-Saxon gold ring, inscribed with what is probably a reference to St Peter along with perhaps a personal name.

Chapter 2

Emissary

Contacts between two courts

Alcuin's involvement with continental affairs was part of a larger network of collaboration that marked the relationship between the English and Frankish churches in the eighth century. The missions of Willibrord and Boniface were the most notable of these initiatives, and both were closely associated with the rise of the Carolingian dynasty on the one hand and with the papacy on the other. In the writings of Bede and in later material, some associated with Alcuin himself, there are glimpses of others who went from England as missionaries to Frisia and Germany in their footsteps.[1] Alcuin's own earlier travels to the continent extended to Rome and Pavia, and also to the monastery at Murbach, early in the 760's; then to the court of Charlemagne probably for the first time in 779, before his famous meeting with the King at Parma early in 781 when he invited Alcuin to join his court. How soon Alcuin responded to this invitation is unclear, and he may not have departed in earnest until after the legatine council in England of 786. On the other hand there may have been other visits to and fro before that, which helped to establish him as a figure of substance at the court of Charlemagne as well as at home in York. The route between York and the Rhineland across the North Sea was one of the principal axes of trade and communication at that time, a relatively easy journey by ship, ensuring close ties between the emergent kingdoms of Northumbria and Francia and their royal centres.

In a poem, written in York between 778 and 781 and probably in 779, Alcuin recalled an extensive visit to members of the entourage of Charlemagne.[2] This poem, beginning *Cartula, perge cito,* is found among poems by Paul the Deacon and Peter of Pisa who were already established at court in a single manuscript of the ninth century associated with the abbey of St Denis in Paris,[3] and it reveals the strength of relationships that Alcuin enjoyed with some of the leading figures in the Frankish church well before he went to join them permanently in the latter part of his life.[4] The style of his poem was modelled on the earlier *encomia* of Venantius Fortunatus and the *Protempticon* of Sidonius Apollinarus: it was written in a confident mode of expression, full of allusion and wit. 'These are not the tentative tones of a newcomer entering an unknown milieu . . . Alcuin wrote in the guise of a shrewd observer of a familiar scene, his sense of decorum betraying the underlying assurance of a trend-setter.'[5] He appealed to Charlemagne as his *protector, tutor* and *defensor* – the arbiter as well as the patron of cultural life at his peripatetic court, a true *rex doctus* as extolled earlier by Venantius, and perhaps alluded to also in Alcuin's York poem in his description of the Northumbrian King Aldfrith as *rex simul atque magister*.[6] The date of the poem can be determined by the names and dates of the bishops of Speyer and Utrecht whom Alcuin mentioned; and his visit to Francia may have been occasioned by political changes in Northumbria, but this is not clear from the poem. The most striking reference is to his sending copies of grammatical works by Phocas and Priscian, presumably from York, to his friend Beornrad, nicknamed Samuel, Abbot of Echternach, where Alcuin's kinsman Willibrord lay buried.

The poem describes vividly the various modes of transport along the Rhine and Moselle rivers and the cultivation in that region. It greets formally but playfully leading members of Charlemagne's cultural court including Paulinus of Aquilea and Peter of Pisa, and also Jonas, Abbot of Kaiserswerth, a monastery of English foundation. It refers as well to an unwelcoming Frisian merchant in Dorestad, the port of entry for anyone travelling to the continent from York. The poem itself is construed as a vocal ambassador from Alcuin to his friends, a symbol of their friendship and intellectual intercourse. This was no empty literary device in Alcuin's mind, however, but rather a vital necessity to bridge the gaps of uncertainty, absence and distance: for him a letter or a poem had an almost sacramental persona as a living token of love. His messenger – his *casta charta* - would have to seek out the king's court, wherever it might be in the Rhine region, in order to salute him as the *rex optime*, whose patronage Alcuin sought and to whom already some of his loyalty and expectation was being transferred. Those others to whom he wrote had become already in his mind and memory 'fathers and brethren', and he hoped his friends too, including Lullus Archbishop of Mainz, the disciple of Boniface, whom Alcuin described as an adornment of the Church, endowed with the splendour of wisdom.[7]

Lullus was in fact an important conduit of communication between the English and Frankish churches: he was the spiritual successor as well as the disciple of the martyred Boniface. Letters remain to him from Cuthbert[8] and later Bregwin,[9] both archbishops of Canterbury, and also from Mildred, Bishop of Worcester; and correspondence remains between him and Abbot Cuthbert of Monkwearmouth-Jarrow monastery as well as with Alcuin's mentor, Aelberht, Archbishop of York.[10] There are further letters to Lullus from the kings of Northumbria and Wessex, and from a bishop of Rochester and a king of Kent.[11] Closely associated with the letter from the King Alhred of Northumbria and his wife Osgifu is one from an unknown Abbot Eanwulf, dated 25 May 773, and directed to Charlemagne himself.[12] It is interesting for a number of reasons: it addresses the King in glowing terms as a good king raised up by God. Using words taken from a letter of Gregory the Great to King Ethelbert of Kent, the Abbot urged Charlemagne to continue his active programme of converting pagan peoples – the Saxons – and building up the moral life of his people 'by great purity of life: exhorting, terrifying, persuading, correcting, and setting an example of good works.'[13] The letter concludes with a request for prayer and safe passage, that Eanwulf may have Charlemagne as his 'protector and patron', bidding him farewell as a 'most beloved lord.'

Its interest lies in the parallels drawn with and from Bede's *History* recounting the coming of Christianity to Kent, and in the confident and articulate way it addressed the King in moral terms. It is a window into the tradition of Christian political morality in which Alcuin grew up, which had already been articulated forcefully by Boniface and others. If this letter were sent along with the letter of the King and Queen of Northumbria, it further demonstrates the active interest shown by the Northumbrian church in affairs in Francia: for one of its purposes was to ask Lullus to facilitate an embassy from Alhred to establish 'peace and amity' between the two rulers.[14] It was also during the reign of Alhred that Aluberht came to be consecrated in York as Bishop to the Old Saxons; and Willehad was sent by a synod of the Northumbrian church to be a missionary among the Frisians and Saxons during this period.[15] The King's letter to Lullus may perhaps be associated with the return of Liudger with Aluberht in 773, as recounted in his *Life*,[16] or perhaps with the obtaining of the *pallium* for Archbishop Aelberht recorded in that year in the York annals.[17]

These York annals are an important source of history for Northumbria in the eighth century, being embedded in the later *Historia Regum* of Simeon of Durham.[18] Fourteen entries pertain to events in Francia or affecting the papacy; others record matters of interest to Northumbria and Francia alike, such as the martyrdom of Boniface and his companions in 754, or the consecration of Aluberht as Bishop for the Old Saxons in 773. They shed vivid light on the political turbulence that dogged Northumbria during Alcuin's adult years. They also record the existence of his letter, since lost, composed for Charlemagne in response to the purported proceedings of the Council of Nicea in 792. 'Against this Albinus [Alcuin] wrote a letter, wonderfully supported by the authority of the Holy Scriptures, and presented it with the synodal book [sent by Charlemagne to the English Church] in the name of our bishops and nobles to the King of the Franks.'[19] If this letter had been preserved, it would have shed crucial light on his attitude towards this controversy and perhaps also to his role along with Theodulf or Orleans and others in combating it.

The York annals record the death of Pope Hadrian I in 794 and the commissioning by Charlemagne of the black marble tablet written in verse and letters of gold and composed by Alcuin himself as his memorial to be placed in St Peter's Rome, where it survives to this day.[20] The annals are also well informed about the progress of Charlemagne's wars, and his imperial coronation by the Pope on Christmas day 800. Often their details enrich the information found elsewhere in the Frankish chronicles, and they therefore reflect a line of knowledge that was immediate and sustained, for example concerning the treasure gained by Charlemagne's victory over the Avars in 795, some of which came to Northumbria as gifts for the church.[21] There is a strong likelihood that Alcuin himself was the principal channel for this information reaching Northumbria from the world of Charlemagne until around 796, the year of his appointment to Tours, after which he never returned to England.[22] There are important parallels between his letters and many of the Frankish and other continental events included in the York annals, and also in some of the language used in them to describe kingship on both sides of the North Sea.[23]

The letter already mentioned of Abbot Eanwulf parallels that of an English priest Cathwulf, written to Charlemagne, perhaps from the royal monastery of St Denis near Paris. This is a more developed piece of Christian political morality, probably composed in 775 in response to Charlemagne's victories over the Lombards, to which the letter from Eanwulf may also allude. Both Englishmen clearly regarded Charlemagne as a rising star, the hope of the Church in the West.[24] This is another text that remains only in a single manuscript, associated with St Denis.[25] Unlike Alcuin, however, Cathwulf asserted that the ruler was God's vice-gerent and therefore superior to the bishops of the Church, a view associated with the fourth century writer called Ambrosiaster.[26] His comparison with the biblical Kings, David and Solomon, became a common-place in later Carolingian political theory, including Alcuin's. 'This letter provides a rare insight into the circulation of insular scholars and ideas on the Continent in the years preceding Alcuin's arrival at the Frankish court.'[27] It is unusual in outlining eight providential foundations to Charlemagne's divinely appointed rule, among which were included his recent victories in Lombardy, notably the capture of 'opulent' Pavia, and his resultant sole rule there as King in Italy. Cathwulf regarded Charlemagne as the winner in the eyes of God, expressing at the same time his own hopes and loyalty in no uncertain terms. His eight proofs of divine favour were mirrored by the eight pillars of a just rule, in terms also used by Alcuin in a letter to Aethelred of Northumbria twenty years later.[28]

It seems that 'Cathwulf was writing for a sophisticated audience and from a well-stocked library,'[29] to an elite familiar with his line of argument and admonition. He may even have served as a tutor to the young Charlemagne.[30] He certainly stands in a firm tradition of insular theological and political writers at the Frankish court.[31] For example, an Irishman called Clemens *peregrinus* also won Charlemagne's favour and was entrusted, perhaps early in the 770's, with the education of the sons of the Frankish aristocracy.[32] The point is that there was nothing unusual about Alcuin's *demarche* to the Frankish court, nor anything intrinsically original in his own articulate application of Christian theology to the moral duties of the ruler. He enjoyed however the personal friendship and favour of Charlemagne. Both men were well-matched in terms of ability and character, and for this reason Alcuin's influence and pre-eminence secured the permanence of his prolific writings, and also the preservation of his many letters, in which his theological and political views were expressed far and wide. But he was not alone, nor without important predecessors. The rise of the Carolingians and their formidable wealth, which derived from both trade and conquest, caused a veritable brain-drain of talent, in which Englishmen and Irishmen led the way, and including those attracted from Italy and Spain. It is in this context that Alcuin's own gravitation towards the court of Charlemagne must be seen.

The legatine councils of 786

As Charlemagne's influence and power grew, so too did his interest in the English kingdoms of Northumbria, Mercia, and Kent. The later eighth century saw the lapse of Northumbria into civil strife and vendetta, much to Alcuin's sorrow and lament. It saw also the rise of Mercia as the dominant English kingdom, ruled by the formidable Offa, with whom Charlemagne had to reckon. Offa dominated London and for a while Kent, and so commanded some of the most lucrative trade routes to the Continent. This brought him face to face, as it were, with Charlemagne's domains and authority. Political interaction was mirrored in the life of the Church, and this is clearly reflected in the arrival of the Pope's legation in 786 to England and the formulation of the decrees of the legatine synods in Northumbria and Mercia, in which Alcuin played an important role.[33] The decrees of these synods are an interesting amalgam of Anglo-Saxon and Frankish influences and their formulation sheds light on the ecclesiastical world in which Alcuin was already well established. The arrival of the papal legates in 786 is attested in the York annals:

> At that time legates were sent to Britain from the apostolic see by Lord Hadrian the pope, among whom the venerable bishop George held first place; and they renewed their former friendship with us and the Catholic faith which Pope St Gregory taught us through the blessed Augustine. They were received with honour by kings and bishops and by the nobles and magnates of this country; and they duly returned home in peace with great gifts, as was fitting.[34]

Their activities are corroborated in a full report of the legates' mission, which lists the members of the mission as George, Bishop of Ostia, Theophylact, Bishop of Todi, and Abbot Wigbod, sent by Charlemagne, to whom he was a close adviser as well as being a leading Frankish biblical scholar.[35] The synods were held in 'English Saxony in the days of the thrice-blessed and co-angelical Lord Hadrian, supreme *pontifex* and universal Pope, and in the reign of the most glorious Charles, most excellent King of the Franks and Lombards and patrician of the Romans, in the eighteenth year of his reign.' The initial tone appears *de haut en bas*, reflecting the energetic reassertion of papal dignity by Pope Hadrian I, in increasingly close alliance with Charlemagne as the emerging pre-eminent Christian ruler in the West.

The report associated the legatine mission with that of Gregory the Great and Augustine, being sent in order to safeguard the church of the English, while asserting that no Roman priest had come as an emissary to England from Rome since that time.

In fact the legatine synods need to be seen in direct succession to the synods of Hertford in 670 and Hatfield in 680, summoned by Archbishop Theodore, who had himself come from Rome, as recounted by Bede in his *History*;[36] and also to the council of Clovesho in 747, which decreed the observation of the feasts of St Gregory and St Augustine as national occasions, and many of whose provisions were reiterated in the legatine decrees.[37] This Rome-oriented synodal tradition was important in giving a sense of national unity to the English church, while respecting the identities and interests of the individual kingdoms. It was a mechanism already at hand and well-accepted, which enabled the legatine mission to proceed effectively. Alcuin and his friend Pyttel, described as *lectores*, came with the legates from Northumbria to Mercia as representatives of their King and the Archbishop of York, and they clearly commanded the respect of the foreign visitors, who described them as 'illustrious'. They probably acted as translators as well as advisers, for the decrees were expounded in both Latin and English.[38] Alcuin forged a strong friendship with George, who was Bishop of both Ostia and Amiens, and he seems to have had a significant influence on Alcuin's thinking. In a later letter, written from England in 790 to Adalhard, Abbot of Corbie, Alcuin asked to be remembered by him to his 'spiritual father', George.[39]

George was a key figure for many years at both the papal and Carolingian courts, holding bishoprics in both domains.[40] His influence upon Charlemagne, as well as upon Alcuin, was likely to have been considerable, as he had accompanied Pope Stephen II on his journey to the Frankish court in 753-4, and had served as an emissary for that Pope and his successor Paul I, participating in the synod of Compiegne in 757. He was granted the see of Amiens by King Pippin, to whom he was close. He then led a delegation of Frankish bishops to a synod in Rome in 769; and was ambassador between Charlemagne and Pope Hadrian I, whom the King came to regard as his spiritual father as well as his ally. Later in the 790s George took part in the dedication of renewed churches belonging to the royal monastery of St Riquier, then under the abbacy of Angilbert; and his last recorded appearance was at a Roman synod in 798 as bishop of Ostia and therefore the most senior figure in the Roman church after the Pope himself. This was a formidable track-record and the quality and nature of his relationship with Charlemagne, as well as with Alcuin, probably sheds light on how the two of them were able later to collaborate so fruitfully. George was thus uniquely well-suited to conduct the papal mission to England in 786, with the support of the Frankish King: it was intended to affirm with all due respect the life and integrity of the English church.

In his report for Pope Hadrian,[41] George outlined the progress of the legates throughout England after a stormy crossing. They were first received in Kent by Jaenberht, Archbishop of Canterbury, to whom they outlined their plans and the Pope's wishes. Then they went to meet Offa the overlord of Kent and King of Mercia, who summoned Cynewulf King of Wessex also to the conference. Offa's devotion to the see of Rome was well known to the legates, being an important component in his claim to overlordship. There remains a later letter of Pope Leo III to one of his successors, Cenwulf, referring to the tribute agreed by Offa with the papal legates on this occasion.[42] The other papal emissary, Theophylact, stayed on in Mercia before proceeding into Wales to visit the British church there, while George with Abbot Wigbod went into Northumbria to meet Eanbald Archbishop of York, and to await the return of the King from the north of his Kingdom. At a synod of both clergy and laity, various weaknesses in the Northumbrian church were addressed that were reflected in the decrees of the legates, which those present duly signed with the sign of the Cross. George and his party, now accompanied by Alcuin and Pyttel, returned to the Mercian court of Offa, and there the southern province of the English church ratified the decrees in the presence of the Archbishop of Canterbury and his bishops, as well as the leading nobility. These decrees therefore afford a comprehensive impression of the church and society in which Alcuin grew up and was operating, painting a picture corroborated in many of his letters concerning the affairs of the English, and particularly the Northumbrian, church.

The legatine decrees need to be read alongside the earlier decrees of the synod of Clovesho,[43] which they appear to some extent to presuppose. There are several angles for approaching such legislation. The first is to consider the issues that they were addressing and what this reveals about the state of the society in which the church was set, and the corrosive pressures it inevitably experienced. The next is consideration of the resources deployed as foundations for the decrees, notably the use of the Bible with other patristic and ecclesiastical precedents. Finally there is the form of the legislation and its likely parallels; for in this area the Anglo-Saxon and Frankish churches marched closely in step in the eighth century, and the legatine decrees mark a particular moment of convergence.

It can be argued that this kind of provision was hard to implement and that is why there is so much repetition from generation to generation. This was probably true to some extent because social conditions and human nature remained little changed throughout the Anglo-Saxon period. But at the same time the continuities within ecclesiastical legislation set forth an ideal tempered by realism, all the more striking for the courage with which abuses in both church and society were repeatedly challenged. There was no hard and fast boundary between church and society in this period, so both bishops and nobles were involved in the conduct of these synods. While the position of rulers was safeguarded in the legatine decrees, their moral accountability was also asserted quite unequivocally on the basis of biblical precedents in the Old Testament. There was therefore a triangular and transformative process underway, whose poles were the law and customs of the people, the canon law of the Church, and the exemplary template found in the Bible. There is thus a clarity and force about the decrees of both synods that is striking still.

The common concern of both sets of decrees was to maintain the integrity of the church and its clergy in terms of their morals and lifestyle, and to regulate monastic life, which was always in danger of becoming dissipated and discredited. There was a common insistence on education of a basic kind, and on uniformity of worship in accordance with the practice of the Church of Rome. The decrees of the synod of Clovesho in particular paint a picture of a society still steeped in paganism and magic; and of clergy prone to drunkenness, gossip and greed. Services in church were too often sung in the style of pagan poems, and Scripture readings were declaimed rather than read in an appropriate manner. Sundays were used for secular business and travel, while monks and nuns had a great appetite for dressing lavishly, their residences becoming centres for gaming, singing, harp-playing and jesting, which undermined their enclosed life. Nuns were especially vulnerable to fraternising with the laity, to gossiping, feasting, drunkenness and luxury. The drinking of alcohol before Terce was therefore forbidden to all clergy and monastics.[44] Even alms-giving was easily corrupted into self-indulgence. No ordained or professed person was therefore to co-habit with laity.

The legatine decrees echoed much of this concern, urging bishops to take action against paganism and not to be lured by greed. Fasting was not to be broken surreptitiously as happened it was alleged, among 'Saracens'.[45] Priests should not stand at the altar in bare legs; cakes should not be used for the Eucharist, or chalices that were made of horn. Bishops were not to participate in adjudicating secular affairs.[46] Firm action was to be taken however against unjust marriages that were incestuous, or made at the expense of religious vows; while illegitimate children were not to inherit property. Judges were to uphold just weights and measures and to prevent usury. The mutilation of horses, eating their flesh, wearing pagan clothes and settling disputes by casting lots were all condemned as unchristian, and in the case of the mutilation of horses as an affront to the Creator.[47]

The challenge facing the Church in the eighth century was clearly to maintain the integrity of its life and of its clergy in a semi-Christian society where ties with families and their lands were inescapable and life was short. One of the keys to this was education, and the earlier decrees of Clovesho are interesting to read in the light of the education that Alcuin and others in his generation received. The seventh decree stipulated that bishops, abbots and abbesses had a special duty to provide education for those under their authority. This required sustained and determined effort, as young people were easily seduced by the instability and false values of the age; but without an educated clergy the Church was vulnerable and ineffectual. 'The love of sacred learning' was also the foundation of sound worship and teaching, in which knowledge of the Creed, the Lord's Prayer and the Mass was central, in either Latin or English or both: for ignorance of the meaning of words denied their spiritual effectiveness.[48] The legatine decrees reiterated this, insisting that fidelity to Nicene orthodoxy, as interpreted by the Church of Rome and the ecumenical councils, was the touchstone of Christianity. Those baptized as infants were to be instructed at a suitable age in the meaning of the foundation texts of the Church. Two of the final sections of the decrees of Clovesho are virtual homilies about alms-giving and the use of the Psalms.[49] They close with an exhortation to unity among all parts of Christian society, emphasising the role of the clergy and monastics as intercessors, not just for themselves but for rulers and nobility, as well as for the well-being of the whole Christian population.[50]

In the legatine decrees, the political dimension of the legislation was much more apparent and developed, probably in response to the turbulence afflicting Northumbria, and the growing assertion of Mercian power in the southern part of England, which directly affected the life of the Church, especially in Kent. Rulers were urged to defend the property and discipline of the Church and to obey in all humility its bishops, who possessed the power of binding and loosing.[51] The exemplary role of the king was emphasised along with his moral responsibility before God for their spiritual welfare. His authority was to rest upon legitimate election by bishops and nobility; his birth must be legitimate because his position is as *'christus Domini'* – the anointed of the Lord. His murder was therefore an affront to God Himself. His duty, along with his nobility, was to administer justice fairly and to resist fraud, rape, violence and unjust oppression of the Church. Throughout these provisions, the principle of moral accountability in the light of biblical standards of behaviour was asserted in no uncertain terms, with reference to both rulers and bishops. Both were called to be shepherds and servants of a Christian people, answerable to Christ for them at the end of their lives.

There is a striking contrast between the two sets of decrees inasmuch as in the earlier ones the use of the Bible is sporadic and for the most part it remains in the background. But in the legatine decrees, there are numerous quotations from both the Old and the New Testaments. The duties of the bishops are defined with reference to the epistles of Paul, as well as to the words of the prophets and the Psalms. Abbots and abbesses are upbraided by the words of Christ from the gospels about being prepared for his coming, while their hypocrisy is condemned by his words. The superiority of bishops over rulers is underpinned by a careful catena of Old Testament texts as well by adapting the teaching of Paul the apostle: the priest is the angel of the Lord and therefore cannot be judged by any secular court.[52] Meanwhile the dignity of a king lies in his love of justice: he is to be surrounded by wise advisers who fear God and are honest, and who set a good example to those under them.

The dignity of the king is further supported by numerous citations from Scripture, many of which became common-place in Carolingian political theology, including references to the monarchy of David and Solomon in the Old Testament. The administration of justice is likewise underpinned by many trenchant references to the Bible; so too is the discussion of marriage, legitimacy of children, and the use of just weights and measures. Tithes are also justified from the Bible; and an opinion attributed to Augustine against usury is cited: 'where there is money gained as interest, there is damnation: such money in the chest means condemnation in the conscience.'[53] The legatine decrees conclude with two short homilies upholding the keeping of Christian vows and the practice of confession and penance, both of which rest on numerous biblical quotations. A distinctive note is also struck by the assertion that 'ancient privileges granted by the holy Roman See to English churches should be respected by all,' unless unjustly obtained.[54]

The form of the legatine decrees of 786 was a careful blending of Anglo-Saxon with Carolingian legal traditions, influenced also by formularies drawn from the papal chancery and reflecting the experience and sagacity of George of Ostia and his coadjutors. In many ways the whole document was like a charter; but its mode of dating clearly allied it with Carolingian and papal interests, falling as it did in the year in which Charlemagne went to Rome to spend the time between Christmas and Easter 787 with Pope Hadrian I. Charlemagne was already acting as 'Defender of the Faith' in the West. The witness lists at the end record those present at the two synods held by the Archbishops of York and Canterbury respectively in Northumbria and Mercia. George of Ostia ratified the document by making the sign of the cross on the Pope's behalf; some of the signatories also marked their names with written crosses, at this time a feature of papal bulls.[55] The decrees were read out aloud in Latin and also in English in order to be understood and accepted by all involved, who solemnly pledged to uphold them. The involvement of clergy and laity together in this ratification may have been an innovation by George, modelled on Frankish practice. The final document was described by him accurately as a 'capitulary', whose closest parallel was the first decrees of Charlemagne at Herstal in 779.

This was the first time that such an instrument was used in England, and George may have been influenced by its earlier use in Lombardy, for example the capitulary of Mantua in 781. After the defining and reforming decrees, called the *Admonitio Generalis*, issued by Charlemagne in 789, in which Alcuin's influence may be detected,[56] the capitulary became a common mode of legislation in the Carolingian realms. 'Although the mission was nominally papal in its origin, the document produced by the legates to fulfil their missionary objectives was Carolingian in typology. Yet the legates' capitulary, which was created in England and ratified by Anglo-

Saxon assemblies, was of a type that, in 786, was still relatively unusual in Francia.'[57] In its development as an instrument of government, it seems that George of Ostia played an influential role. In its contents, however, it represents an amalgam of local and wider issues: it was the Franco-papal response to the problems primarily of Northumbria, but it was also a response to Mercia as the emerging power in England, whose ruler, Offa, had no qualms about overturning existing ecclesiastical arrangements in his own interests, shortly after the legatine visitation, by creating for his own purposes an archbishopric at Lichfield at the heart of his domains. The legatine decrees were thus an instrument for holding together the English church as an entity in the face of changing political tides, while keeping it in step with the dynamic developments on the continent in which Alcuin would play a significant part.

The substance of the decrees addressed in the first place the state of the Northumbrian Church and there is much in them that echoes the known views of Alcuin in his many letters to English churchmen in the years after these synods, when for the most part he was based abroad.[58] The final document is of a high quality, lucid and balanced in its approach, and relatively succinct; it surely represents a consensus in which more than one mind was at work. There are close parallels with the *Admonitio Generalis* of 789, especially in the second part of each set of decrees, where theological argument backed by biblical references is prominent and a more homiletic tone is struck.[59] Many of the same issues were raised and addressed, sometimes in identical terms, on both occasions. Were the legatine decrees a model for the *Admonitio Generalis*, and was Alcuin an important link between the two? It is in the legatine decrees 11-14 that it has been argued that Alcuin's influence is most apparent in the light of his subsequent letters, notably the one he wrote to King Aethelred of Northumbria in the aftermath of the Viking raid on Lindisfarne in 793.[60] Alcuin's view of bishops as superior to kings was very different from Cathwulf's but it is inherent in the structure of his York poem; he shared with Cathwulf however a belief in the moral accountability of rulers as being fundamental to the prosperity of the people.[61] His thinking about bishops and kings may have its roots in the political theology of Pope Gelasius; or it may reflect Alcuin's own understanding, perhaps after discussion with George and Theophylact, of the sacrosanct nature of papal authority, which he would assert to Charlemagne to be beyond human judgement in the dispute over the succession of Pope Leo III in 799.

In the last part of the legatine decrees two themes emerge that were dear to Alcuin's heart: *concordia* or 'peace' in the Christian state, often mentioned in his letters, and penitence in the life of the Church. There are close parallels between decree 20 of the legatine provisions and Alcuin's teaching about penitence and confession in his *Liber de virtutibus et vitiis*, and also his letter to the boys at St Martin's at Tours.[62] In addition many of the passages from the Bible that are cited in the more homiletic decrees were widely used by Alcuin elsewhere, even though which version of the Bible was being used is not always clear. The most likely explanation of this collaboration is that the papal legates were open to the concerns of the Northumbrian churchmen, who were faced with a deteriorating political situation and anxious about the rise of their midland neighbour, Mercia, and any possible disruption to the English church that might be consequent upon it. 'The report of the papal legates in 786 looks therefore very like an Alcuinian prescription for the evils of Northumbria',[63] which were perhaps already incipient in Mercia and elsewhere.

Alcuin's growing connections with the court of Charlemagne, however far they were established by this date, might have reinforced the King's determination to exert his influence across the sea, as well as confirming his judgement of Alcuin's ability and usefulness to him. But it is unlikely that Alcuin was alone in articulating such moral and political concerns: his York poem was written for an audience already receptive to such a vision of a Christian church and society. It was for the benefit of this ecclesiastical elite that these decrees were promulgated, with the authority of the Pope himself, and backed by the declared interest of Charlemagne, with a view to their reception and application throughout the English church.[64]

'The evidence for Alcuin's influence over the legatine decrees has important implications for our understanding not only of the legatine mission, but also of Alcuin and his early career. It documents a period of his life when evidence is sparse, suggesting that his standing was already high in both England and Francia, and sheds special light on the formation of his political ideas. . . . His years in Northumbria moulded not only his scholarship but also his political theory.'[65]

It is also evidence of how since the time of Boniface, 'English and continental law-making could proceed in tandem: that the stimuli that produced the one could also inspire the other.'[66] The Church faced the same challenges in each society, and the fostering of Christian kingship was a common enterprise.

Working with George of Ostia clearly left its mark upon Alcuin's thinking and vision, equipping him for the role that fell upon him when he moved permanently to the court of Charlemagne shortly after these events. He may also have enjoyed the friendship of Theophylact, Bishop of Todi, if a poem Alcuin wrote describing him as *sophiae doctor honestus* and a pillar of the Roman church was in fact dedicated to him.[67] It is however in his many letters to his English friends that the development of his political and moral thought can be discerned in the years following the legatine synods of 786. These demonstrate that the English Church, and Northumbria in particular, were never far from his heart, despite the disasters at home that rendered Alcuin a voluntary if reluctant exile after 796 until his death in 804.

Chapter 3

Letters to England

The letters that Alcuin wrote from the continent during the last decade of his life to English rulers and to the church centres of Lindisfarne and Monkwearmouth-Jarrow, York and Canterbury, shed much light on three major episodes that rocked the English church in the last decade of the eighth century: the Viking assault on Lindisfarne in the summer of 793, inducing a sense of vulnerability from the sea and fear of what it might portend; the mounting political crisis in Northumbria, which culminated in the murder of King Ethelred in 796; and the repeated attempts by Offa of Mercia to subdue the Church and Kingdom of Kent to his will, partly through Ethelheard, his nominee as Archbishop of Canterbury, and the inevitable violent and sustained reaction which this policy provoked. They also shed light on relations between England the continent at that time, and on Charlemagne's interest in and concern about the course of English affairs, knowledge of which came to him by several channels, and not just from Alcuin himself.

These particular letters illuminate the framework of political and moral theology that Alcuin shared with those to whom he was writing, some of whom he had educated while in England. As such they open a window onto the context in which his own thinking was formed, and reveal the deeper nature of the theology upon which he built his subsequent writings, while at the court of Charlemagne or at Tours. His letters were collected in his lifetime at Salzburg, as well as subsequently at Tours itself, and much later in England, and they were regarded in his lifetime and long afterwards as exemplars of letter-writing and theology on both sides of the Channel. They are therefore a monument to the very real measure of freedom of thought that he enjoyed, and also to his moral courage. In the case of each English Church centre to which Alcuin was writing there is also an intimate connection between the relevant letters and some of his poetry.

Lindisfarne and Monkwearmouth-Jarrow

The Northumbrian monasteries of Lindisfarne and Monkwearmouth-Jarrow lay on the North Sea coast and were the cradles of northern English Christianity, one created by saints Aidan and Cuthbert, and the other graced by the learning of Bede. Lindisfarne lay on a tidal island overlooked by the royal fortress of Bamburgh; Monkwearmouth-Jarrow was a double monastery at

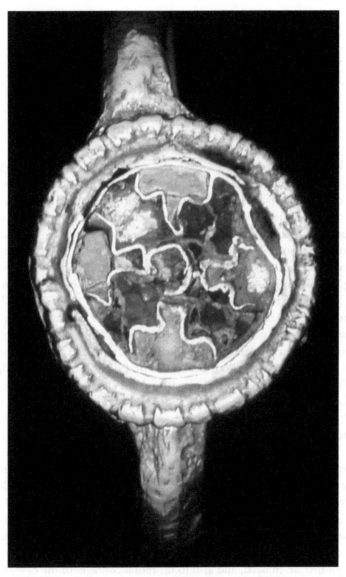

A Carolingian finger ring of the late eighth or early ninth century wrought
in gold and enamel.

the mouth of the river Tyne, with a fine library. They were both places well known and beloved by Alcuin, as his writings make clear. The Viking assault on Lindisfarne on 8 June 793 assumed cataclysmic significance in his mind and perhaps in the minds of others too. It demonstrated the vulnerability of the long narrow Kingdom of Northumbria and its monasteries to sea-borne attack. Perhaps it also reawakened the ancient insecurity of the Northumbrians towards those whom they had violently supplanted, the British, still living in the upland regions, and their allies the Picts. Threatened now on three sides because of the aggressive rise of Mercia as well, the prosperity of the Kingdom centred on York, in which Alcuin had grown up, began to appear fragile. Indeed its very economic wealth may well have attracted Viking interest and settlement for some time, in their double guise as traders and raiders. Compounded by the political turbulence within the Kingdom, Alcuin sensed a turn of the tide and a loss of security, which haunted him to the end of his days, and which certainly impinged on the life of the Northumbrian Church. His judgements were sometimes as severe as they were harrowed. The world he had known and loved was coming to an end, he feared; and where were God's saints who had allowed such a debacle to occur?

There is no doubt that the sack of Lindisfarne was an atrocity comparable to a terrorist attack in its impact and nature. It is mentioned in the Anglo-Saxon chronicle under the year 793, in version D that draws on northern sources. According to the northern annals embedded in the later writings of Simeon of Durham, the raiders came in the summer by sea to plunder, trampling the holy places, destroying the altars, digging up the relics and stealing the treasures of the monastery. Worse still they murdered some of the monks, enslaved others, and expelled the rest 'naked and laden with insults'. Some drowned in the sea, perhaps caught by the tide while trying to escape across the sands to the mainland. This was a deliberate act of terror and desecration, aimed at the spiritual heart of Northumbria; it was followed by other sea-borne raids, including one on Monkwearmouth-Jarrow itself.[1] Lindisfarne was not immediately abandoned at this time, however, but its position was no longer secure or sacrosanct. For Alcuin, the shock was compounded by the fact that he was now abroad, having visited both places only recently. His sense of powerlessness is palpable in his writings to his friends in response to the calamity.

In a letter of 793 to Ethelred, King of Northumbria and his court, written from abroad, Alcuin set out his initial response to the news.[2] Drawing on the Bible, he castigated the ruling elite for their corruption, portraying a slide into immorality and rapacity since the days of King Aelfwold, who had reigned briefly in 778 and whom Ethelred had displaced. Alcuin had clearly said much of this before and he reminded them of their double citizenship as Christians, which was the basis for his own loyalty and concern. He reminded his readers also that study of the Bible and of other 'ancient histories' revealed 'that for such crimes, rulers lost kingdoms and peoples their homeland', while rapacity overturned all law and order. Alcuin mentions portents, also mentioned by the chroniclers, which signified impending calamity and famine.[3] He expressed his horror at the desecration of Lindisfarne, the sanctuary of St Cuthbert that was now bespattered with blood. After 350 years of settlement, the English people were prey to a seaborne menace: 'the inheritance of the Lord was now abandoned to a people not His own.' He challenged the allure of Viking customs and dress for the people of York, lambasting also the extremes of wealth and poverty in Northumbrian society: 'this opulence of the rulers means poverty for the people.' His first criticism may well indicate the extent to which a Viking presence had already established itself among the traders in York, like the community of Frisian merchants already living there.

For all this, divine judgement had fallen first on the holy places of God: further calamities must surely follow, unless repentance should occur first. Prayer and acts of charity were the best defence of a Christian nation. The ruling class were bidden to be shepherds and not plunderers, to be obedient to the teaching of their clergy, and to remember their accountability to God as their judge. It seems that this formal charge was accompanied by a more personal approach to the King.[4] In this Alcuin appealed to his personal friendship with him, setting before him a 'mirror' of what was required of a ruler: submission to the will of God, abandonment of a 'rustic' lifestyle, commitment to reason and mercy, rather than anger and cruelty; the King was to set an example of moral life and to avoid excess. He urged the King, 'never, never plunder others, lest you lose your own possessions.' He reminded him of his accountability to Christ as his judge. These letters reveal in the mind of Alcuin a strong grasp of morality and a fearless capacity to write to those in political authority, who knew him well, albeit from the relative safety of the Continent. They reflect a disturbing picture of Northumbrian society, booming economically, but sliding morally. Speaking as a prophetic voice, Alcuin sensed the shaking of the foundations of his homeland.[5] 'With Alcuin, the theory and practice of power appears inextricably linked. His correspondence was dictated by a commanding need to converse and to exhort.'[6]

In the same year, Alcuin wrote to Ethelheard, the new Mercian Archbishop of Canterbury; the letter concludes with a poem extolling the spiritual significance of the Church of Canterbury.[7] In describing the attack on Lindisfarne as a *flagellum* or chastisement from God, he referred again to the interval of 350 years since another cleric, Gildas, had castigated the British Church and people for their apostasy. The advent of the Anglo-Saxons had been their *flagellum*.[8] In his York poem, Alcuin portrayed the Anglo-Saxons as God's chosen people, like Israel of old, displacing those who had proved faithless.[9] Now the English were under a similar judgement and threat. In the face of this spiritual challenge, and addressing an existing friend whom he obviously respected, Alcuin directed a formidable pastoral charge to the new Archbishop, urging him to be a true pastor and preacher, and no time-server. He was to monitor the administration of justice and not to fall silent. He was to maintain his reading and to stand in prayer as a mediator between God and men. His office was to be a light to the *whole* of Britain, an interesting emphasis that occurs elsewhere in Alcuin's thinking. He asserted: 'there is a distinction between secular and spiritual power: one carries the sword in hand to administer death, while the other holds the key to life in its tongue.' Secular power should therefore defend the Church, while spiritual power should guide it and intercede for it.[10]

This long and major letter reveals the range and depth of Alcuin's theology of the episcopate, as well as his expectations of the Archbishop of Canterbury as head of the English Church, with an active influence in political affairs and the confidence of the overlord Offa. It is a letter studded with citations from the Bible, revealing the way in which Alcuin was so adroit at welding together both the Old and the New Testaments to develop a cogent political and pastoral theology.[11] There is no sense that he regarded Canterbury itself as being under any immediate threat of Viking attack at that time, however. He distilled his vision in the elegant poem with which the letter concludes, which expressed the special place which Canterbury held in his heart and mind as the mother church of English Christianity. It was also a tribute to Ethelheard, who would remain a good friend until the end of Alcuin's life, as well as to the community at Canterbury, which by implication Alcuin seems to have known well. The poem is likely to have been carefully composed well before the sack of Lindisfarne, probably to mark the enthronement of the new Archbishop, whose nomination Alcuin seems to have supported.[12]

> *City of the eternal God, salt of the earth, light of the world!*
> *Twelve are the signs of the zodiac and the months of the year,*
> *Twelve also are the hours of the day and the jewels in the crown of Christ.*
> *Your tongue can open or close heaven itself.*
> *Teachers of life, great ones wielding the medicine of salvation,*
> *Living fountains of life and sacred rivers of Paradise.*
> *You are the glory of the Church, the hope of the people, the door of life:*
> *A distinguished race and the noble temple of Solomon.*
> *Through you, O fathers, all Britain now flourishes,*
> *Full of virtue and merits in our time.*
> *With one mind you defend the strongholds of Christ:*
> *With the shield of faith you overcome the webs of evil.*
> *I, Alcuin, say this, one who is devoted to your love.*
> *May you fare well forever, beloved shepherds and fathers;*
> *And may you, holy father Ethelheard, devoted priest,*
> *Prosper and flourish forever by Christ's grace.* [13]

It is however, in his letters to the monastic communities of Monkwearmouth-Jarrow and Lindisfarne that Alcuin reveals his innermost feelings, and also his beliefs about monastic life, which he always encouraged (even if his own life was only partly monastic) and whose principles he was eager now to reassert in response to the catastrophe. In a letter written to the monks at Monkwearmouth-Jarrow shortly after the attack on Lindisfarne in the summer of 796, Alcuin speaks of his deep love of the place and his spiritual affinity with it.[14] Its library must have been an important source of his knowledge in addition to the one at York. He cites words from the first book of Augustine's *De Doctrina Christiana* about the four natures of love and calls for unity in the life of the community: 'for God is a God of peace and love.' He urges fidelity to the rule established by their saintly founders, Benedict Biscop and Ceolfrith, emphasising the significance of the monastic vow as the foundation for personal and communal stability. The rule is to be expounded in English so that all may understand it. Integrity of religion is the only defence against enemies, within and without. Alluding to the recent attack on Lindisfarne only some sixty miles north on the same North Sea coast he said, 'you also live by the coast whence this pestilence arose.' Alcuin asserts that 'it is because of interior enemies that external ones gain the upper hand.' This was his theodicy, his explanation for the sudden upheaval of their life, as well as of the travails afflicting the Northumbrian Kingdom and its Church.[15]

As in his letter to the King, Alcuin drew a biblical parallel with enemies coming from the north. He condemned meanwhile the lure of luxury and entertainment, lavish clothes and hunting, citing the authority of Gregory the Great on the matter. The monks were to cherish their rich inheritance of books instead and, remembering Bede, to make sure that the young were properly educated: 'for he who does not learn while young can hardly teach when old.' The pupils are 'to open the books, recognise the letters and understand their sense.' This letter is therefore an important clue to Alcuin's own inner psychology in coping with the implications of the sack of Lindisfarne. His first reaction was to return to the roots of his own formation in faith and theology, remembering a community from which he drew much inspiration. What other foundations were there for faith apart from the living tradition of a holy place, which was also a precious centre of learning? He wrote to keep up morale, his own, as well as that of his readers.

Alcuin wrote to Higbald, Bishop of Lindisfarne and head of the community there, shortly after the attack in the summer of 793 in another letter, and also in a lengthy poem.[16] He recalls his fond memories of the island and expresses his grief at their calamity. His letter and his poem are haunted by his anxiety about the apparent abandonment of the English Church by its saints.[17] Once again he could only counsel fidelity to the footsteps of the fathers in order to achieve security by their prayers. Divine chastisement could be seen as a sign of divine love, however, and Alcuin recalled the devastation of places in history such as Jerusalem and Rome, and more recently much of Europe, and their eventual recovery. The exemplary role of the Bishop was pivotal: 'Let Christ be clothed and fed in the person of the poor . . . for the redemption of humanity is true riches . . . so love should be for what is eternal.' The bishop's role was a form of martyrdom, a spiritual warfare in the front line.[18] This was a brave defiance of the situation, an expression of hope against hope. Meanwhile Alcuin promised to approach Charlemagne to seek his intervention in order to secure the release of monks and others taken captive from Lindisfarne to the continent.

In his poem about the sack of Lindisfarne, Alcuin develops the themes of his letter to the full.[19] It comprises a sustained blend of biblical and classical themes, reflecting on the changing fortunes of the world of nature and the history of mankind. His view of the transitoriness of human achievement and glory is coloured by the Wisdom literature in the Bible, notably Ecclesiastes. It may also reflect knowledge of Boethius' *De Consolatione Philosophiae*, evidence of which certainly appears in some of Alcuin's later writings. At the heart of this conspectus lies the haunting question, posed in reflection upon the attacks of the Huns on Western Europe: 'Why, Jesus, do you permit such events in the world? Your judgement is so obscure – I cannot discern it.'[20] Alcuin drew the sad conclusion that no-one can put their trust in the permanence of joy: saints are forged only in affliction. He prays that his readers will love Christ more than gold. He reminds the community of their inheritance and of the miracles wrought by their saints Aidan and Cuthbert, as Bede recorded. Alcuin regarded the violent death of some of the monks as a form of martyrdom and he encouraged Higbald to 'bear Christ's sad burden with patience,' taking Job as his example.[21] It is a fine and moving poem, probably intended more for private contemplation than the letter, which it exceeds in length. They both reveal the depth of Alcuin's sorrow, compassion and faith.[22] Alcuin's concern also included individual friends, such as the priest Cudrad, now a lucky fugitive from the stricken island community.[23] He urged him to consider taking up a solitary and contemplative life, sending greetings through him to others of his brethren, while drawing comfort from the stories of Jonah and Job in the Bible, and commending him to the prayers of St Cuthbert.

What emerges from these letters and this important poem is the forging of a full-blown eschatological dimension to Alcuin's vision: he was witnessing, he believed, in his own times, in the tragic events befalling his homeland, the biblical pattern of divine judgement heralding the End. This perspective coloured much of his correspondence in the last decade of his life. Addressing both churchmen and rulers, using a similar theological vocabulary of morality and warning, Alcuin fearlessly applied the template of biblical history to the choices confronting his contemporaries. 'The opposition between the riches of this world and interior wealth, the ephemeral character of political power, the *rationem reddere* – giving of account – as the horizon determining all political action, the overwhelming moral responsibility of the ruler and the teleological implications of his power, these are the *leitmotivs* which pervade these letters, whether they be addressed to religious figures or to rulers – *potentes*.'[24] The important thing to note is that they emerge in dialogue with those already well known to Alcuin in England. They reflect therefore an established framework of Christian political morality, whose roots lay in the approach of Bede in his *History,* and before that in the teaching and letters of Gregory the Great.[25] Christian history in all its turbulence was to be seen and endured *sub specie aeternitatis,*[26] for which it was an all too brief and precarious preparation. In this as in much else, Alcuin was a true disciple of Augustine, whose great book on this theme, the *City of God,* became one of the common bonds between him and Charlemagne.

York

Alcuin's letters to the community of the church in York during the last decade of his life abroad have to be seen against the double background of his own intimate association with the place, which has already been discussed, and his mounting anxiety about the turbulent course of political affairs in the Northumbrian Kingdom and its impact on the church. In a letter already discussed and probably written in the year 794, Alcuin waxed nostalgic about his debt to their nurture of him from his childhood and youth.[27] He reported his prayers for them during his pilgrimage to 'the shrines of the holy martyrs and confessors of Christ,' probably in Rome. He pledged his loyalty to them in glowing terms: 'O most beloved fathers and brothers, remember me, for I will be yours, whether in life or death.' It is in this letter that he expressed for the first time his hope to be buried in York, sensing perhaps that he might not be, and mentioning the friend of their youth, Seneca. As in his letters to Lindisfarne and Monkwearmouth-Jarrow, he emphasised fidelity to the paths of the saints, 'our predecessors', whose memory and significance he had extolled at length in his York poem, urging his friends not to succumb to the blandishments of a life of luxury, drinking and lavish dress: 'Let the discipline of life under rule order your lives.'[28] This letter was followed by another in response to correspondence received from his friend Eanbald, who would become Archbishop of York in 796. Alcuin's feeling of absence was keenly expressed and his letters became surrogates for the personal meetings and communication that he so missed. This sense of loss focused on the relics of the saints of York, their common fathers in God, whose footsteps they were called to follow. Charity and prayer are the foundations of the common life and angels frequent the hours of prayer, as Bede had taught. The pressure of secular life and its brazen prosperity were the particular form of martyrdom to which they were now subject. Alcuin prays for them as a devoted son, moved by compunction as well as by his friendship for them. Taken together, these two letters reveal the strength of the bond between Alcuin and his community; but they reveal also the beginning of a process of growing apart, which he reluctantly accepted with unease, and in due time with regret.

Alcuin retained a close friendship with both Archbishops of York, Eanbald I and his successor Eanbald II. He wrote, perhaps in 794, to Archbishop Eanbald, his contemporary and fellow-disciple, about whom he had received news from the younger Eanbald, to explain why illness and

Charlemagne's absence at war in Saxony had prevented him from returning home as planned.[29] His devotion to the older Eanbald is evident, as is his concern for his succession, which Alcuin clearly considered was imminent. His anxiety concerned any plundering of the church's lands during an interregnum, or attempts to prevent a free election of his successor. He reminded him that his days were numbered and that all human glory is transient and flees like a shadow.[30] He signed off by describing Eanbald as his 'most beloved father'. It is a moving letter of valediction to one whose face Alcuin would dearly love to have seen again. Closely associated with it is a short letter to a sick bishop or abbot accompanying medicine, sent by Alcuin via his younger friend Eanbald. In it he laments the death of their mutual friend and doctor, Basil, while on a pilgrimage to Rome.[31]

Another letter to the community of the church of York, written in 795, addressed the matter of the election of a new archbishop head on.[32] Alcuin was anxious about an election being completed before he could get home, and he warned them in no uncertain terms against the sin of simony – bribery to gain ecclesiastical office. He described it as the worst form of heresy.[33] Citing the example of Judas, Alcuin described such corruption as violation of the Church as the Bride of Christ: 'for Christ and the Church are one Body.' His tone is quite shrill and his sentences are brief and to the point: Alcuin wrote here as if he were speaking directly. It may imply that he sensed that things were slipping and that he was powerless to avert something lamentable from happening. The election of Eanbald II as Archbishop of York may in the end have been soundly conducted. But the fact that Alcuin had to write in this abrupt and forceful manner belies his unease at unhelpful influences affecting the community back home. It implies that he was still an active player in the affairs of the church in York even while he was away; but it might imply also that his advice, while heard, was not necessarily heeded in his absence by his friends. It would certainly indicate that there was considerable wealth circulating in York at that time, affecting the integrity of the church's life. Whether it reflects a frustrated hope for his own election as Archbishop of York is not at all clear and is probably unlikely; he was anyway not free at that moment to return to England.

Alcuin wrote a long and warm letter to his former pupil Eanbald II on his election and consecration on 15th August 796 as Archbishop of York, describing himself as his spiritual father.[34] He recalled their common inheritance of 'the treasury of wisdom' created by their beloved Archbishop and mentor, Aelberht. Alcuin poured a great deal into this letter, revealing his vision of episcopacy and his high hopes for his younger friend. The letter implies that Eanbald was in his forties, as Alcuin reminds him that the normal span of life was only fifty years. Its message may be summed up in the injunction: 'Be a model of salvation to all.'[35] Alcuin warned Eanbald against pressures to exercise a secular pattern of patronage, giving way to the claims of kinship. Instead the Archbishop was to care for the poor and pilgrims, safeguarding the work of the guesthouse in York. The letter contains no less than twenty-one citations of Scripture: it is a formidable pastoral charge. Eanbald was to wear the *pallium*[36] as Archbishop only with the support of deacons, and he was to teach and uphold Roman liturgical practices and customs. He was to segregate the masters from their pupils, safeguarding their concentration in order to master books, liturgical chant and the work of the scriptorium. Alcuin promised his support from afar, mindful of his own advancing age. His letter was to be a token of friendship and spiritual guidance – the voice of a spiritual father. In a subsequent letter, written shortly after, Alcuin referred to this earlier letter, expressing anxiety about the influence on the Archbishop of apparent 'friends', whose ambitions might be more secular in their intent. He warned Eanbald that not all friends make good advisers.[37]

Another cluster of letters to and concerning Eanbald II date from the last part of Alcuin's life when he was far from well, being written in the years 800-801, when the Archbishop was clearly under some pressure. According to the annals recorded later by Simeon of Durham, there was conflict within the ruling Northumbrian elite, and also vast gales and floods in the winter of 800. In 801, war broke out between Northumbria and Mercia, which was only brought to a negotiated end by the intervention of the bishops.[38]

In a letter written in the spring of 801, Alcuin offered encouragement and commiseration in equal measure by letter to his beleaguered friend and Archbishop in his illness, reminding him that all the saints passed through tribulation in this world.[39] Alcuin had a lively sense of heaven as the true goal of all human labours and relationships. The letter is also interesting because of the gifts sent by Alcuin via his friend and disciple, Cuculus Dodo: they included wine, a hundred pounds of tin for the cathedral roof, drinking vessels, and bells for domestic use. Eanbald had asked Alcuin for more up to date Mass books, to which he received a brisk response, asking whether he did not already have an ample supply of Roman sacramentaries: 'Why was it necessary to pursue novelties when the old books sufficed?' Once again Alcuin urged fidelity to Roman practice by all in York. Eanbald was also to insist on regular reading of the Bible by his clergy, 'lest our work in collecting so many books should perish' from disuse. Alcuin's personal conclusion was 'that a multitude of wise men is the health of the world and the praise of a city.' Mindful of his own unremitting illness, he drew comfort from the faithfulness and labours of his disciple the Archbishop.

Closely related to this letter is another, written around the same time to Eanbald, reporting the visit of Archbishop Ethelheard of Canterbury to Alcuin's own monastic cell at St Josse-sur-Mer on the Channel coast, accompanied by two fellow-bishops and others *en route* to Rome.[40] Alcuin referred directly to the political difficulties experienced by the Archbishop of York with King Eardulf of Northumbria, urging him to stand firm, but indicating his fear that his situation may have arisen from his harbouring some of the King's enemies: 'Do not think of flight, but hope for the crown.'[41]

Alcuin reminds him of earlier rulers who fell foul of the Church and duly perished. He sees the Archbishop as a general leading the forces of Christ in a spiritual battle. He speaks again of his sense of his own impending death, and confirms news already sent by Cuculus that he has retired on health grounds from the active pastoral care of the monastery at Tours. This letter was supported by one directly to Cuculus and another disciple and friend, Calvinus.[42] Alcuin urged them to assist the harassed Archbishop. 'Let him take care that there be in him no other cause of trial than his preaching of the truth,' words that imply unease that Eanbald might have been compromised in some way by political entanglements, or by his desire for wealth, or on account of the size of his armed retinue. 'He has, as I hear, far more retainers than his predecessors had.' Was Eanbald turning into a second Wilfrid, provoking the King and his nobility to jealousy and unease?

More light is shed on this situation in a long letter to Calvinus, who was described as living in the cell of St Stephen, possibly at York, where he seems to have been a senior cleric of some influence.[43] Alcuin alludes to the material wealth in and around the York church, which threatens the true wealth of Christian life: the care of the poor and of pilgrims, and the cultivation of learning. In the midst of this there was the need to support Archbishop Eanbald, whom Calvinus had helped to elect in the face of his adversaries 'both wolves and serpents.' He was to warn him about the dangers of worldliness, flattery and the claims of kinsmen: 'It is surely better to have Christ as friend and kin.' Calvinus was to read carefully and repeatedly Pope Gregory I's *Pastoral Rule* alongside the Bible. He was to be a light in the house of God by which many might be illuminated. He was to inscribe the gospel and the Psalms in his heart, and especially that of John, for which Alcuin was preparing a commentary which he would send him when it was complete. 'Discretion is the mother of all virtues among monks . . . for in all things temperance is to be served, which is the royal way of our whole life.'

These letters are all that remain now; but they were probably part of a rich correspondence between Tours and York that persisted until the end of Alcuin's life. It is sad that none remain directed to Alcuin. But they afford a valuable window into the world of his friendship, into the range and depth of his theology and pastoral experience, and into his abiding loyalty to the place he regarded as home.

York was probably commemorated in the beautiful poem that he wrote at Tours towards the end of his life, beginning *O mea cella*, lamenting the lost world of his youth, with its congenial companions and love of learning.[44] Its authenticity is no longer in doubt, though there is debate whether it describes York or Aachen, or whether it portrays some idealised location rich in association, a *locus amoenus*, embodying the ideal of the spiritual life and the pursuit of learning.[45] It is close in spirit in some ways to his poem lamenting the sack of Lindisfarne, both of them capturing a wistful sense of lost security and apprehension about the future. Both poems are monuments to a transmutation of faith from something certain and seen in some sense, to something more fragile and unseen. 'The two elements of admonition and of underlying uncertainty which can be discerned in these poems distinguish them . . . from the overriding optimism of his epic poem on York . . . Stunned by the devastation of Lindisfarne, Alcuin recognised that even the ability of the saints to defend their own might be doubted.'[46] This mood can also be detected in his many letters from this time, as has been shown.

The poem itself paints a rich picture of a cell set in a garden, a rural Arcadia full of life and beauty and music, an enclosure probably modelled in part on the Song of Songs in the Bible, but drawing on the classical tradition of a *locus amoenus*.[47] 'A key feature of Alcuin's landscape is its stability.'[48] In a letter to Charlemagne, written from Tours in 797, Alcuin described York as a garden of learning from which he wished to retrieve some of his books, with the King's permission.[49] It draws directly upon the Song of Songs, wishing that as York was a 'garden enclosed', so Tours might become a place full of 'the plants of Paradise', full of fruit, an orchard in which God might be encountered as the Beloved One.[50] The parallels of language and imagery between the letter and the poem are striking. In the poem *O mea cella* the place in Alcuin's mind and memory is portrayed as a lost paradise, where the big book of nature shed radiant light on the little book of the Bible: 'for in you sounded the beloved voice of the teacher, handing on with sacred utterance the books of wisdom.'[51] In such a place liturgy and learning, love and prayer, were intermingled.

Now, however, all had changed and Alcuin the poet has changed too. *Ichabod* – the glory has departed, taking with it the inspiration of the poets. 'Nothing remains eternal, nothing is truly unchanging: murky night obscures holy day.'[52] Alcuin probably portrays himself when he describes 'an old man leaning wearily on his stick' watching the scenes of his youth recede. In the spirit of Boethius, he lamented the transience of all things, reaching out solely and forlornly to the love of Christ, who in his mercy is 'our glory, life and salvation.' Both faith and hope now have to reach beyond this life and experience, yearning for the safe haven of the love of Christ. It is a most lovely and reflective poem, one that recalls in its ending the *Confessions* of Augustine. It encapsulates Alcuin's sensitivity and aspirations as he sensed the waning of his earthly life with all its memories and loves.

> *How wretched we are! O world, why do we love you, ever fugitive?*
> *You flee from us, always rushing onwards.*
> *Flee away then, ever fleeing one!*
> *Let us always love Christ:*
> *May the love of God hold fast our hearts!*
> *May He, who is loyal and tender, defend His servants from their dreadful foe,*
> *By snatching our hearts towards heaven.*
> *Let us praise and love Him equally with our whole heart:*
> *For He alone in His kindness is our glory, life, and salvation.*

Chapter 4

Alcuin and Offa

The letters that reveal most about Alcuin's personal political influence in England and his aspirations are those that he wrote to members of the Mercian court, including to King Offa himself. While the Carolingians were establishing their ascendancy on the continent in the eighth century, Offa was creating a powerful and dictatorial *imperium* that dominated southern England and which posed a powerful challenge to Northumbria, whose power was gradually declining in Alcuin's later years partly as a result of internal strife. Connections between the two English kingdoms were close, both politically and ecclesiastically. Alcuin was not unusual therefore in having links with both societies. But in the later part of his life, from the time of the visit by the papal legates to England in 786 onwards, his ties to Mercia appear to have become closer, and they persisted during his time on the continent. As a result he found himself sometimes participating in diplomatic exchanges between Charlemagne and Offa, who sustained an uneasy amity.[1] To some extent Alcuin's own hopes, and perhaps his loyalties also as an Englishman, began to switch from Northumbria to Mercia before the traumatic events of 796.

One of the outcomes of the papal visitation in 786 was the anointing of Offa's son, Ecgfrith, as co-ruler and, in order to achieve this, the creation of an additional primatial see at Lichfield, at the heart of Offa's domains. Offa's relationships with Jaenberht, Archbishop of Canterbury, were bad, partly because of resistance in Kent to his rule with which the Archbishop was implicated. Offa's own nomination as Archbishop in 792, Ethelheard, had a rough ride as a result. The creation of an amenable archbishopric under his direct sway was a comprehensible proposition, and reflected the new political realities in England, even if it transgressed the blue-print laid down by Gregory the Great as recorded by Bede in his *History*. The legatine decrees articulated the sacrosanct nature of anointed monarchy in return for close co-operation between a king and his bishops. Both these developments were ratified at a 'contentious' synod held at Chelsea on the Thames shortly after the legates' departure, in 787, and both shadowed comparable happenings within the Carolingian realm. For in 781, Pope Hadrian had anointed the sons of Charlemagne, Pippin and Louis, as co-rulers of Italy and Aquitaine in their father's lifetime, even as Charlemagne himself had been anointed alongside his brother Carloman by Pope

A silver coin of Cenwulf of Mercia (796 - 821).

Stephen III on his visit to St Denis in 754. Offa, like the Carolingians, was obsessed by the need for legitimacy, generating suitable coinage and an elaborate genealogy to assert this as well as leaving his great Dyke along the Welsh border as a mark forever on the landscape of the assertion of his power.[2] Alcuin himself was in Rome in 780 to collect the *pallium* for Archbishop Eanbald I of York, encountering Charlemagne at the Lombard capital, Pavia, on his way back to England, when he was invited to join the Carolingian court, according the *Life of Alcuin*.[3] Whether he actually witnessed the papal anointing of the two princes in 781 is unclear and seems unlikely; but he would certainly have known about it and probably sensed its potency and significance.

Friends at the Mercian court

A letter written by Alcuin to a nun called Hundrad at the Mercian court around the year 795 reveals how close he was to members of the royal family, notably to Offa's Queen Cynethrith and her anointed son Ecgfrith, who would shortly if briefly succeed his father.[4] He regarded this nun as a pillar of integrity, living a devout religious life under rule in the midst of the court. She was to be his emissary to the Queen, to whom he pledged his personal loyalty. Ecgfrith may perhaps have been a pupil of Alcuin's for a time, for he wrote to him earlier at some length about his duties in the wake of his anointing as co-ruler. He urged him to learn from his parents' example which was tactfully summed up as 'authority from your father and piety from your mother.'[5] This letter was an epitome of a whole tradition of moral advice to Christian rulers, recalling the example of Solomon in the Bible, and quoting words from Proverbs: 'A wise son is the glory of his father.'[6] It would seem that Ecgfrith was still quite young, probably an adolescent, whom Alcuin had to warn against the excesses of luxury and a 'rural lifestyle', which meant too much hunting, reminding him that he had been born in a palace not a barn! He signed off by addressing the prince as his 'most dear son', though Alcuin usually began his letters to such royal contacts by describing himself as a humble deacon.

  Alcuin's closest friendship seems to have been with one of Offa's daughters, Ethelburh, who was an abbess, to whom he wrote several letters.[7] In the first of the letters[8] Alcuin encouraged her commitment to the celibate life by reference to passages in the *Apocalypse*,[9] reminding her that one who conquered nature would share fellowship with the Creator of all. He upheld the angelic vocation of virginity despite the social pressures upon a young princess. Subsequent letters to her were occasioned by the murder of King Ethelred of Northumbria on 18 April 796, whose widowed Queen, Ethelfled, was sister to Ethelburh. Alcuin expressed the hope that she would follow her sister into the relative safety of religious life. He expressed also his horror at what had befallen his homeland, to which he now feared to return, recalling the lamentations of Jeremiah in the Bible. He also asked her to pray for him and for Charlemagne's Queen, Liudgard, whose friendship would be both honourable and useful to her, and who had sent her a dress as a gift. As a token of his spiritual friendship for her he sent her an *ampulla* and a paten for use at the Eucharist. He asked her to use it regularly at the altar with a prayer for him: *Christe miserere Alcuini servuli tui*, asserting apostolic authority for receiving Holy Communion daily.

Alcuin's final remaining letter to her reflected more troubled times in both kingdoms, Mercia and Northumbria, as both kings, Cenwulf and Eardulf, brought pressure to bear upon her and her interests. [10] This reveals well the vulnerability of female members of Anglo-Saxon royal families, even if they were professed nuns. [11] In response Alcuin poured forth a torrent of biblical references to support his friend in her tribulations, saying that: 'The Cross is to be borne so that by patience tribulation might be overcome.' [12] She was clearly being put under pressure to renounce her vows and to marry. Alcuin reminded her again of her heavenly loyalty and vocation. He addressed her disappointment at being unable to make a pilgrimage, probably to Rome, urging her instead to use the money to care for the poor. These are quite intimate letters, revealing Alcuin's close friendship with the princess and her immediate family, whose affairs had been plunged into insecurity by the murder of the Northumbrian King and then the death of Offa himself and shortly after of his son, all in the fateful year of 796.

It is in this context that Alcuin's letters to Etheltrudis, the mother of King Ethelred of Northumbria are best appreciated. She was by now abbess of a nunnery, perhaps at Crowland, and his first letter was clearly written to her before her son's murder in 796. [13] It reflects a mature and established relationship with an older woman who had perhaps afforded Alcuin some patronage at the Northumbrian court. It is an interesting letter because of the way he addressed her with a carefully composed piece of pastoral theology, supported by numerous biblical references. [14] It is interesting too because it reflects the ease with which he wrote to noble women about theology and their moral duties: this in turn sheds light on their influence behind the scenes at court and in the Church. Pastoral rule mirrored political authority and her duties now were a continuation of her royal ones, but in a different context. Alcuin charged her to cultivate the love of God in her heart not secular ambition in her mind. He also warned her against lapsing back into a luxurious lifestyle: 'for Christ was buried in a tomb, not a temple.' It was a robust line of argument, taking seriously her intelligence and status. It reflects her own grasp of Christian theology that he was able to write to her so easily in these terms. This quality of dialogue between intellectual equals reflects also the richness of lay devotional life in Mercia and Northumbria in the eighth century, which found expression in the prayer-books that emerged from this period, such as the *Book of Cerne* and the *Nunnaminster Codex*.

The strength of Alcuin's relationship with Etheltrudis enabled him to write a very different letter after the murder of her son, Ethelred, briefly king of Northumbria in 796.[15] Once again it has a dozen biblical references, this time designed to comfort a mother in her loss and to give some spiritual direction to her in her bereavement. He urged her to receive comfort from Christ in place of her murdered son. He hinted that perhaps the King had died as a result of his sins, for which her intercessions and almsgiving could make amends, reminding her, not altogether felicitously, of the penitent thief on the cross in the gospels. Her grief could assuage her son's sins, for 'large and unfathomable indeed is the mercy of our Lord Jesus Christ.' Her generosity was the best memorial for her son, for 'we should be trustees of this age and not the possessors of it.' Her untimely loss was a call to her own repentance and spiritual preparation. It was a bold and heart-felt letter to an old friend from someone who felt the deeper implications of such a murder, and feared them too.

Alcuin was clearly in contact with a number of bishops and nobility in the Mercian Kingdom. Three letters are particularly interesting. The first was addressed to a priest called Beornwine, written from Francia before the death of Offa in 796, in which Alcuin professed his continued loyalty to the King despite his absence abroad.[16] It reflects the difficulty experienced in moving from realm to realm without creating suspicion, and also the uneasy relations between the Mercian King and Charlemagne with regard to harbouring enemies who had fled abroad. Alcuin was not to be numbered among such company.[17] But he alludes to some earlier disagreements and hopes that his friend will make peace and exert a positive influence on his behalf. The context of this letter remains obscure however.

In another letter, written in 797 after the sudden death of Offa's son, King Ecgfrith, Alcuin addressed the bishop of Leicester, Speratus,[18] who had been one of the signatories to the decrees of the papal legates in 786.[19] It was a weighty letter to someone of substance in Mercian church and society, sombre in its tone with regard to the upheavals of the day, and anticipating imminent divine judgement. Alcuin exhorted his friend, and possibly a former pupil,[20] to stand firm and to speak out: for the tongue of a bishop was a key to the kingdom of heaven. He urged him to read frequently the *Pastoral Care* of Gregory the Great as the indispensable guide to being a bishop. In his reference to the recent death of the young King, he rather cryptically alluded to Offa's hopes that had now been dashed, reflecting on the uncertainty of human planning in secular affairs. He concluded by reminding the bishop of his duty towards the poor, while cautioning him against keeping too large a retinue. The letter closes with a four line poem of commendation in which Alcuin asked for the prayers of his friend.

The third letter was sent to another signatory of the legatine decrees, the nobleman Osbert, also in 797.[21] It is a very revealing letter of considerable historical significance and it clearly rests upon a close and strong alliance of friendship between Alcuin and Osbert. Alcuin expressed sympathy for the political crisis that had engulfed Mercia after the death of Offa and his son, placing it within the wider context of the deterioration of affairs elsewhere in England, some of which he traced back to the manner of Offa's rule. 'For truly that noble young man [Ecgfrith] did not die for his own sins, but out of revenge for the bloodshed by which his late father sought to secure the Kingdom for his heirs. This has proved not the girding of his Kingdom but its undoing.' Alcuin expected Osbert to wield a strong and positive influence in both Mercia and Northumbria over their new kings, Cenwulf and Eardulf, steering them in a Christian and moral direction, urging them to maintain their marriages. Alcuin was scathing about the ease with which Eardulf had apparently set aside his lawful wife for a mistress. He drew a very pessimistic general conclusion: 'It seems that to some extent the happiness of the English is coming to an end.' Repentance and moral reform were the only hope, and Alcuin referred to the legacy of laws left by Offa 'of blessed memory'. The internecine strife that was pulling down Northumbria was an awful warning. But Alcuin remained uncertain whether the new king, Cenwulf, would be amenable to such advice.

What this letter reveals is Alcuin's ambivalence towards Offa, whom he admired as a strong and effective king and law-giver, while not mincing his words – after his death at least – about his ruthlessness. Yet could any king at that time be strong without being ruthless? Charlemagne was the same. For without the protection of law backed by force, the life of the Church, learning and education could hardly survive. Alcuin was caught in a moral dilemma, and ever haunted by the fragility of society as he experienced and sensed it on both sides of the Channel, as his letters and some of his poems make clear. He was therefore a critical and sometimes rather fraught friend to those in authority, racked by the discrepancy between political realities and the demands of divine order. It is perhaps remarkable that his fearless, and at times prophetic criticisms, were tolerated and preserved in his letters as exemplars. Political rule that was at times quite arbitrary and bloody did not quench his freedom of speech; and this must reflect something creditable and moral about the Christian rulers whom he felt able thus to address. His letters reflect a universe of discourse that subjected political affairs to well-informed moral and theological critique, a lively dialogue between elite laity, both men and women, and some of their more educated clergy, about the implementing of Christian values in a turbulent society. Alcuin did not stand or speak alone in his fearless articulation of Christian theology in its bearing upon politics and morality but neither was what he said repudiated or, it seems, resented. Whether it would be heeded however was another matter, for then as now politics was the art of the possible, and also often the expedient too, as kings themselves seldom felt secure for very long and life was short.

Offa

Alcuin's correspondence with Offa himself has to be placed within the context of other letters that remain between Charlemagne and the Mercian king. One concerned a 'Scottish' (i.e. Irish) priest working in Cologne, who had scandalised people by eating flesh in Lent and whom the bishop wished sent home to be disciplined. Charlemagne described himself as King of the Franks 'by the grace of God' and the 'defender' of the Holy Church of God, and he addressed Offa as his beloved brother and friend.[22] The other letter asked Ethelheard, the Archbishop of Canterbury whom Charlemagne had met, to intercede with Offa on behalf of some exiles from England who had followed lord Hringstan abroad and whom the Frankish king had sheltered 'for the sake of reconciliation, not out of enmity.'[23] The point is that it is almost certain that these two letters were drafted by Alcuin himself, probably around the year 794, on behalf of the King, using his intimate knowledge of the political environment and persons to whom Charlemagne was writing.[24] The words, 'It is better to live in exile than to perish, to serve in a foreign land than to die in one's own,' proved prophetic for Alcuin himself after 796. No less striking was a brief letter which Alcuin sent to Offa in his own name at an unknown date but probably from abroad, commending one of his pupils of Mercian origin whom he was sending back at the King's request.[25] Alcuin asked the King to protect him from idleness and drink, and to provide him with pupils whom he was to teach with due diligence. Alcuin hailed Offa's commitment to education, acclaiming him as 'the glory of Britain, a trumpet of Christian proclamation, a sword and a shield against enemies' of the Church. He urged the king to obey the commandments of Christ and to pursue justice, love and mercy.

Alcuin's vision of Offa's vocation seems rather far-fetched perhaps in the light of how Offa actually conducted his affairs, political and ecclesiastical. What it reveals is that Alcuin regarded himself as in some way under Offa's patronage, even while abroad or away from Mercia.[26] He was clearly anxious to maintain his links and his reputation with the court of the pre-eminent king in his own homeland. In another letter to an unknown Mercian abbot, Alcuin promised to write to Offa on his behalf to ask him to protect him from lay persecution.[27] The most important evidence for Alcuin's close association with Offa was a letter written while he was in England, sometime it seems between the death of Archbishop Jaenberht of Canterbury in August 792 and the consecration of Offa's nominee, Ethelheard in July 793, confirming to the King that it was appropriate for the new Archbishop of Canterbury to be consecrated by the existing Archbishop of Lichfield, where Offa had created an additional primatial see in 788.[28] Citing precisely the plan of Gregory the Great as recorded in Bede's *History*, Alcuin clearly had no qualms about the novelty of Offa creating an additional archbishopric to the original ones of Canterbury and York. The point he makes explicitly to Offa is his duty to supervise an orderly consecration, as both southern archbishoprics lay within his Kingdom. Once consecrated, the new primate was to seek his *pallium* from Rome.

Two famous letters remain that are often cited. The first was directly from Alcuin to Offa shortly after news of the murder of King Ethelred of Northumbria had reached the court of Charlemagne in early summer, sometime after 18 April 796 and before Offa's own death at the end of July.[29] This assassination clearly touched a raw nerve and Alcuin reported directly Charlemagne's alarmed and angry reaction against 'that perfidious and perverse race, murderers of their lords.' The stability of Northumbria was of concern to him because of the important and lucrative trade route from the Ouse to the Rhine, and Charlemagne was a great business-man. But there was also fear in this remark, perhaps of a copy-cat assassination and the subversion of loyalty and fidelity that dogged even a strong ruler like Charlemagne, causing him to react so ruthlessly against the pretensions of his kinsman, Tassilo of Bavaria. Charlemagne immediately recalled the gifts that he had intended to send to the Northumbrian court and threatened dire action. Meanwhile Alcuin himself no longer felt secure about returning to a home that he described in dark colours, fortified by words of the prophet Isaiah in the Bible.[30] He feared lest his own return would contribute to disturbing 'the peace of my people', an interesting phrase which raises the question of whether his own close links to the royal family of the late King Ethelred, now plunged into mourning and grief, were too close, and that he was perhaps *persona non grata* with those taking over the reins of power.[31]

Instead, in this letter, he pinned his loyalty and hopes on Offa, shortly himself to die, pleading with him to rule justly so as not to provoke the divine wrath that had fallen upon Northumbria: for 'the throne of a kingdom is strengthened by truth and mercy'.[32] This letter began by mentioning the lavish gifts that Charlemagne was sending to Offa and his bishops; and it concluded with commendations to the Queen and to the heir apparent, Ecgfrith, vouching also for the *bona fides* of his own pupils who were accompanying the embassy from Charlemagne. For Alcuin was anxious at the start of the letter to assert Offa's good standing with the Frankish king, mentioning envoys sent to Rome for the judgement of the Archbishop of Canterbury, Ethelheard, and of the new Pope, Leo III.[33] The letter is also important because in it Alcuin reported that he had recently been given charge of the monastery of St Martin at Tours, where he would continue to pray for Offa, and where he would in the end die. There is pathos about this particular letter, inasmuch as both Offa and his cherished son would be dead within months of receiving it. It would be Alcuin's last personal letter to the King and it marked the beginning of his sense of involuntary exile from his homeland, Northumbria.

The second letter cannot have been sent much later in 796 and may actually have preceded the first or been drafted before it, because it mentions the gifts intended for Ethelred of Northumbria, and it seems to have been composed by Alcuin on behalf of Charlemagne, in whose name it was sent to Offa.[34] It is interesting because of its mode of composition, being a portmanteau of paragraphs addressing a range of topics that had clearly been the subject of earlier correspondence, to which allusion is made. It was also intended to establish peace between the rulers after a period of some economic disputes. The first item concerned the *bona fides* of pilgrims on their way from England to Rome, challenging the subterfuge of certain merchants 'seeking gain, not serving religion,' and trying to evade royal tolls in Francia. The second sought to put royal protection of merchants in each country on an equal and reciprocal footing. The third item related to certain exiles from England, whom Charlemagne had sent on to Rome for adjudication by the Archbishop of Canterbury, Ethelheard, who was then with the Pope. Then there is a fascinating glimpse of Offa's building activities, as his request for special black stones, probably some form of rare marble, from the royal quarries abroad, was granted. In return he was to guarantee English cloth lengths that had been recently curtailed. Finally Charlemagne explained that the gifts that he was sending to the Mercian and Northumbrian courts and to the English bishops were intended to secure their intercessions for Pope Hadrian, 'our father and your friend', who had died on Christmas day 795. They included 'a belt, a Hunnish sword and two silk palls' for Offa personally, part of the great Avar treasure that Charlemagne had obtained in his victory over them in 795.[35] There is a third letter which corroborates these and completes the picture.[36] It was written by Alcuin himself to the English bishops, deploring the murder of the Northumbrian King in 796 and asking them to pray for Charlemagne as well as for the soul of the late Pope Hadrian. He urged them 'to preach truthfully, correct in a virile manner, and to exhort persuasively,'[37] concluding his letter by affixing his own seal to vouch for its authenticity, presumably his seal as the new Abbot of Tours.

This trio of letters affords a vivid and fascinating insight into relations between Mercia and the Kingdom of Charlemagne at the end of the eighth century, referring as they to do to regular correspondence and many points of economic and political contact and exchange. They reflect also the close relationship that Alcuin enjoyed with Charlemagne, which helped to secure their preservation. Taken alongside the Northumbrian annals included within the writings of Simeon of Durham,[38] which themselves contain a high level of information about Frankish affairs, they are a monument to the close community of interest that existed at many levels between the English kingdoms and the emergent *imperium* on the continent.[39] Alcuin's direct involvement in their composition reflects the trust in which he was held by parties on both sides of the Channel. They are steeped in his own theology of Christian political rule with which he framed what he had to say, either on his own behalf or that of Charlemagne.

They also mark the resolution of various disputes between Offa and Charlemagne that are recorded elsewhere. In the *Acts of the abbots of Fontenelle* (i.e. St Wandrille) there is report of how Abbot Gervold of St Wandrille, who administered royal trade taxes and tolls at the important port of Quentavic[40] and elsewhere along the Channel for Charlemagne, enjoyed a close friendship with Offa and acted as a trusted emissary for the Frankish King to and fro.[41] Around the year 790, Charlemagne proposed a marriage alliance with Offa, but on his terms.[42] Offa resisted this and insisted on a reciprocal arrangement, which enraged Charlemagne and led to a trade ban being imposed against English goods for a while, to which the English retaliated, until Gervold persuaded Charlemagne otherwise. This implies some parity of value to this trade across the Channel to Hamwic, near Southampton, and into the Thames estuary, past Thanet and Canterbury and on to London. It was clearly of great importance to both rulers, who profited from its control and the taxes it paid them.

Charlemagne was essentially a big business-man commanding huge resources and dominating the principal trade routes of Europe; and it was this preoccupation that determined his close interest in the stability of the English kingdoms, which he could influence but never control directly. The language of royal ideology backed by Christian theology cannot conceal this underlying reality, which was the source of the great wealth that he could command. Offa's drive to ascendancy in England had a similar motivation in addition to his desire to create a lasting dynasty. The quality of commissioned art remaining from this period and the building projects both kings indulged in, more obviously now from the Carolingian realm, but evident still in fragments remaining from Mercia at this time, reflects the scale of this intercourse of trade, craftsmen seeking patronage, and ideas. Alcuin was a direct beneficiary of this tide of wealth and a participant in it: the monastic houses that came his way in Francia all lay on important trade routes; and in case of Tours it had vast land-holdings.

Alcuin referred to such a trade dispute in a letter written early in 790 to his friend Colcu, an Irish cleric who may have been based for a time at York.[43] In it he gave a glowing account of Charlemagne's military successes on various fronts but refers with some anxiety to a 'certain dissension' between the two kings, whose causes were apparently unknown to him, 'so that on both sides the passage of ships has been forbidden to merchants and is ceasing.' English fear of exclusion from trade with the continent had its beginnings here and would prove perennial and endemic for centuries. Alcuin was also apprehensive that he and some others of his English friends might be drawn in as peace-makers. Perhaps they were, for in another letter written later in that year, when he was back in Northumbria assisting with the establishment of Ethelred as King there. Alcuin wrote to his friend Adalhard, Abbot of Corbie in northern Francia explaining his delay, reporting a settlement between Charlemagne and Offa, and encouraging the abbot to act as a peacemaker if necessary too: 'for we should be sowers of peace among Christian peoples.'[44]

Part of the background to this dispute was probably Offa's determination to dominate Kent against the wish of the Archbishop of Canterbury, Jaenberht and the people there: Canterbury was an important and lucrative *entrepot*, close to the Wantsum channel through which shipping passed safely into the Thames estuary, thus avoiding the perils of circumnavigating the Isle of Thanet. Dominance of Kent and Wessex gave Offa a monopoly of much of the trade across the Channel and so brought him face to face, as it were, with the Carolingian domain as a trading zone. Abbot Gervold found himself in the front line, as indeed did Alcuin as well when Charlemagne gave him the monastic cell of St Josse-sur-Mer near Quentavic, where most English traders and pilgrims landed.[45] Relations between these two ascendant kings even caused anxiety to Pope Hadrian in distant Rome at one stage, who heard rumours that they were colluding, allegedly at Offa's instigation, in his replacement by a Frankish nominee.[46] Had there been a land frontier there would have probably been war between Offa and Charlemagne: instead they squared off using trade and diplomacy as their weapons. Alcuin found himself, with others, squeezed at times between their conflicting interests. Yet some of the credit for their eventual amity, revealed in Alcuin's letters of 796, may lie at his door, as he clearly had the trust of both kings, and was strong enough to deal with them effectively, as well as to serve them as an articulate intermediary.

After Offa

The year 796 was calamitous for England and for Alcuin personally. The murder of Ethelred of Northumbria, the death of Offa himself, and barely six months later of his son, Ecgfrith, and the death of Archbishop Eanbald I of York left Alcuin feeling bereft and apprehensive about returning home to England: indeed he never did. But his contacts and concerns remained active as he reacted to the fall-out from these events. For several decades England was turbulent in its various kingdoms and this impacted upon the life and stability of the Church, as Alcuin lamented in his letters to his homeland. The fluctuating situation in England remained of concern to Charlemagne also, who some time after Alcuin's death in 804 had to intervene in 808 with the help of the Pope to restore Eardulf, King of Northumbria, acting as the overlord of all Christian people in Europe.[47] 'Towards the end of the eighth century, some sections of the Frankish political elite may have regarded Anglo-Saxon England as an outlying cog of the Frankish machine.'[48] This may in a way be comparable to the earlier relations between the Merovingian kings and Kent at the end of the sixth century, the time of the mission of Augustine to Canterbury, which occurred with Frankish support and in the context of an existing marriage alliance.[49] Now in a more developed political situation, Alcuin may well be seen as part of a process of active political affiliation, which was cemented by the elaborate exchange of gifts, contributing to it by his diplomatic skills and initiatives, while giving it theological and moral justification.[50] At stake were not only mutual economic interests, however, but also the authority of Christian kingship on both sides of the Channel, with all its moral implications for churchmen like Alcuin and those around him, and those who succeeded them. The inherent fragility of monarchical rule, evident in England in the last decade of the eighth century to Alcuin's chagrin, would be demonstrated dramatically on the continent in the years after the death of Charlemagne.

This concern is evident in the letter that Alcuin wrote to the new King of Northumbria, Eardulf.[51] In 790 he had had a narrow escape when captured by King Ethelred and nearly executed at Ripon.[52] Now he had returned from exile and been made King in the cathedral at York on 26th May 796; but as the northern annals indicate his reign was hardly secure. Alcuin appealed to their 'old friendship' and reminded the new King of the vicissitudes of fortune that he had experienced, urging him to put his trust in God as his best protector. Once again he cited the words of Proverbs: 'The throne of a kingdom shall be established in mercy and justice.'[53] He reminded Eardulf of the fate of many of his predecessors who had perished for their sins. All the recent calamities that had befallen Northumbria were signs of divine judgement. The King was therefore to labour wholeheartedly in pursuing the will of God for the salvation of his soul, the prosperity of his country as well as of the people committed to his charge. The letter contains Alcuin's theodicy and his moral theology of Christian kingship in a nutshell.

No less striking is the letter Alcuin wrote around the same time to the nobleman Osbald, who for a month had usurped the throne of Northumbria after the murder of Ethelred.[54] The royal household and his fellow noble conspirators deserted him, however, and he had to flee into exile, first to the island monastery of Lindisfarne and then among the Picts.[55] Alcuin reproached him for not fulfilling his command to him to become a monk two years earlier, which would have spared him his present plight: 'turn again and fulfil what you once vowed.' Alcuin challenged him to repent and seek the friendship of God rather than be condemned by association with king-slayers. 'Do not heap up sin by ravaging the land and spilling blood. Consider how much blood of kings, princes and ordinary people has been shed by you and your kinsmen.' These are extraordinary words that reflect vividly the turbulence and violence in Northumbria during these years, recorded in such detail in the northern annals.[56] Alcuin was armed with prophetic courage as he urged his former friend to repent and save his soul, and perhaps, by his example, some of his associates and kinsmen too. Osbald could not read, however, so Alcuin asked that his letter be read to him often as a reminder of Alcuin's care for him. Alcuin's prayers were clearly answered because the death of Osbald 'formerly an ealdorman and patrician, for a while a king, and finally an abbot' was recorded in the northern annals for the year 799: he was buried in the church of York.[57]

Alcuin wrote also to the new King of Mercia, Cenwulf, shortly after his accession at the end of 796. His concern was to put his kingship on a sound moral footing as Cenwulf lacked the legitimacy of dynastic succession. He was to summon wise counsellors and to take warning from the untimely death of his predecessor, Ecgfrith, and the general state of the country. He was to obey the Church because Christ alone was the true King who could exalt him as a ruler. There is more than a hint of reticence by Alcuin towards someone whom he may have regarded as an upstart of doubtful reputation, as he hinted in his letter to the Mercian nobleman, Osbert.[58] What is interesting is that a copy of this letter to Cenwulf was sent by Alcuin to his friend Paulinus of Aquilea at the same time, as parts of it appear word for word in his *Libellus exhortationis*, which was probably composed in 798. Alcuin's approach was once again rooted in Proverbs and the Psalms, insisting on mercy and truth as the foundations of kingly rule. He also appealed to the verdict of 'ancient histories'. Cenwulf was to be a ruler, pastor and dispenser of the gifts of God, rather than a lord and exploiter of his people. He was to respect and consider the laws and customs of his great predecessor Offa, supporting the good and prosecuting the wicked, and so enabling the Church to grow and advance. This letter was an epitome of Alcuin's admonitions about Christian kingship and its moral purpose, and that was no doubt the reason why he sent it to Paulinus as an exemplar.

When Cenwulf became King of Mercia there was immediately a rebellion in Kent against Mercian rule which caused Archbishop Ethelheard to flee. Alcuin roundly condemned this *demarche* from the safe distance of Tours, writing first to the church of Canterbury and the people of Kent.[59] After a long peroration urging them to maintain their pre-eminence as the fount of Christianity in England and a seat of learning, he warned them about the dangers of division and conflict, reminding them of the strictures of Gildas towards the faithless British. He urged them to recall their Archbishop and to ensure his safety, for it was not right that the See of St Augustine should be without its pastor. The rebellion soon collapsed and the Archbishop was able to return to his post, whereupon Alcuin wrote to him a stern remonstrance in 798, chiding him for his flight and questioning his motives, recalling the words of Christ about the duties of a good shepherd.[60] He encouraged him to read again the homilies of Gregory the Great and to do open penance with his people for such a dereliction of duty. Ethelheard was to give priority to establishing learning and singing in the community of Christ Church, the cathedral at Canterbury, and proving himself to be a true pastor of the flock. Once again Alcuin revealed his deep sympathy with the poor and his sense of a bishop's duty towards them. Then he turned to the vexed issue of the archbishopric of Lichfield, which he discerned had been created by a desire for power rather than more rational or principled considerations.[61] Alcuin urged proper consultation with the archbishop of

York and asked that the Archbishop of Lichfield, Hygberht, should not be humiliated by being deprived of the *pallium* in his lifetime, even if the consecration of new bishops reverted to the Archbishop of Canterbury. It was a careful letter, cautious about trespassing on a friendship, but frank and encouraging too. It is quite possible that Alcuin had a hand in resolving the matter behind the scenes, helping perhaps to secure the agreement of the Pope; for he wrote to Ethelheard in 802 congratulating him on the Pope's agreement to suppress Lichfield and to restore the ancient rights of Canterbury.[62] Earlier in 801 he wrote congratulating him on his successful collaboration with Archbishop Eanbald II of York, describing the two primates as the two eyes of the English church.[63] The significant thing is that it was Ethelheard who took the lead in resolving the matter peacefully, presiding over a synod of the southern province in 803.[64] Thereafter all new bishops in the southern province of England swore an oath to uphold the primacy of Canterbury.

Alcuin's friendship with Ethelheard was evident to the very end of his life. In 801 he wrote to Charlemagne commending Ethelheard and his companions on their way to Rome to resolve the dispute over the see of Lichfield.[65] The Archbishop was accompanied by a former thegn of King Offa called Ceolmund and also the faithful companion of the murdered King Ethelred of Northumbria, Torhtmund, who had avenged his lord's death.[66] Alcuin described them as 'very true friends to me and helpers on my journey, and the protectors of my pupils as they hastened hither and thither.' He commended them to the King as his 'very close friends'. This is firm evidence for Alcuin's roots in both kingdoms, and it accounts for the clutch of other letters to his friend Ethelheard that still remain, touching on various matters, including the perennial battle against pagan superstitions and customs among the people of Kent.[67] Alcuin died in 804 knowing that the primacy of Canterbury was secure and that the rift in the southern province of the English church had been mended by his friend, Ethelheard, the Archbishop of Canterbury.

Part Two
Charlemagne
Chapter 5
Charlemagne

It is unlikely that the writings of Alcuin would have been preserved to the extent that they were had it not been for his close association and friendship with Charlemagne. In some ways the King's moral authority and political prestige lay behind them. It is notable that the overwhelming bulk of the material remaining from Alcuin's hand dates from his years on the continent while in the retinue of the King and, after 796, at Tours. His many letters from the last period of his life open a fascinating window onto the court of the great Christian Emperor, as he became, and there is no doubting the respect and affection that flowed between Alcuin and Charlemagne.[1]

This was fully recognised by the two biographers of Charlemagne.[2] The first of these, Einhard, was himself an intellectual and courtier, being close to the King in the latter years of his reign, and also to his son, Louis the Pious. He was educated at Fulda, the monastery created by Boniface and where the saint was buried, and soon after 791 he went to join the royal court around the same time as Alcuin himself, whose friend he became. After Charlemagne's death, Louis gave Einhard several monasteries including Seligenstadt where he built a remarkable church. He retired there and died in 840. His *Life of Charlemagne* was written at the end of his life and it benefits from hindsight. It is modelled on Suetonius' lives of the Roman emperors - most notably his *Life of Augustus*, which Einhard follows closely. It is a judicious encomium, well informed, though in places inevitably selective out of his deep loyalty to the late King, who was his friend and patron.

Einhard was therefore well placed to portray the King's interests and also his friends and he paints a vivid picture of a powerful and energetic personality, noting that Charlemagne spoke 'easily and fluently', not only in his native language but also Latin; he even had a limited reading knowledge of some Greek. 'He paid the greatest attention to the liberal arts, for he had great respect for men who taught them, bestowing high honours upon them.'[3] His initial teacher was Peter, a deacon from Pisa; 'but for all other subjects he was taught by Alcuin, surnamed Albinus, another deacon, a man of Saxon race, who came from Britain and was the most learned man anywhere to be found.'[4] This was high praise indeed from Einhard who was no less able in his own way, and equally close to the King. Under

A clasp made either for a sword or harness out of gold and copper alloy
from the time of Charlemagne.

Alcuin's tutelage, Charlemagne studied rhetoric, dialectic and astronomy, each of which clearly fascinated him, as is evident in some of the letters that passed between the King and Alcuin. Charlemagne also tried his hand at learning to write, but without great success, having embarked on it too late in life and amidst too many distractions of duty. Like Alfred the Great later, Charlemagne's commitment to learning was personal and sincere, if at times frustrated by the limitations of his own education and lifestyle. He was a person of high ability in every way, and in Alcuin it would seem that he met his match.

This relationship between King and scholar is also evident in the second *Life of Charlemagne*, written later in the ninth century at the monastery of St Gallen, probably by Notker the Stammerer, around the year 884. By this time, and in the midst of the turbulence of the second part of the ninth century, the memory of Charlemagne had already begun to take on legendary proportions as a 'golden age.' Nonetheless this *Life* contains many valuable reminiscences, including two concerning Alcuin and the King. The *Life* starts with an interesting story about two Irish scholars who arrived at the court of Charlemagne: 'these men were unrivalled in their knowledge of sacred and profane letters, at a time when the pursuit of learning was almost forgotten throughout the length and breadth of Charlemagne's Kingdom.'[5] This was of course a generalisation; but it recalled the decisive role played by insular scholars during the rise of the Carolingians in the eighth century, and at the court of Charlemagne himself. It is in this context and in the second chapter of the *Life* that the monk of St Gallen mentions the arrival of Alcuin, attracted by the patronage of the great King. He described Alcuin as 'a man more skilled in all the branches of knowledge than any other person of modern times, . . . a pupil of Bede, that priest of great learning, himself the most accomplished interpreter of the Scriptures since St Gregory.' The recognition of a direct line of intellectual descent from Gregory the Great through Bede to Alcuin is significant and accurate, even though Alcuin was not a personal disciple of Bede's, being born around the year that he died. It is quite clear that the author knew of the close friendship between Alcuin and the King: 'the Emperor went so far as to have himself called Alcuin's pupil and to call Alcuin his master.' It also asserts that the reason why the King gave Alcuin the abbacy of Tours was so that he would have a base for his teaching of 'all those who flocked to him' there. 'His teaching bore such fruit among his pupils that the modern Franks came to equal the Romans and the Athenians,' a conceit which encapsulated the aspirations of the Carolingian reformers, and that was deployed by Alcuin himself occasionally in his letters.[6]

In his comments about Alcuin, the writer appears to have known the *Life of Alcuin*, adding in chapter nine the comment that 'of all his pupils there was not one who did not distinguish himself by becoming a devout abbot or a famous bishop.' He alleged that his own master, Grimald, had studied the liberal arts under Alcuin;[7] even if were not so precisely, he and his monastery were close to the memory of Alcuin and his disciples. He also records a fine joke between Charlemagne and Alcuin.[8] Despite all his efforts to revive and proliferate Christian learning, Charlemagne on occasion expressed his frustration: 'If only I could have a dozen churchmen as wise and well taught in all human knowledge as were Jerome and Augustine!' To which Alcuin shrewdly replied, with some irony and perhaps suppressed irritation: 'The Maker of heaven and earth Himself has very few scholars worth comparing with these men, and yet you expect to find a dozen!' The writer observed that Alcuin 'considered *even himself* ignorant in comparison with these two': this is probably a genuine reminiscence of both men and of their rapport. What was also remembered was Alcuin's boldness before a king who struck terror in many of his other courtiers. The Gallen *Life* is therefore a testimony to the power of oral tradition across a couple of generations, often highlighting what was significant in relationships and the developments they inspired, even if not always precisely accurate in some of its details. Taken together, the two biographers of Charlemagne emphasise the unique importance of Alcuin in relation to the king's personal life as well as to some aspects of his policy. Their almost *viva voce* judgement is to be respected inasmuch as what they say can be confirmed from the documents that remain which are associated with both men.

The reign of Charlemagne

Before examining the precise ways in which Alcuin interacted with Charlemagne and his court, some outline of his reign must be sketched in order to provide a context for understanding Alcuin's place and his role. Englishmen before him had played a significant role in justifying and supporting the rise of the Carolingians and their accession to royal power in the course of the eighth century.[9] Most notable among these were St Willibrord and Boniface. To their influence may also be attributed to some extent the alliance forged between the new Carolingian dynasty and the Papacy in the middle of the eighth century, as it sought to emancipate itself from Byzantine control and to protect itself from the Lombards in northern Italy. Charlemagne came from a militant and assertive tradition, founded by his great-grandfather, Pippin of Herstal, who wielded supreme power among the Franks after his victory at Tertry in 687 until his death in 714. He was the first patron of Willibrord. His son, Charles Martel, fought the Saxons and the Frisians on the borders of his realm, and in 732 he defeated an Islamic incursion from Spain at Poitiers in 732. The aggressive behaviour of the Frisians and the Saxons, and the rapid defeat of the Christian Visigoth kingdoms in Spain, however, haunted the Carolingian enterprise for many years.

In 741, Charles Martel was succeeded by his brother, Pippin the Short, who assumed control of the whole Kingdom after his brother retired to a monastery in 747. During his reign, the leadership of Boniface and others strengthened the influence of the Roman church and its practices, as part of a reform movement with which the Carolingian dynasty increasingly identified itself to its profit and to enhance its political control. In 752, Pope Zachary confirmed the legitimacy of Pippin's kingship, setting aside the last representative of the Merovingian dynasty. In 753, Pope Stephen II crossed the Alps to secure Carolingian military support against the Lombards, who had seized Ravenna and most of the Byzantine territory in north-eastern Italy. Pippin agreed to this alliance in 754 and in return the Pope consecrated his two sons, one of whom was Charlemagne himself, as co-rulers, calling them and their father 'patricians of the Romans' and therefore protectors of the Holy See. In 755 and 756, Pippin invaded Italy and conquered Ravenna, handing over the lands of the Byzantine exarchate to the Papacy. In the 760's, Pippin waged continuous war against the south-western provinces of Aquitaine in order to secure their submission as a bulwark against the threat from Spain. He died in 768, and in that year Charlemagne and his brother Carloman inherited the Kingdom.

Between 768 and 771, Charlemagne shared rule with his brother but their relations were not good, failing to collaborate in the subjugation of Aquitaine in 769. Pippin's widow, Bertrada, played an ambivalent role, creating an alliance for a while between Charlemagne, Tassilo of Bavaria and the Lombard King Desiderius, whose daughter was Charlemagne's first wife. Carloman was isolated and in vain did his followers in Rome raise an abortive revolt in 771, bringing the Lombard King to the gates of the city itself, to the unease of Pope Stephen III. Carloman died in the winter of that year, however, and Charlemagne assumed rule of the entire Frankish Kingdom, which he exercised until his death in 814. His Lombard wife returned home to Italy, whither the widow of Carloman also retreated with her children and their retainers.

In 772, a new Pope took office, Hadrian I, who was to play a decisive role in the restoration of Rome and in encouraging Charlemagne in his policies and reforms. Their relationship became one of the anchors of his rule. Meanwhile, Desiderius challenged the lands of the papacy and sought the consecration of Carloman's sons. But it was a bluff, and in 773 he retreated from his assault on Rome. Charlemagne was initially loath to intervene but finally did so, and with some difficulty got his forces through the Alps to besiege the Lombard King during the winter, securing the fall, first of Verona and with it the widow of Carloman, and finally of Pavia in 774, and then becoming ruler of the Lombards in place of Desiderius. Having established his political position, he had his son Pippin consecrated King of the Lombards in 781. Irreversibly, the Carolingian ruler was now caught up in the complex jostling between Byzantium, the papacy and the various Lombard and other Italian rulers.

While Charlemagne was thus engaged beyond the Alps, his hereditary enemies seized their advantage and in 774 the Saxons launched heavy raids against the Carolingian borderlands. According to Einhard, the border was ill-defined and hard to defend: the Saxons lacked any united command or political authority and so proved intractable to deal with politically. War with the Saxons therefore dominated the reign of Charlemagne, and its tortuous and bloody course brought out the worst and the best in the King. By 777 he was in a strong enough position to summon the annual assembly of the Franks to his new headquarters at Paderborn. It was seen as a turning-point: the triumph of Christianity over paganism. In the same year he embarked on an assault on the Islamic rulers of Pamplona and Saragossa in Spain. Returning home, his rearguard was decimated by an ambush in the Pyrenees at Roncesvalles, the setting for the later *Chanson de Roland*. It was a major setback and Charlemagne never again invaded Spain. As a result, in 778 the Saxons rebelled and destroyed his fortress at Karlsburg near Paderborn. Charlemagne reacted with great determination and force and secured the temporary submission of the Saxons in 779 and 780. Over the winter of 778-9, he stayed at his family home at Herstal, and from there issued the second capitulary of his reign, which set out the aims of his rule and reforms as a Christian monarch.

Another capitulary, however, to assert Frankish rule over the Saxons, issued perhaps in 782, incited further rebellion, led by Widukind. It was seen as harsh and alien in some of its demands, including the forcible imposition of tithes, against which Alcuin would later protest. Charlemagne's revenge was ruthless, executing 4000 captive Saxons at Verden on a single day. Violent resistance continued for a number of years until the submission of Widukind and his baptism in 785. Trouble flared up again in 792 and continued until 804, culminating in mass deportations of Saxons in the closing years of the eighth century. Behind the war banners of the King followed the mission of the Church as an integral part of royal policy. But a brutal pattern was created that would be replicated in the treatment of Slavs and others in subsequent centuries. It was well observed by Edward Gibbon that 'so intimate is the association of the throne and the altar that the banners of the Church have seldom been seen on the side of the people.' But Charlemagne's policy did not go completely unchallenged, not least by Alcuin, as revealed in some of his letters. For compulsory conversion to Christianity had been eschewed by the missionaries to the English under the guidance of Gregory the Great. Therein lay one of the secrets of its success to the extent that within a hundred years Christianity had become so acculturated and had given such fertile expression to Anglo-Saxon culture that the *Lindisfarne Gospels* could be produced along with the writings of Bede.[10]

From time to time Charlemagne faced challenges from within his own ruling clan and most notably from Tassilo of Bavaria, who still retained considerable autonomy from direct Frankish rule. He was created a duke by his uncle, Pippin III, in 749, and at his majority had sworn allegiance in 757 to the King, his heirs and successors. But in 763 he broke free and the old King died in 768 before he could reassert his over-lordship. It seems that the young Charlemagne tolerated the situation for a full decade, while Tassilo founded monasteries[11] and defeated the Slavs of Carinthia in 772. But in 781, Charlemagne and Pope Hadrian insisted that Tassilo obey his oaths and so he came to Worms to renew them. It seems that there was a joint determination to rein him in lest he conspire with the King's enemies, the Saxons, Slavs and Avars, and so weaken the support that the Pope hoped to receive from Charlemagne. In 787 Tassilo fell out with the Pope and refused to attend another Frankish assembly at Worms. Charlemagne invaded with three armies and the Duke capitulated. He surrendered his duchy along with his son as a hostage and then received it back as a royal fief. But in 788 he was arraigned at a further assembly at Ingelheim, again on grounds of treachery and collusion with the Avars, and was condemned to death. Charlemagne instead showed clemency and Tassilo was banished to a monastery, to appear before the synod of Frankfurt in 794 as a penitent.

It seems that in 787-8 the Byzantines collaborated with the Avars while attacking Charlemagne's domains in southern Italy, and relationships between the Franks and their warlike eastern neighbours remained fraught until the King attacked them in force in 790-1 by way of a crusade of revenge, a holy war. They put up little resistance and as a result the King added much of what is now Austria to his domains. In 795-6, one of the Avar leaders came to Aachen to submit to Charlemagne, and in the same year the duke of Fruili, Eric, a friend of Alcuin's, attacked the headquarters of the Avars and despoiled them of a fabulous hoard of treasure. According to Einhard, no war so enriched the victorious Franks, and booty from this hoard was sent by Charlemagne far and wide, including to the English kings, as signs of his prowess. Meanwhile Alcuin urged his friend, Arno of Salzburg, and others to evangelistic activity among the Avars, though not this time by compulsion.

After Alcuin's death in 804, the King intervened on behalf of his Avar subjects against the Slavs of Bohemia in 805-6, and he waged war further east in Pannonia in 811. Charlemagne had to face challenges from the Bretons, whom he subdued, and also from the Danes in the later years of his reign. These he withstood until the Danish Kingdom collapsed from within. His ascendancy north of the Alps was therefore never in doubt. His alliance with the English kings held good to their mutual profit, as it secured the North Sea coasts and the narrow seas of the English Channel and sustained the trade between them, with occasional interruptions. On the other hand, the proverb of the Greeks, cited by Einhard, probably applied to the English: 'If a Frank is your friend, then he is clearly not your neighbour.'[12] The lack of a land boundary protected both sides from each other. The threat from the Vikings, despite Alcuin's forebodings about the sack of Lindisfarne in 793, was still only a distant cloud on the horizon. While Charlemagne commanded significant fleets in the northern seas as well as in the Mediterranean his vast realm might seem secure. His sheer energy as a war-leader never abated until the end of his life.

His engagements south of the Alps were different and in some ways more complicated. Lombardy retained its identity and integrity under Frankish colonial rule. It was the strategic key to Charlemagne's influence in Italy. It also exerted a significant influence on Carolingian culture. In 774, Charlemagne paid his first visit to Rome where he was received by a wary Pope Hadrian, who extracted an oath from the King before permitting him actually to enter the city of Rome. On this occasion, however, Charlemagne made a solemn commitment to endow the papacy with extensive land grants across Italy. Although the text of this no longer remains, it became a bone of contention between the Pope and the King as its implementation was tardy and incomplete. Charlemagne did not bend to the Pope's will with regard to the claims of the see of Ravenna; nor did he hand over Spoleto, which he visited in 775 rather than Rome itself. Further planned visits in 776 and 778 fell through to the chagrin and frustration of Hadrian.

Charlemagne's presence in Italy drew him into direct confrontation with Byzantine power, which claimed the exarchate of Ravenna and which still ruled extensively in southern Italy. By 781, however, the Byzantines were seeking a marriage alliance with the rising power in the West. In that year, the King visited Rome again, having installed his son Pippin as ruler of Lombardy. It was also the year in which the King and the Pope collaborated against Tassilo of Bavaria. On a further visit in 787, Charlemagne exerted his authority over Benevento, which had been a thorn in the side for him and the Pope for a number of years. He also met ambassadors from Byzantium who confirmed that the marriage alliance was off. War broke out in 788 in the south of Italy and for a time Grimoald, the Frankish appointee ruling Benevento, stood firm with the King against the Byzantine forces. Later he reneged and was attacked by Pippin from Lombardy twice early in the next decade. The Byzantines discovered that the Frankish ruler and his empire were a force to be reckoned with as their own influence in Italy continued to wane.

The failure of the marriage alliance meant that Charlemagne was on a collision course with the Eastern Roman Empire, which is part of the background to his own assumption of the imperial title in 800 at the hand of Pope Leo III. It was also part of the background to the Carolingian criticism of the decrees of the second council of Nicea of 787, which sought to reverse the policy of iconoclasm in the Byzantine realms. This resulted in the preparation of the *Libri Carolini* by Theodulf of Orleans and others in 792 and its adoption by the Synod of Frankfurt in 794, despite the justifiable protestations of Pope Hadrian, who pointed out that it had completely misunderstood the decrees of the synod of Nicea due to a faulty translation. The Latin word *adorare* had been used to translate both the 'worship' due to God alone and the 'veneration' that might be offered his saints to and through icons. Despite Charlemagne's respect and friendship towards Pope Hadrian, his sense of his own duty and authority stood firm on this issue.

It was during the 790's that the imperial cult of Charlemagne began to gain ground, and in this Alcuin was to play a hidden but perhaps decisive part in the years immediately leading up to Christmas 800. The King's new title reflected primarily the extent of his rule. His authority lay behind the *Libri Carolini* and his other capitularies of reform as that of the defender of Christian orthodoxy in the West. The palace complex that he began to build at Aachen became his fixed winter capital after 794. Its chapel imitated Ravenna and Rome, from which some of its decorative materials were pillaged – or purchased. By the end of the decade, Pope Leo III portrayed Charlemagne as a modern counterpart to Constantine in a mosaic flanking the apse of his *triclinium* in the Lateran palace in Rome.[13] To some extent the synod of Frankfurt in 794 was Charlemagne's answer to the synod of Nicea seven years earlier. It asserted his authority to judge the heresy of Adoptionism in Spain, which much preoccupied Alcuin, and it condemned image-worship in the East as the Frankish ruler perceived it to be.

The new Pope, Leo III, looked to Charlemagne as his protector and perhaps as the co-ruler of Rome itself. He certainly needed that protection for he was nearly killed in 799 by his enemies and had to flee across the Alps to his northern patron at Paderborn. Meanwhile, in Byzantium itself, the Empress Irene ruled alone, having blinded her son in 797. The plight of the Pope drew the King to intervene in Roman affairs, ordering a commission of enquiry to exonerate the Pope and securing his restoration. Alcuin was one of the advisers who in 799 urged Charlemagne to assume formally the imperial role apparently being offered him by Leo at Paderborn. To mark the King's elevation, Alcuin sent him a specially prepared copy of the Bible. So on Christmas Day 800, Pope Leo III crowned Charlemagne as emperor in St Peter's basilica, an event much discussed by historians and with hindsight pregnant for the future of Europe. Einhard asserted that the King accepted this with great reluctance, but this is most unlikely in reality. He was however crowned first and then acclaimed, and this may have irritated the King though why remains unclear unless it was that he felt that the hapless Pope had presumed too much authority in the matter.

Nonetheless a new political fact was created, which Charlemagne exploited to the full in his title and in his actions. It gave him renewed moral authority as a political and religious reformer, and this was reflected in various capitularies issued at Aachen in 802. This encapsulated his whole vision of a Christian empire and a well ordered Church, enjoining new oaths of loyalty to himself and to the standards of justice and Christianity. It was also at this synod that the *Rule of St Benedict* was laid down as a norm for monastic life. Further war with Byzantium broke out, after Alcuin's death, in 806-8 over the territories of Venetia and Istria at the head of the Adriatic, which had fallen under the lordship of Charlemagne. During peace negotiations in 812, envoys from Byzantium acclaimed Charlemagne as 'emperor'. The coasts of Spain and the inroads of pirates in the Mediterranean also required the King's attention throughout his reign. Moorish attacks from North Africa into Sicily and southern Italy also posed a challenge which was successfully met in 799. Naval power was the key to relative political security and also to trade, in which the Carolingian dynasty had a keen interest.

Byzantine ascendancy in the western Mediterranean was no more however, and the focus of European development now lay north of the Alps.[14] The impact of Charlemagne's *imperium* was therefore of decisive importance for the subsequent history of Europe. Although effective control of such a wide domain proved impossible under his successors, and the northern borders of the Frankish realm became under increasing Viking attack throughout the ninth century, the model of Christian monarchy and reform of the Church remained as a tangible ideal, with education, liturgy and monasticism at its heart, to inspire their restoration under the Ottonian kings as well as in England in the tenth century. In the formulation and dissemination of this vision and its practical implementation, Alcuin and his writings played a decisive part, during his lifetime and long afterwards.

Chapter 6

Alcuin and Charlemagne

Both the ninth century biographers of Charlemagne emphasised the close relationship that Alcuin enjoyed with the King, and his many letters open a window onto the nature and depth of that personal relationship. They were not, of course, private and intimate letters: they were written for a wider audience who would have heard them read aloud to Charlemagne, within which stood others with a good claim on his friendship as well. Some were also part of a network of communications in letters and poems between the entourage of learned men and women assembled at various times and places around the King.

Before using these letters for an evaluation of Alcuin's influence on the King's policies at various times, they should be examined first for the light that they shed on his personal relationship with Charlemagne insofar as it emerges from them. For within the bond of patronage, and at times subservience, there was a strong tie of friendship, and often a real affinity of interest. Some of the occasional letters have personal dimensions; others treat of scientific and theological interests shared by Alcuin and Charlemagne with others. Some address policy issues of the day directly. There are also important dedicatory letters, alongside the poems that Alcuin composed for the King. Finally there are letters addressed to royal women, with some of whom Alcuin enjoyed close spiritual friendship. His sympathy and respect for learned and devout women was very evident in all his correspondence and reveals an important side to his character.

The quality of a fascinating exchange of scientific letters between Alcuin and the King, written in 798-9, reflects the vigour with which Alcuin could engage the King's genuine interest and knowledge, as well as some of the contrary influences at court which Alcuin perceived to be at work while he was away from there as Abbot of Tours.[1] In these letters Charlemagne was portrayed as a second Solomon, an arbiter of wisdom, and the defender of truth against error and heresy alike. In his appeal to both classical and patristic authority, Alcuin identified the King with the maintenance of due order, both at court and in the state. Meanwhile they were as friends united in their common pursuit of truth, even if they felt that resources at hand were sometimes limited both at Tours and at Aachen.

The rigour and intensity of some of these letters reflects also a frustrated spirit of scientific enquiry, evident elsewhere at times in the patristic and early

An intaglio of rock crystal carved delicately with a Crucifixion scene,
probably from Metz in the early ninth century.

medieval period. The near obsession with the correct calculation of time, shared by Charlemagne and his advisers, as well as by Alcuin, encapsulated their sense that their apprehension of truth and reality was fragile yet vital, and that this was the goal of learning and the purpose of royal patronage that made it possible. In a letter written in the midst of this exchange in July 798, Alcuin asked the King to correct him where he was wrong rather than let his alleged errors become the butt of jokes at court: 'for there are those who seek praise at the expense of others. But this is weak praise indeed and not truly laudable: it is surely better to correct a friend than to rebuke him, to put him right wisely than to put him down bitingly.' Only on this basis had Alcuin written to the King about the matter under discussion in the first place.[2] But perhaps from a distance it was becoming harder for Alcuin to hold his own, confronted by a rising generation at court. His own approach was well summed up in a subsequent letter: 'I am no mere defender of my own words, but rather a devoted seeker after truth.'[3]

Occasional letters

The letter that reveals most clearly the depth of affection and rapport between Alcuin and Charlemagne was written shortly after 4 June 800 to the King on the death of his Queen, Liudgard, during a royal visit to Tours.[4] She was duly buried in the abbey church there. She had been Charlemagne's third Frankish wife by choice, succeeding Fastrada sometime after her death in 794; but she bore him no children. It would seem that Alcuin knew her well, as she appears in several of his letters.[5] In 795 he wrote to her affectionately, enquiring about the King's likely return from his war with the Saxons. He wrote shortly afterwards to a monastic community at Montamiata in Francia, reassuring them of her patronage of their interests at court; and he mentioned her gifts of two gold bracelets in a letter written around the same time to Paulinus of Aquilea. In a letter, also written in 796, to Ethelburh, daughter of Offa of Mercia, Alcuin commended the Queen's friendship towards her, referring again to an exchange of gifts. In 798, he wrote to his friend, Arno, in Salzburg, hoping to meet up with him during the summer at Nivelles, where Queen Liudgard would be staying with some of the royal children by Charlemagne's earlier marriage. This earlier correspondence provides context for and corroborates the authenticity of this particular and very personal letter, which certainly breaks the bounds of formality in dealing with a personal tragedy for Charlemagne in his bereavement, as well as addressing the loss of a good friend of Alcuin's.

In the more intimate letter,[6] Alcuin invoked directly the promise of Christ in the gospel: 'Come to me all who labour and are heavy laden, and I will give you rest.'[7] He referred also to the conclusion of Romans 8, where Paul affirmed God's solidarity with all who suffer within the love of Christ. Alcuin bowed before the absolute sovereignty of God, who kills and makes alive again, reminding himself as well as the King of the afflictions of Job. All is God's gift – in life and in death: in the words of God, 'all that you have are my gifts, not your own.' They have been prepared as a *via dolorosa* that will lead to the joys of heaven. In this letter, Christ summoned to himself his bride, his sister, addressing her in words drawn from the Song of Songs: 'the eternal king loves your beauty.' Alcuin reflected that death is the condition of our fragile mortality as a result of the Fall: 'we are born in order to die, but we die in order that we may live.' This encapsulates the heart of Alcuin's theology of bereavement, evident in some of his other consolatory letters. For a Christian, death is the gateway to eternal life: so why weep about something that cannot be avoided? Often it is time alone that will heal what the mind never will. So let us offer works of charity and prayers for those whom we love who have departed: 'let us have pity on the wretched so that God may have pity on them. For what we do in faith for them also profits ourselves.' There can be no doubt that if Alcuin was comforting the King, he was also comforting himself, opening his heart with an unusual intensity and directness, even for him. The letter concludes with a very loving prayer:

> Lord God, Jesus kind and merciful, take pity upon her whom you have taken from us. Hear our prayer by your healing wounds, who once hung upon the tree, but now sit at God's right hand to intercede for us.
>
> I know the extent of your mercy, who desire that all should be saved. Forgive whatever sins she committed after her baptism: forgive them, Lord, forgive them we pray! Do not enter into judgement with her: may mercy triumph over judgement. For your words are true, by which you promise forgiveness to the wretched: you have given them to her so that she might live.
>
> Have mercy O Lord upon your creature, for you will show mercy to those whom you deign to forgive, so that she may praise you and sing of your mercies forever. Then her soul, which will prove victorious, will ever say: 'I will praise the Lord while I live, and sing psalms to my God as long as I have breath.'
>
> *So may she live forever in eternity.*
> *I wish you blessedness,*
> *My beloved daughter,*
> *Who is, I trust, beloved also to God.*

What is striking about this letter is the adroit way in which Alcuin deployed a rich tapestry of Biblical references – twelve in all, hand-picked and briefly referred to, giving resonance and depth to his own words and thoughts, by appealing to the memory of those hearing or reading his letter, and so weaving his faith and theirs into the liturgy and worship of the Church.

The letter that follows it in all three manuscripts is another letter of consolation to the King, but in a very different tone, marking perhaps the death in battle of two of his key nobles, Eric of Friuli and Gervold of Bavaria, about whose demise Alcuin wrote to Arno in Salzburg at the end of 799.[8] It is much more formal in tone, almost a sermon, well supported by biblical quotations, many from the Psalms, and it was undoubtedly preserved as a fine exemplar. It is a classic piece of theodicy whose pivot was the words of Christ to Mary and Martha in John's gospel.[9] 'May the words of Truth serve as our consolation . . . the death of a good person is a migration to a better life, not a cause for lament but for congratulation . . . For by the death of Christ, death died . . . therefore this life is the way for pilgrims to their homeland.' With this in mind, Christians are called to imitate the life of the angels. The letter closes with a two-line poem to the King, whom Alcuin described as 'beloved David', his usual sobriquet for Charlemagne.[10] Firm and direct in its tone, it was a letter to put backbone into a situation that weighed on the King in a more than personal way, as it probably affected the security of his realm.

Others shared in Alcuin's close relationship at times with Charlemagne, one of whom was his pupil and colleague, Candidus Wizo. In a letter written either in 794 or 795, or perhaps somewhat later,[11] he served as emissary between them, as Alcuin apprised the King of the shape of the theological challenge emanating from Spain – Adoptionism. He expressed his deep appreciation of the King's good wishes in personal as well as more formal terms. He praised the King for his concern to uphold Christian orthodoxy: 'Blessed are the people whose God is the Lord and blessed are the people exalted by such a ruler, fortified by sound preaching!' Charlemagne was called by God to wield the sword in one hand while preaching the Catholic faith in the other. Alcuin drew a straight parallel with King David in the Bible, 'chosen by God and beloved of God': he was the ruler and teacher of the people of God.[12] With that in mind, Alcuin proceeded to give Charlemagne a concise summary of the principal errors of Adoptionism, assuming that the king with his advisers would readily understand the theology involved, which revolved around the reality of the risen human body of Christ. 'For we preach one true God, and one Son of God in two natures, divine and human, our Lord Jesus Christ, who reigns with the Father and the Holy Spirit.' This letter was the harbinger of much more theology on this matter by Alcuin and others, directed to Charlemagne at his request and sometimes for his approval too.

When Alcuin became Abbot of Tours in 796, he felt remote at times from court, and his letters from that time onwards remain as only fragmentary evidence for the quality of his continuing relationship with Charlemagne, who had given him the ancient royal abbey of Tours with its shrine of St Martin to reform, and also as a base for his teaching as he grew older. Alcuin referred to this in a notable letter, written perhaps early in 797, which after a florid encomium alluded to his 'exile' at Tours and the educational programme he was attempting to establish there, and for which he sought the King's permission to send to York for some of his books.[13] It was a letter in which he reminded Charlemagne of their common commitment to Christian education and learning, and its significance, both at Aachen and at Tours. He referred to the consistency of his own vocation as an educator, first in Britain and more recently in Francia. His advancing years had not blunted his determination as a teacher. He cited a letter of Jerome, asserting that only growth in wisdom could counteract physical ageing. In his farewell, he commended the King to the protection of Christ, who was 'the power and the wisdom of God.'

In a much later letter[14], commending the archbishop of Canterbury, Ethelheard, to Charlemagne as he made his way to Rome, Alcuin described himself as the King's *matricularius* or beneficiary, as he indeed he was, presiding over one of the wealthiest abbeys in Francia.[15] By this stage, 801, his letters served as proxies for his absence due to the onset of old age and infirmity. In other letters from around the same time, Alcuin refused a summons to attend court on grounds of his illness.[16] His prayers for the King would have to reach where he could no longer be. His affection for his royal friend was unabated, while his own dread of impending divine judgement as his life drew to a close was pressed home upon the King too. To the end he could write moving small poems for Charlemagne to attach to his letters: 'may the grace of Christ be with you, David, forever.'[17] He prayed that the King's generosity towards him would be repaid many times over in heaven.

Theological letters

According to Einhard, one of Charlemagne's favourite books was *The City of God* by Augustine. 'He also learnt Latin so well that he spoke it as fluently as his own tongue.'[18] Whether he could actually read it unaided is unclear, as he had great difficulties attempting all his life to learn how to write as an adult. It would seem that he could only read parts of the Bible from memory; but Einhard says that the King had some understanding of oral Greek, and emissaries from Byzantium were often at his court, on one occasion proposing a marriage alliance. Einhard, who knew the King and Alcuin well, emphasised Charlemagne's real devotion as a Christian, building as he did the great royal chapel at Aachen as an expression of this, as well as the expression of the prestige of his rule.[19]

The King went to church twice each day and also regularly to Mass and to some of the night vigils. Many stories of Charlemagne in the St Gallen *Life of Charlemagne* actually occur in church, some of them as amusing as they are revealing. Even if they may be *bene trovato,* they support the picture painted by Einhard of Charlemagne's religious devotion, and also his demands upon his clergy in terms of their preaching and the quality of worship. It seems that on occasions he personally supervised the scriptural readings during the divine office in the choir at Aachen, indicating who was to read and when they were to stop, even if it were mid-sentence, which would seem to confirm the limitations of his own literacy. There is a charming story of how a strange monk came into the choir one day and did not know what do to, trying finally to sing while the others laughed at him. At the end of the service, however, the King called him over, thanked him for his efforts and gave him a pound of silver to relieve his poverty.[20] Notably he showed no sign of distraction by this debacle when it occurred in the course of the service. Charlemagne was an active churchman, therefore, whom his bishops and clergy feared and respected.

There is therefore no reason to doubt his ability to hold his own theologically and intellectually with people like Alcuin or Theodulf, as the record of his comments recorded in the margins of the *Libri Carolini* indicate. The letters of Alcuin to the King, which addressed matters of theological concern, therefore reveal another facet of the relationship between them, as well as the King's active engagement in the great religious issues of the day, such as the role of images, Adoptionism in Spain, or the nature of papal authority. Alcuin and Charlemagne shared a common love of Augustine, whose theology was seminal for their own belief and thinking. To judge from the wealth of biblical references in these letters, the King had a good knowledge of the Bible too and he certainly revered its authority. The seriousness of Charlemagne's religious purpose was reflected in the high quality of the theology that he commissioned from Alcuin, which often went first to the King for his approval. The research that underpinned Alcuin's main treatises against Adoptionism, for example, represented a major investment of effort and money, not least in terms of books for use as resources by Charlemagne and his advisers as well as by Alcuin. The commissioning of the *Libri Carolini* by Theodulf was on a similar scale, as was the copying of many lavish and beautiful Bibles and other manuscripts. These were of course expressions of royal prestige; but they were first and foremost expressions of the king's commitment and personal belief as the paramount Christian ruler of Western Europe.

The nature and significance of Alcuin's theology will be discussed elsewhere but the measure of rapport between himself and the King in this area of theology can best be gauged from the dedicatory letter that he composed in 801 or 802 as the preface to his treatise *De fide sanctae et individuae Trinitatis*.[21] Addressing Charlemagne as 'the most august and Christian emperor', to whom God had committed both power and wisdom surpassing his ancestors, this letter was a characteristic encomium, replete with Alcuin's vision and expectations of Christian kingship as embodied in his royal patron and friend. His treatise on the Trinity was intended to assist Charlemagne in defending and preaching Christian orthodoxy. It was sent to the King as *refulgens rector* for his personal approval, because he had responsibility for the right faith of those subject to him. As ever with Alcuin, adulation paved the way for moral accountability. Moreover royal authority, accurately informed, was to undergird the effective preaching and teaching mission of the Church. Alcuin's treatise also demonstrated how important dialectic was to a proper understanding of Christian theology, and why it should be taught. His letter concluded with a tribute to Charlemagne in the form of a short poem:

> *O king, worthy of most noble and august honour,*
> *Our leader, teacher, and glory of empire.*
> *May the Father and the Son of the Father and the beloved Spirit*
> *Protect, exalt, save and love you.*

Four other letters reveal the range of theology that concerned both the King and Alcuin. In one probably written in 798 or 799 in response to a letter sent from Charlemagne by Candidus Wizo, Alcuin went to great lengths to explain the precise meaning of certain key theological words to the King and those around him, linguistically and metaphysically, supported by seventeen biblical references.[22] Alcuin concluded with the important principle that:

> the words which we speak are nothing unless they signify those things which we conceive with the mind, by which we wish to arrive at an understanding of things: for words lead nowhere rightly unless they signify what is true.

He also asserted that 'truth is natural to human beings insofar as they never wish to hear anything that is false.'

In another letter, Alcuin outlined his understanding of the significance of the word 'sword' in the Bible, in response to various lay enquiries.[23] It later circulated as a distinct treatise entitled *De Gladio*. In expounding the range of use of such a word in the Bible, Alcuin affirmed that 'the Word of the Lord is full of apertures and may be penetrated in many ways, such is the depth and height of the mysteries of God: who can investigate all His secret ways?' It was a lengthy attempt to move from the familiar to the profound. In it Alcuin addressed Charlemagne as 'the beloved and honoured defender and ruler of the churches of Christ', urging him to rebuke those bishops who prevented priests and deacons from preaching in church, and insisting that altars should not be left open to birds and dogs. There are thirty-nine references from the Bible in this lengthy letter, in which Alcuin took very seriously the beliefs and enquiries of the laity at court.

The third letter is a very interesting piece of biblical exegesis, written in response to a question from Charlemagne sometime between 801 and 804.[24] The address is interesting: *regi regum Deo Christo donante Carolo regi, imperatori Augusto, optimo, maximo, perpetuo.*[25] Alcuin praised the king for his intellectual enquiry in the midst of his public duties, commending the example he set to the younger generation at court. He cited various classical examples in support of the study of philosophy. He then tackled the question raised by the King about the hymn sung by the disciples after the Last Supper and why it was not included in the gospels. Alcuin sketched in as background the likely psalms that would have been included among the hymns sung at Passover. Then he discussed how the evangelists proceeded, commenting on the variations in their accounts of the Last Supper. He asserted that the great prayer of Jesus in John 17 is in fact the hymn alluded to in the other gospels. It is a very original and perceptive piece of writing, reflecting the depth of dialogue between himself and Charlemagne as well as his own sensitivity to the text of the Bible and its composition and interpretation.

The last letter is most interesting and important: it was composed at the very end of Alcuin's life in response to a question about the nature of the Atonement from Charlemagne, prompted by a visiting Greek.[26] It was one of the most significant pieces of theology that Alcuin wrote, clearly the fruit of long reflection, and rooted in his understanding of Augustine and other Latin Fathers. It sums up his whole approach to theology and assumes a fair range of knowledge on the part of his hearers. Alcuin began by defining wisdom as the knowledge of things human and divine, revealing first-hand acquaintance with Boethius' *De Consolatione Philosophiae*. His letter constitutes in fact the most important consideration of the Atonement in the early Middle Ages in the West before the writings of Anselm. It stressed the self-surrender of Christ to his sufferings as the key to understanding the doctrine, challenging current Christian misapprehensions, as well as the limitations of Greek philosophy in dealing with Christian theology. In many ways it is a *tour de force*, rich in biblical references and distilling in a distinctive way the theological inheritance of Western Christianity as Alcuin had mastered it. As such it could only be written as a contribution to a deep dialogue with the King that was already well established.

Reviewing these letters, the thorough and even intense nature of Alcuin's responses was striking, prompted by the King's enquiries. It must be assumed of course that these letters are now only a small part of a much wider correspondence and prolonged dialogue over many years. Notable is Alcuin's insistence on the correct use of language in order to access the Bible and to think straight about Christian doctrine. His range and mastery of biblical quotations is also striking and most effective: his argument in many places is so often a dialogue with scripture. He presupposed familiarity with the Latin Fathers of the Church on the part of his hearer, and expounded the proper use of philosophy and its tools, such as dialectic. Alcuin is at his best as an exegete of the Bible and as an eloquent communicator of its relevance and moral authority, which he regarded as the foundation of Charlemagne's rule and duty as well as of their whole society. It is very apparent that Alcuin's own grasp of theology was always deepened, sharpened and elucidated by question and debate, of which these letters are merely a fragmentary glimpse. His approach to the Bible and to the Fathers was interrogative and energetically engaged: there was a creative process of interpretation and 'innovative deference'[27] underway that was never merely derivative. By their very subject and depth and in some cases their length as well, they were the product of a strong and demanding relationship, of a true meeting of minds over more than a decade of active collaboration between Alcuin and Charlemagne.

The carmina for Charlemagne

Another window into their relationship may be found in some of the poems that Alcuin composed for Charlemagne on various occasions. These were part of a wider tapestry of poetry produced in court circles during his reign.[28] One of the most striking was composed around the year 780, quite early therefore in their relationship and collaboration. It is a sophisticated acrostic poem, beginning *Crux, decus es mundi*, fashioned around a Cross, within which is held a diamond shape. The lines across the top and bottom and down the sides, as well as those marking the Cross and the diamond, constitute prayers to the Cross, superimposed on the whole poem that is suspended within them.[29] In the manuscript it is preceded by the line *'Alcuin the abbot composed the verses which are contained on this page.'* Alcuin revived and consciously imitated the Latin court poet of Constantine the Great, Publilius Optatianus Porfyrius, setting a pattern for others.[30] In its theological content and emphasis, its roots lie deep in the tradition of Anglo-Saxon poetry about the Cross that found supreme expression in *The Dream of the Rood*. It mirrors too the elaborate stone carvings of the Cross in England from this period. It is a poem about the kingship and victory of the crucified Christ; but embedded within it is a reference to King David the harpist, a direct allusion to Charlemagne himself and to the cultivation of music and poetry in the circles around a king. Alcuin's indirect portrayal of him as a second Constantine, for whom such an elaborate poem was fitting, connects with the way in which Charlemagne was described in some of the papal letters and other writings during the earlier part of his reign.

   Closely connected to this poem is another acrostic creation by Alcuin for the King, which begins *Magna quidem pavido*.[31] It was probably composed a decade or so later in 790 and uses a Roman imperial title for the King, *Flavius Anicius Carlus*, which appears three times in highlighted lines across the poem. This represented Alcuin's conscious emulation of late antique models and was probably intended to portray Charlemagne once again as a second Constantine. These two poems, by their visual form and intricacy, associate Alcuin directly with the brilliant artistic flowering underway at the Carolingian court during the last decade of the eighth century. Others were occasioned by friends in common, for example one written in 792 celebrating the arrival of good news about the King brought to Alcuin by Angilbert, the King's nephew and Abbot of St Riquier.[32] This poem is actually quite intimate in tone, hailing the king as 'David' and associating him in Alcuin's heart with Christ himself. The young boy being sent back as an emissary was to serve as 'song, heart and hand' - a tangible bond between them.

   In 796, Alcuin wrote a long and elaborate response to a letter from Charlemagne, hailing him as 'the glory of the Church, its ruler, defender and lover;' it also addressed various members of the court including the doctor and the steward.[33] It is a vivid and witty piece, a window into a world of mutual entertainment and parody. Alcuin was now absent from court, hence perhaps the ironic line 'was the poet Virgil the only one to do wrong at court?' He also refers to Einhard as Bezaleel, the builder of the Tabernacle in the Bible,[34] hoping that he would step up to the mark as a teacher of poetry at court. Close on its heels went another more private poem to Charlemagne and his immediate family.[35]

Two further poems were written just before the momentous year 800 when Charlemagne was crowned as emperor by Pope Leo III in Rome. In the first, Alcuin continued to address Charlemagne as king and 'most noble consul', the 'ornament of wisdom'.[36] Clearly feeling his advancing age, he implored the King's protection against unnamed critics. The other poem caught the tide of anticipation in Alcuin's mind as the King embarked on his journey to Rome.[37] It referred to the vicissitudes of Pope Leo III whom Charlemagne had to rescue from his enemies and reinstate. Only Charlemagne could secure justice and order, and echoes of Virgil are apparent towards the end of this poem, as in another letter from Alcuin to the King at this time. Not everything that Alcuin expressed in his poetry however is directly interchangeable with what he said in particular letters; as ever the precise context holds the key.[38] Charlemagne was bidden 'to raise up the oppressed and dethrone the arrogant, so that holy peace and piety might everywhere prevail.' In this poem Alcuin carefully affirmed the supremacy of the one who alone could wield the power of an emperor in Rome, thus safeguarding the position of the Pope. His aspirations expressed in this poem found their fulfilment in the coronation of Charlemagne in 800.

It is a rich and interesting poem, redolent with many images by which Alcuin extolled and encouraged Charlemagne's Christian kingship. What is striking is the way in which Christian pastoral imagery, normally applied to abbots and bishops, was transmuted into the ethos of a universal moral rule, which Charlemagne seemed at that moment uniquely equipped to wield. The Pope was to be put right by the King: 'may the ruler of the Church be ruled by you rightly;' for the King was the mighty hand of Christ himself, surely an extraordinary and highly revealing assertion. The poem concludes with the lines: 'O father, pastor and ruler, beloved hope of your people: to you be life and health without end – so farewell!' This is a highly revealing letter in so many ways, the monument to a unique friendship and alliance of interest. Charlemagne's own estimate of Alcuin as a friend may perhaps be glimpsed in a poem attributed to, or commissioned by him, greeting Alcuin as 'father and master' and 'beloved teacher.'[39] If so, it sounds as if it was written towards the end of Alcuin's life when he was largely absent from the King at Tours.

Alcuin and the royal family

Einhard, who knew Charlemagne and his family closely, portrayed the course of his private life in some detail in the third book of his *Life of Charlemagne*.[40] Initially in 770, the King married the daughter of Desiderius,

King of Lombardy; but this was at his mother's behest and after one year he dismissed her and married Hildegard, by whom he had three sons and three daughters. She died in 783, and by his next wife, Fastrada, he had two more daughters and yet another one by a concubine. When Fastrada died in 794 he married Liudgard, who proved to be childless; and after her death in 800, he took a succession of four concubines by whom he had a further five children. His own mother, Bertrada, lived to a great age and, apart from an inevitable rift over the dismissal of the first Lombard wife, whom he had married for crudely diplomatic reasons, she was held in high honour by her son: she died in 783 and was buried in state at St Denis near Paris, which became the royal mausoleum.

His beloved sister, Gisela, became Abbess of Chelles and a great friend of Alcuin's; she lived almost as long as her brother. Charlemagne educated all his children, giving his son and also his daughters 'a proper training in the liberal arts, which had formed the subject of his own studies.' When some of them died early he was greatly and visibly distressed 'for his emotions as a father were very deeply rooted.' His children were his constant companions, at the baths in Aachen, on journeys and at table; but he denied his daughters marriage, 'maintaining that he could not live without them.'[41] They had inevitable liaisons, the most important of which for Alcuin was the relationship between one of the royal daughters, Bertha, and the King's nephew Angilbert. He was a close friend of Alcuin's and the lay Abbot of St Riquier in northern Francia, which he rebuilt in a spectacular manner.[42] Alcuin called him *Homer* for he too was a gifted poet.[43] Alcuin enjoyed familiarity and friendship within the royal circle as some of his poems and letters reveal.[44]

There is an interesting poem, probably by Alcuin, written to one of the sons of Charlemagne, perhaps Pippin King of Italy around the year 800, extolling the flowering of the virtues of nobility in his life in a manner comparable to his royal father.[45] The charming poem to Charlemagne and his children has already been mentioned.[46] Angilbert again featured in another poem as a 'living letter' of affection to the King, being addressed himself as *dulcis Homer*.[47] There is also a poem in which Alcuin drew a parallel between the King's generosity to him and Christ's generosity to Charlemagne; it also addressed one of his daughters, perhaps Bertha.[48] Elsewhere he addressed each of the royal children in a personal poem, encouraging them in their education.[49] Another personal piece was a short poem to Gisela, Abbess of Chelles, in which Alcuin hailed her as a noble sister in the bond of sweet love, assuring her of the prayers of the brethren at Tours.[50] The intimate tone of this clutch of poems is very revealing of Alcuin's character and it is corroborated by some of the letters that remain.

Those letters that relate to Queen Liudgard have already been discussed. A brief letter remains from Alcuin to Charlemagne's son, Pippin King of Italy, written between 790 and 795 and commending a priest who was travelling through his domains.[51] This was followed in 796 by another more substantial letter in which Alcuin, referring to the clemency of his father, painted a picture of the Christian prince to which Pippin should aspire.[52] He was among other things to be 'large-hearted to the wretched, pious towards pilgrims, devoted to the servants of Christ' who in turn would pray for his welfare as their ruler. He was also to be 'honest in conversation and chaste in body' – not perhaps the most welcome advice, with its explicit admonition to remain loyal to the wife of his youth; and to listen to mature counsellors while retaining the active service of the young, a familiar balancing act for kings. Alcuin commended his letter as an expression of his affection for Pippin. Two similar letters were sent to the King's eldest son, Charles, who was anointed King in 801: the first, written perhaps in 797 and before this event, commended him for his virtuous life, following the example of his father.[53] Alcuin warned him against flatterers and referred to letters he had sent to Louis, Charlemagne's other son who was then ruling Aquitaine and who would succeed him. None of these now remain. The second letter congratulated the prince on his papal anointing.[54] It too is an early form of a 'mirror for princes' that extolled the figure of Charlemagne as the exemplary 'ruler and emperor of a Christian people.'[55]

Alcuin's letters to the royal women reveal a different side to his sympathies and disposition.[56] There is a very kindly and gracious letter to the daughters of Charlemagne, Rotrudis and Bertha, written in the first half of the last decade of the eighth century.[57] In it Alcuin said that 'the devotion of my heart specially tends towards you both because of the familiarity and dedication that you have shown to me.' He signed off by bidding farewell to his 'most beloved daughters.' Sometime between 793 and 796, he wrote to Gisela, Abbess of Chelles, from the court at Aachen during a major festival. In it Alcuin thanked her warmly for the gift of a hat – *cappa*. He anticipated the visit to her of Angilbert and remembered her sister Ava, who later gave a Bible to Chelles to which a poem of Alcuin's was attached.[58] He also sent greetings to *Columba* the nickname for Rotrudis, to whom, with Gisela, Alcuin dedicated the last two books of his commentary on John's gospel. There is another gracious letter to Gisela, written in September 798 from Alcuin's monastery at St Loup de Troyes.[59] In it Alcuin lamented that an acute fever had detained him from being able to come and see her, and it might yet impede his planned meeting with the King. He encouraged her leadership in rebuilding the church of St Mary at Chelles and also in building up its library: he would send his pupil and friend Fredegisus to assist her.[60] He thanked her for the gift of a cross, produced it would seem at her monastery. He bade her farewell as a most beloved sister.[61]

One of his most moving letters was written to Gisela and Rotrudis sometime in 801, lamenting that he had not heard from them for a while.[62] It contains one of the most heartfelt expressions of his theology of Christian friendship and of the inspiration of the Bible: 'the child of love is a child of God,' he said, for 'someone who reads the most sacred words of the Lord handed down to us by his saints hears God speaking; and the one who prays speaks with God.' Alcuin prayed that they too might sense the presence of the Holy Spirit in their hearts. The letter that he had written was a sacramental sign of the reality of their friendship in Christ.[63] Taken together with the fact that he dedicated his commentary on John's gospel to them,[64] this is a profound insight into the intensity and depth of Alcuin's spiritual relationship with noble women who were his personal friends. It would seem that to the royal family, Alcuin was always a steady friend and spiritual father.

Chapter 7

Statesman

The last of the capitularies of the synod of Frankfurt, which met in 794 to respond to the twin challenges of the reversal of iconoclasm in the East and the rise of Adoptionism in Spain, recorded that 'Charlemagne recommended that the holy synod should receive Alcuin into its religious fellowship and prayers inasmuch as he was a man learned in ecclesiastical doctrines. So the whole synod gave approval in accordance with the Lord King's instruction and received him into their fellowship and prayers.'[1]

In Byzantium an attempt had been made at the second council of Nicea to restore the veneration of images or icons. The decrees of this council had reached the court of Charlemagne in a faulty translation that muddled veneration with worship. It provoked a sharp reaction which was only reined in by Pope Hadrian I. In Spain, a variant form of Christology had sprung up which asserted that in his human nature, Jesus was the 'adopted' son of God and therefore only 'nominally' God in that respect. Alcuin devoted his best energies in the last decade of his life to repudiating this heresy as he saw it on behalf of Charlemagne and his bishops.

The rest of the decrees of the synod of Frankfurt dealt with the reform and good ordering of the Church, having first condemned the two heresies and ratified the public deposition of Tassilo of Bavaria, whom Charlemagne pardoned and confined to a monastery for the rest of his life. Alcuin's position as a visiting scholar under the patronage of the King was consistent with Charlemagne summoning him back from a lengthy visit to England in order to deal with the Adoptionist crisis. He may have had some influence upon the drafting of the last stages of the *Libri Carolini*, which was produced by Theodulf of Orleans at royal command to rebut the decrees of the second council of Nicea concerning the veneration of icons and his reported letter on this subject is now lost. Alcuin's role as an emissary also made him to some extent a representative of the English Church, to which Charlemagne looked for support at this time on these theological issues.[2] He had had first hand experience of legislating alongside papal representatives for the reform and good order of the English Church during the legatine visitation to England in 786. Two representatives of Pope Hadrian I were present at Frankfurt in 794, the bishops Stephen and Theophylact, along with the archbishops of Milan and Aquileia. The synod of Frankfurt was of fundamental importance for Charlemagne's programme of reform and leadership of the Western Church.[3]

The Cross in the form of either an amulet or a brooch, of Irish workmanship but similar in style to the Tassilo chalice, being made out of silver, gold and glass.

The 'Admonitio Generalis' and the 'De litteris colendis'

Alcuin's influence on Charlemagne's church policy can however, be detected earlier in the *Admonitio Generalis* issued in 789.[4] This important statement of royal policy was clearly a collaborative and fully worked project of reform, one of the most influential of the Carolingian capitularies. Charlemagne was hailed as a second Josiah, the King in the Old Testament who had recovered the book of the Law and reformed the Temple.[5] Josiah had 'striven by visitation, correction and admonition to recall the kingdom which God had given him to the worship of the true God.' The words 'visitation, correction and admonition' sum up very well the tenor of the Carolingian renewal of the Church, which had the furtherance of Christian education at its heart. Much of the material included in the *Admonitio Generalis* was drawn up using and abridging canonical legislation sent earlier from Rome by Pope Hadrian I to Charlemagne.[6] Alcuin's influence appears evident in the phraseology of the address clause to the King, the first part of the prologue about the role of bishops and kings, where parallels with his letters to various bishops are very striking; in chapter 60, which is a second prologue, and from chapter 61 to the end.[7] This last part reads more like a sermon steeped in the Bible, with a strong moral appeal. The overt biblical dimension was not repeated in subsequent capitularies, however, giving to this one its programmatic character. The titles given to Charlemagne by Alcuin were also very significant: he was called to be the 'ruler, defender and helper' of the Church, terms Alcuin reiterated in some of his letters to the King. In Alcuin's judgement, the legal and moral force of these decrees had its root in the Law of the Old Testament, hence the comparison with Josiah. The authority of the king was therefore backed by the authority of the Bible itself as the Word of God, insofar as he was obedient to it, and ensured that his people were too. The whole document is also a vivid window into the state of the Church at that time, and it provides an ample context for understanding Alcuin's own writings as well as his authoritative contributions to the life of the Frankish church in the 790's.

The elements in the *Admonitio Generalis* that may be attributed to the influence of Alcuin are very close in tone and content to another document that remains from that time, the famous letter *De litteris colendis* of which only a single damaged manuscript now remains in Oxford.[8] Both documents place great emphasis on education in the life and reform of the Church.[9] *De litteris colendis* was a letter apparently addressed by Charlemagne to Bagulf, abbot of Fulda, and it seems to have been composed in advance of the *Admonitio Generalis*, being a product of the ferment of thought that coalesced in that decree. It may therefore be dated before 789, reflecting perhaps Alcuin's growing influence at court after his departure from England sometime following the legatine visitation in 786.[10]

Initially the letter *De litteris colendis* was probably circulated more widely, perhaps at the behest of Angilram, Archbishop of Metz and principal royal chaplain, who was a friend of Alcuin's.[11] It is topped and tailed by formulae common to the royal chancery, with a couple of additional clauses at the end, directing it to all suffragan bishops and monasteries, and precluding monks from involvement in secular courts. The actual text contains many phrases common to Alcuin's other writings, notably the assertion that *discere* is the foundation of *docere* – to learn is to become able to teach. It is of particular interest also in its reference to the *Rule of St Benedict* that was to become subsequently of central importance to Carolingian reform of the monasteries led by Benedict of Aniane, who had a close relationship with Alcuin.[12] 'Charlemagne's letter contains elements of Alcuin's style, and educational ideas which, like those of Alcuin, belong to the tradition of Anglo-Saxon humanism.'[13] It seems that the lost manuscript that was destroyed in 1944 in Metz contained the original draft of the letter intended to be circulated in the King's name, probably by Angilram of Metz, who may have pressed Alcuin into service in the first place. The present damaged but earlier manuscript was a version adapted for a particular monastery, in this case the strategically important centre of Christianity at Fulda, founded by Boniface, which became an active centre of mission among the conquered Saxons. *De litteris colendis* may therefore be the first of Alcuin's known contributions to the reform of the Frankish Church, as he stepped into the shoes of his predecessors, Willibrord and Boniface, drawing on the experience and traditions of the English Church, and of York in particular with its long involvement in missionary work.

De litteris colendis repays close reading in order to appreciate the contribution that Alcuin was able to make to the Carolingian reform movement at a crucial formative stage in the years immediately before the issuing of the *Admonitio Generalis* in 789. It helps to explain why he was 'head-hunted' by Charlemagne in the first place and it reflects what he had to offer in terms of his learning and experience cultivated at York. For learning was to be based upon a stable rule of community life, in a monastery or a cathedral. To achieve this, the teaching of the study of letters was essential. Learning of language was the prerequisite to its correct use, so that 'those who seek to please God by right living may not neglect to please Him also by right speaking.'[14] Knowledge was the foundation for right action; error in worship was to be avoided at all costs. The letter remonstrated against the evidence on every hand of low standards of Latin literacy, which had troubled the King and his advisers for some years. They like Alcuin himself feared that this would undermine the ability of clergy and monks to read the Scriptures, leading to errors of understanding and heresy arising from ignorance and carelessness.[15] Learning was therefore the key to penetrating the mysteries of the Bible, some parts of which deployed 'figures of speech, tropes and the like' for which training was required in their comprehension. 'The more fully anyone is instructed beforehand in the mastery of letters, the more quickly he will gain spiritual understanding.' The willingness to learn was also the foundation for effective teaching. Both reading and singing in church were signs therefore of effective discipline in the common life, both in terms of chastity of life, and also of scholarly speaking by which wisdom might be imparted. This letter is therefore a fine distillation of the heart of the reform and an epitome of what Alcuin himself believed, practised and commended on many other occasions.

In the *Admonitio Generalis*, the chapters that deal with education in the life of monastic and other communities are of a piece with *De litteris colendis*: 'Let schools for teaching boys the psalms, musical notation, singing, computation and grammar be created in every monastery and episcopal residence.'[16] This was a bold hope. Books were to be carefully corrected lest people pray to God improperly: copying was to be supervised with due diligence by older men and not by boys. Those admitted to monastic life had first to be properly instructed before being allowed out into the affairs of the world: as in England, monks were not allowed to participate in secular judicial assemblies.

Alcuin's contribution to the last part of the *Admonitio Generalis* not only defined the role of the king, it also put moral backbone into a fairly standard list of traditional canonical prescriptions. He appealed to the conscience of the bishops and their clergy, insisting on the central importance of their teaching and preaching ministry, citing the great commandment reiterated by Christ in the gospels in which he added emphasis on the love of God with the mind.[17] The letter also enjoined the keeping of the peace, and urged judges to become properly informed, so that their judgements might be just and public oaths be administered properly and effectively, and not to those under-age. There followed a series of chapters that were clearly based on the Ten Commandments as they applied to Frankish society. Finally the clergy were to be tested regularly as well as instructed properly in order to ensure their intelligent orthodoxy, so that services might be conducted with understanding. They were not to carry weapons. Churches were to be secured against weather, dogs, and gossip. Weights and measures were to be standard, and provision made everywhere for pilgrims and the poor. At every point, direct reference was made to the Bible.

Furthermore abbesses were not to make the sign of the Cross in blessing, nor themselves to veil virgins; nor were clergy to dress as monks if they were not so professed or settled. Wandering monks and freakish religious penitents were to be restrained. Roman chant was to be learnt as the norm, and Sunday respected as the Lord's Sabbath: only carrying stuff for the army or of vital provisions was permitted, along with carrying and burying corpses. Preaching was to be supervised in its content as well as in its form to ensure orthodox belief and the avoidance of novelty, a distinct preoccupation of Alcuin's. Following the teaching of the apostle Paul in Galatians chapter 5, a sombre list of sins was balanced by an encouragement to preach the love of God and of others. The final note was homiletic, even apocalyptic: 'Let us prepare ourselves with all our heart in knowledge of the truth so that we may be able to resist those who oppose truth.'[18] All these prescriptions were to be a foundation for the decrees of the Synod of Frankfurt in 794, by which time Alcuin had visited and returned from his visit to England on Charlemagne's behalf to consult about the icon controversy.[19]

Alcuin and the Synod of Frankfurt

Alcuin threw his whole weight behind the rebuttal by the Frankish and Italian churches of the Adoptionist theology emanating from Spain. This was a heresy much closer to home than the quarrel with Byzantium about icons; and given the lukewarm response of the papacy to that issue, it was a new challenge that re-united Charlemagne and Pope Hadrian. Alcuin produced his most important and significant theology in dealing with this variant Christology, generating three major treatises in the process.[20] The first chapter of the decrees of the synod of Frankfurt rejected utterly any idea that Christ was the 'adopted' Son of God, and later on included a short form of the Creed that emphasised the equality of persons in the Trinity and the divine initiative in the Incarnation.[21] The second chapter rejected a single aspect of the icon controversy: the belief that Nicaea II had decreed that the same worship should be offered to saints and images as was offered to the Holy Trinity.[22] Meanwhile Pope Hadrian had already repudiated Adoptionism in a letter dated 786, and this may have influenced how the Frankish and Italian bishops responded at Frankfurt in 794.[23] Charlemagne's own reaction was severe, both in public and behind the scenes: for he regarded heresy as a peculiar form of public disorder, which it was his duty as the paramount Christian ruler in the West to crush. It may also have given him an opportunity to override the set-back from Rome that had led to the sidelining of the *Libri Carolini*. Adoptionism was an issue within his own remit and political interest, as he still sought to secure his position in the marches and to extend his influence across the Pyrenees into Spain.

There is, however, no evidence of Alcuin's hand directly in any of the decrees issued by the synod of Frankfurt, although some looked back to the *Admonitio Generalis*; but he was entrusted with the writing of two important letters on behalf of the Frankish bishops to their Spanish counterparts, the second of which was addressed to Elipand Archbishop of Toledo directly.[24] These were identified long ago by Wallach as work of Alcuin's drafting, on the grounds of their close similarities to his main treatises against Adoptionism and his other letters on the subject. Along with the papal condemnation and the decrees of the synod itself, the Frankish and Italian remonstrances constituted the first wave of reaction and challenge to these perceived Spanish errors.

In his letter to Elipand Alcuin challenged the Spanish Church for departing from the *via regia* of the Catholic faith – that which all Christian everywhere and at all times had believed about the nature of Christ: for only within this fortress of faith lay true peace.[25] The union in Christ of his divine and human natures was a mystery to be worshipped, not something to be subjected to rational analysis or explained away. He described Christ as King and Redeemer, Lord and God. Characteristically he appealed to his hearers: 'Let us follow in all charity the venerable precepts of our holy fathers.' In fidelity to the Catholic tradition, Charlemagne had summoned representatives from across the Western church, including Britain, to a synod at Frankfurt, having first informed the Pope in Rome of his concerns. With their collective authority behind him, the King, or rather Alcuin proceeded in this lengthy letter to dismantle the assertions of the Spanish bishops along lines that would be developed much more fully in Alcuin's three treatises against Adoptionism.

The episcopal letter concluded with a remarkable composite and amplified form of the Nicene Creed, which conflated additional material from the *Quicunque Vult*, the creed of Pelagius (then attributed either to Jerome or Augustine) and the creed of Toledo of 675.[26] It has important similarities to the Creed inserted into the *Libri Carolini*, and the King affirmed it at his own belief as well as that of the Catholic Church. It was notable also for affirming the *Filioque* more than once, in relation to the Trinity and to the Incarnation. It affirmed that Christ was 'perfect God in his divinity and perfect man in his humanity – the true Son of God in both substances.' It was a highly significant and revealing monument to the unity and theological vigour of the Frankish Church and its Italian and British supporters.[27] Charlemagne concluded by urging the Spanish bishops to return to the bosom of Mother Church, and to regard him and his bishops and other theological advisers, like Alcuin, as 'co-operators in your salvation and helpers in maintaining Catholic peace.' It was an eloquent, lucid and balanced pastoral instrument, 'illustrative of Alcuin's position as an adviser to Charlemagne and of his influence on royal government.'[28]

Closely related to this letter to Elipand in timing, style and substance was the fuller synodical letter sent by the entire Frankish episcopate to Spain, which it accompanied and explained. In the drafting of this letter Alcuin also had a key role, and there are important and close parallels between the two documents.[29] It was a full and detailed response to the *libellus* sent by the Spanish bishops and read aloud at the synod. It may be that the initial letter to Elipand was the draft upon which the Frankish bishops proceeded to formulate their own collective response, which Alcuin then wrote up for them shortly afterwards. Its contents clearly recorded the proceedings of the synod by someone who was an active participant and an ally of the bishops, commended to them and authorised by the King with their consent, as the final chapter of the synod's decrees made clear. Alcuin's role as a special adviser and a learned deacon was clearly and irrevocably established by these events: confronted by Adoptionism, his hour had come. His consistent approach in this document, as in his other writings, was to challenge Adoptionism as a novelty within the long tradition of Christian belief. He referred obliquely to the status of the synod of Frankfurt in two of his later letters: in a long letter written in 798 warning the monks in Septimania on the borders of Spain about the dangers of Adoptionism; and in another letter written late the next year to Arno, Bishop of Salzburg, lamenting the persistence of the Spanish errors.[30] He at no time made any direct mention however of his own pivotal role in the proceedings at Frankfurt.[31]

The synodical letter of the Frankish bishops, drafted by Alcuin, runs to 26 chapters. It was a weighty and detailed rebuttal of the Spanish case, point by point.[32] Its first charge was that of novelty, their book having been read out loud in its entirety, sentence by sentence, in the presence of the bishops. The second charge was that of transgressing the boundaries of doctrine established by the Catholic Fathers of the Church. The third charge was that of prying in a rationalistic manner into the divine mystery of the Incarnation: 'for divine realities are better venerated by faith than investigated by reason.' The Spanish bishops were criticised for their slack use of texts, not offering accurate references to their authorities, and often making selective use of the writings of the Fathers. Thereupon Alcuin proceeded with a systematic demolition of their arguments and their use of patristic texts, in whose mastery he showed himself adept. This was to be his standard approach in his three theological treatises against Adoptionism. It presupposed access to a full library, as well as a long familiarity with classical Latin patristic theology on his part. Large extracts from the Spanish *libellus* were cited, only to be picked apart ruthlessly. No less striking was the encyclopaedic use of biblical texts in support of his critique and argument.

Alcuin left no stone unturned, nor was he at any point distracted: his intention was clearly to produce, on behalf of the Frankish bishops, and with their united support, a definitive and authoritative statement of orthodox Catholic belief around which the Western Church could rally. It was a weighty and exhaustive treatment of the core of Christian belief about the nature of Christ. Alcuin drew parallels with the heresy of Nestorius, whom he alleged that the Spanish were reluctant to repudiate alongside other notorious heretics of the early Church. Central to his concern was his utter repudiation of the term *adoptivus* – 'adopted' when applied to Christ himself as the Son of God. He accused the Spanish bishops of failing to understand the teaching of the apostles and the Fathers, citing the gospels very fully in support of belief in the divine nature and origin of Jesus as God-become-man. The letter concludes in the same tone as Alcuin's letter to Elipand, with a sincere, charitable and heartfelt appeal for a change of heart on the part of the Spanish bishops.

Alcuin's letter was a condemnation determined throughout by reasoned argument and relentless appeals to biblical and patristic texts and theology, warning towards the end against any division of the unity of the Church, which was certainly Charlemagne's principal concern, as it was the Pope's: 'may it suffice you to follow the footsteps of the Fathers, and by faith to hold fast to their sayings.' Alcuin appealed also to the scandal caused to non-Christians, perhaps with the Muslim population of Spain in mind, which was attracting many converts from Christianity as its influence and political control spread:

> Consider what a scandal this is among pagan peoples, that it may
> be said that the God of the Christians was in fact an adopted slave;
> whereas it is we who are adopted by him, not he along with us.

Were Christ's divine nature not united in himself with our humanity, he could hardly be the only mediator between God and human beings and their saviour. Alcuin's final argument rested upon the words of Jesus in the gospel of John: 'If the Son shall make you free, you will be free indeed.'[33] These two documents, produced with such skill, determination and care, were the first salvoes in what would be the sharp conflict that would preoccupy much of Alcuin's time and energy in the last decade of his life.

Detailed research has also confirmed the existence of other letters written by Alcuin on behalf of Charlemagne.[34] Two have already been discussed because they were sent to England. One went in 795 to Ethelhard Archbishop of Canterbury and Ceolwulf Bishop of Lindsey, seeking their mediation with Offa of Mercia on behalf of some exiles at the Frankish court.[35] The other letter was written from Tours to Offa sometime after Alcuin's arrival there as abbot in 796 and was a portmanteau response to various issues outstanding between the two kings, probably settling diplomatic tensions between them.[36] It dealt with the safety of pilgrims and merchants on a reciprocal basis and the adjudication by the Pope Leo III of the exiled priest Odbert in the presence of the Archbishop of Canterbury. It dealt also with a request by Offa for certain black marble stones and treated of the length of English cloth on sale on the continent. It asked for prayers for the soul of the late Pope Hadrian and mentioned gifts sent by Charlemagne to Offa. Close examination of the style of these letters reveals many features common to the known letters of Alcuin. They need to be seen also in the context of Alcuin's own correspondence with Offa and with the Archbishop of Canterbury. They demonstrate the trust placed in him by Charlemagne in matters of which he was particularly well informed in relation to English affairs. One thing that is notable about these diplomatic letters however is the complete absence of any biblical references. Both letters played on the existing friendship between Alcuin and correspondents as a means to achieving Charlemagne's ends.[37] In the case of the letter to Offa, there are close parallels with Alcuin's own letter of the same year upon hearing of the murder of King Ethelred of Northumbria, which he wrote reassuring Offa of Charlemagne's continued goodwill.[38]

The third letter, also written in 796, was in the name of Charlemagne to the new Pope, Leo III, congratulating him upon his election, and commending Angilbert of St Riquier as the royal envoy bearing gifts intended for his late predecessor.[39] It is closely related to a letter of instruction to Angilbert composed for the King by Alcuin.[40] The King's letter to the Pope contained

the famous definition of the role of Charlemagne in defending the Church
of Christ and strengthening its grasp of the Catholic faith, while the Pope,
like Moses, was to raise his hands in prayer for the victory of the Franks as
'the Christian people' over all their enemies. Once again the absence of any
biblical references is striking when compared with Alcuin's own letters. Alcuin
was also commissioned by Charlemagne to compose around this time the
epitaph for Pope Hadrian I that may still be seen in the portico of St Peter's
in Rome, as the Frankish King's tribute to his older mentor and friend.[41] This
letter has also to be seen in the context of several subsequent letters from
Alcuin to Charlemagne and others about the plight of the papacy between
the death of Hadrian I in 795, the restoration of Pope Leo III in 798-9, and
the King's subsequent coronation in Rome as Emperor by that Pope in 800.

Conquest and evangelization

Charlemagne's wars against the Saxons dominated much of his reign and
went on for thirty-three years, as Einhard described in his *Life of Charlemagne*:
he painted them in barbarous terms, emphasising the porous border-land that
lay between the Saxons and the Franks, 'nearly everywhere flat, open country,'
and prone to repeated incursions. The hatred and impatience felt by the Franks
for their pagan neighbours is palpable in Einhard's account. This conflict,
more than any other, had a hardening effect on the Franks, who believed that
they were God's chosen people conducting a virtual crusade of conquest and
assimilation.[42] The continual militarization of Frankish rule left its mark on the
liturgy, in which the Church endorsed the wars at the King's command with
lengthy litanies and fasting, acclaiming the king as an instrument of divine
purpose.[43] 'The God of the Frankish army was close indeed to that of ancient
Israel, and the liturgy provided the link;'[44] and this belief was reflected in some
of Alcuin's letters to the King. It was also endorsed by Pope Hadrian I, who
praised Charlemagne's 'conversion' of the Saxons in a letter written in 786. The
Saxons posed a permanent economic and cultural threat to the Rhine trade
route, which was of central importance to Charlemagne's kingdom, its wealth
and its power. Charlemagne's coronation by Pope Leo III in 800 as Emperor
of the Christian West was in part therefore a device for subduing the Saxons
to his legitimate rule, as they had no uniting kingship in their own society. It
represented also papal endorsement of the naked imperialism and ascendancy
which Charlemagne consistently, and at times ruthlessly, pursued on every
frontier of his broad domains and from which the papacy clearly profited.[45]
With regard to the Saxons in particular, 'it was hard enough to defeat the Saxons
in war, let alone find a way of ruling them, which saved their faces and gained
their consent.'[46] Without this reluctant consent the missionary advance of the
Church among the Saxons could hardly proceed in safety or become established.

Some time, either in 782 or 785[47] or perhaps as late as 795,[48] the first Saxon
capitulary was promulgated:[49] it was a shrill instrument of brutal repression.

It smacked of ruthless desperation, commanding capital punishment for a whole range of offences – attacking churches, contempt for the Lenten fast, murdering one of the clergy, witch-craft and cremation, and most notoriously for refusing baptism. Conspiracy against the King and the Frankish nobility, and any violence towards Christians was equally punishable by death. This code was a determined effort to stamp Frankish Christian culture onto an alien and sullen people, who had been savagely treated by Charlemagne on numerous occasions. Its spirit was drawn from some of the grimmest pages of the Old Testament. It allowed little autonomy for Saxon customs. The argument for the earlier date would connect it with the submission and baptism of Widukind, the Saxon leader, in 785, or perhaps to an even earlier attempt at subjugation and imposition of Frankish direct rule at Lippspringe in 782. The argument for the later date, even 795, rests on the sense that this code was born of frustration and was probably unenforceable, a final prelude perhaps to the necessary accommodation embodied in the second Saxon capitulary of 797, which clearly reflected a broader consensus among both Franks and Saxons. On the other hand it would represent a rapid change of policy and this may be unlikely given the fundamental hatred of the Franks for the Saxons and the problems of communication and implementation. Either way, the second capitulary definitely represented a new approach and its background may be illuminated by Alcuin's letters.

The later date for the first Saxon capitulary might be supported indirectly, however, by a letter written in 789 to an unknown abbot or bishop working in Saxony as a missionary, in which Alcuin sent greetings to his friend Willehad, the titular Bishop of Bremen, asking for news about the progress of Christian missionary work in Saxony and also among the Danes.[50] He made no mention then of any forcible conversions, though perhaps he did not know the full scope of Frankish repression; yet he was close to the King and his court at that time before his return to England in 790.

Alcuin, who took an active and most seminal role in formulating Charlemagne's policy and in drafting official documents on behalf of the Frankish king, was not the kind of man to sit quietly and ignore such colossal misconduct, especially when it had some important theological implications.[51]

It may well be that this fearsome first code was part of Charlemagne's last major campaign against the Saxons and that it back-fired. Certainly in 797, a second Saxon code was issued with the full support of the court at Aachen, which was more conciliatory and pragmatic in many ways.[52] It spoke of agreement between the Franks and the Saxons, naming specific groups among them, outlining its detailed provisions in order to create a consistent framework for dealing with theft and violence throughout the lands under Charlemagne's overlordship. Monetary recompense between Saxons and Franks was to replace capital punishment and retribution, utilising customary means of legal settlement among the Saxons.

It would seem that Alcuin himself may have had some hand in this reversal of royal policy.[53] In a series of letters, he was quite outspoken in his condemnation of forcible baptism and conversion and the immediate and greedy imposition of tithes upon the Saxons, lamenting to friends the alienating impact of such an approach politically and its spiritually deleterious nature. In this he was a true disciple of Gregory the Great, whose own approach to mission among the Anglo-Saxons was recorded explicitly in his letter in Bede's *History*[54] and portrayed by Alcuin in his *Life of St Willibrord*.[55] It was a measure of the strength of his relationship with Charlemagne and the respect in which he was evidently held that Alcuin could articulate such a firm and public moral criticism of a policy central to the King's concerns. It was a credit too to Charlemagne that he did not silence his critic as no doubt he could have done. It is notable too that these letters were soon copied and preserved as exemplars by sympathetic friends who presumably shared Alcuin's views.[56] Alcuin had immediate knowledge of the whole range of missionary activity in which other Anglo-Saxons were engaged at that time and he was in regular contact with them. He could therefore speak with authority and probably on their behalf too, on a matter that was close to their hearts and which would certainly impinge upon their safety as well.[57] It remains a striking fact of English church history that there was no forcible conversion recorded by Bede or anyone else. Instead education was the handmaid of evangelism in England, maintained however within the framework of social and political support by the local royal family and landed nobility, without which neither churches nor monasteries could have been created or protected. This was of course a form of social pressure, but it was not obviously violent in its method, intention or impact.[58]

After his victory over the Avars, Alcuin therefore wrote to Charlemagne a strong letter of remonstrance about the policy enshrined in the first Saxon capitulary.[59] This was one of a group of letters dealing with the treatment and baptism of newly conquered people – the Saxons and the Avars.[60] It was addressed to Charlemagne sometime after August 796 and it referred to Augustine's work *De catechizandis rudibus*.[61] Alcuin criticized the practice of premature and compulsory baptism and the immediate levying of tithes on newly conquered and 'converted' people, outlining instead the classic Christian approach to catechism prior to baptism. He praised the King 'for leading so many from the paths of error into the way of truth,' referring to the Saxons and the recently vanquished Huns. He urged genuine evangelism and challenged directly the imposition of taxes, asserting that it would be better to forfeit them for a while than for Charlemagne's new subjects to resent and so reject the Christian faith: for true belief must always precede baptism[62].

Closely related to this letter was one to Megenfrid, the King's treasurer, in which Alcuin expressed his concerns and views even more forcefully.[63] It set out Alcuin's thinking and its theological basis at some length, which presupposed therefore a high level of literacy in his hearers at court: for both letters were probably intended for public consumption as well as constituting a trenchant contribution to an ongoing debate about policy towards the Saxons and other conquered peoples. It addressed the nature and importance of lay Christian vocation and duty on the basis of the parable of the talents in the gospel. It then set out the theology of evangelization, based on the gospels and the teaching of the apostle Paul.[64] Alcuin also cited Augustine: 'Faith is something voluntary never compelled.' If faith were received falsely no true salvation could occur; therefore preachers to pagan peoples should teach the faith by careful and peaceful words: they were called to be 'preachers and not predators.' Alcuin sought Megenfrid's sympathy and active support with the King in restraining the forcible imposition of tithes and baptism upon the conquered Saxons as a way of attempting to override their natural resistance. He urged Megenfrid to use his influence on Charlemagne in this matter 'as a most faithful dispenser of royal treasure and his devoted helper and counsellor.'[65] Alcuin also challenged careerism and the pursuit of worldly wealth and honours by senior clergy, warning of the danger of lack of effective leadership in the Church, and trusting that his reader would warn the King of this also. It was one of his most outspoken letters.

At the same time, he expressed his concern to his friend Arno, Bishop of Salzburg, about a repetition of such harsh policies towards the newly conquered Avar people.[66] He urged him to engage in a mission of preaching to them as his diocese bordered their lands; and a second letter shortly after set out in full, as requested and promised, his theology of baptism, evangelization and education.[67] After a short homily about the nature of episcopacy as fishing for souls and a symbolical analysis of the 153 fish caught in John chapter 21, Alcuin built his argument on the Lord's command at the very end of Matthew's gospel. His fear was that the wretched Saxon people would lose altogether the benefits of their baptism because they did not have the fundamentals of the faith in their hearts. According to Augustine, baptism must rest upon choice, not compulsion: 'a person can be compelled to baptism but not to faith.'[68] He drew comparison with the obstinacy of the Adoptionists who had departed from the Catholic faith.[69] Careful and sensitive education was the only sure foundation for effective evangelism: a person must co-operate with the Holy Spirit in the salvation of people; the priest washed the body with water, but it was the Holy Spirit that justified the soul through faith.[70] Baptism therefore had a visible and an invisible component. He cited the gradual transformation of the apostle Peter and the Lord's humility towards the woman taken in adultery as examples of the fragility of human nature and therefore of the need for a more patient approach towards conversion. There were similarities here with the penitential teaching of Theodore of Tarsus, Archbishop of Canterbury. Alcuin cited the authority of Gregory the Great, who in his *Pastoral Rule* enjoined accommodation to the differing temperaments of individuals. He urged his friend to have this book as an *enchiridion* in the hand and in the heart. He anticipated eagerly the time when distance would no longer separate friends, and letters would therefore be redundant.[71] Alcuin's concern for the plight of the Avars was also expressed in a subsequent letter to Charlemagne in which he urged the King to show mercy to his captives and erstwhile enemies.[72]

These letters of Alcuin's were preserved as potent models of a tradition of moral challenge to rulers that had a long tap-root stretching back through Boniface and Willibrord to the writings of Bede and the letters of Gregory the Great; they also accorded with the fearless evangelism of the early Irish missionaries like Columbanus, who followed the example of the prophets in the Bible. Alcuin appealed however to the King's own knowledge of Christian theology, and could therefore place this particular issue within a wider context with which Charlemagne and those around him were familiar, notably the authority of the Bible and also of Augustine, whom the King especially revered.

The practical impact of such letters is impossible to assess, however: Alcuin was surely heard; but was he heeded? They probably mitigated a severe royal policy to some extent, and they certainly called it openly into question in the minds of others; and they may lie behind the change of policy expressed in the second Saxon code. But one of the sad contrasts between England and the continent during these early medieval centuries was the readiness with which coercion was used in Europe as a weapon of Christianization alongside military conquest for many centuries to come.[73] It proved a baneful legacy of Charlemagne's reign.

Chapter 8

Rome

Rome loomed large on the horizon of western Christian Europe throughout the eighth century, and especially for Anglo-Saxon Christians.[1] Part of Alcuin's intention in his poem about the city and church of York was to incorporate Northumbrian history within the wider ambit of Rome and its legacy, both spiritual and tangible.[2] His attitude towards the holy city, which he visited on several occasions, and in particular towards the authority of the papacy, emerges throughout his writings and letters; and it was to exert an significant influence in the events leading up to the coronation of Charlemagne as Emperor by Pope Leo III in St Peter's basilica on Christmas day 800.

The English Church saw itself as an outpost but also an integral part of Roman Christianity, as exemplified in its own apostle, Gregory the Great.[3] Bede made this very clear in his *History* as well as in his gospel homilies, which complemented those of Gregory himself. The monastery at Monkwearmouth-Jarrow in which he grew up and was educated was consciously modelled on Roman practices, notably in its singing, its internal decoration and in book production: the *Codex Amiatinus*, one of three great pandects of the Bible produced there in Bede's time, was closely and consciously imitative of Italian models. Benedict Biscop, its founder, like Bishop Wilfrid, made many visits to Rome, as well as to monasteries throughout Gaul, bringing home works of Christian art and books, as well as the experience of varying monastic practices. Relics too played an important part in this process: these were normally items that had been in close proximity to the tombs of Roman martyrs rather than actual fragments of their bodies, and these martyrs were celebrated in the liturgical calendar in England. The topography of a monastery or a cathedral environment was sometimes designed to replicate the sacred geography of Rome, actually imitating in some situations, for example at Canterbury, the pattern of church dedications around the Lateran itself. Anglo-Saxon sculpture reflected this Roman influence too, for example the Northumbrian crosses at Ruthwell and Bewcastle. Many English church dedications were to St Peter; and from the middle of the seventh century pilgrimage to Rome became a desirable goal, attracting kings, churchmen and pilgrims, as well as merchants and women of doubtful repute. Monkwearmouth itself claimed a papal privilege from Pope Agatho; and by the end of the eighth century there was the *schola Saxonum*, a place of lodging and settlement for Anglo-Saxon pilgrims to

An ivory panel portraying the Crucifixion of Christ, flanked by St Mary and St John: one of many ivories generated in the Carolingian milieu and emulating those of Byzantium and late antique Rome.

Rome that lay between the basilica of St Peter on the Vatican hill and the river Tiber, in the area now called Santo Spirito in Sassia. The Frisians and Lombards had similar enclaves; so too did the Franks at a slightly later date.[4]

The missionary activities of Willibrord and Boniface enjoyed papal blessing and support, and they in turn helped to inculcate respect for Roman practices and papal authority in the Frankish Church. Perhaps the most striking example of Bede's own reverence for the authority of Rome may be found not only in his description in his *History* of the synod of Hatfield in 679,[5] which was summoned by Archbishop Theodore in response to a mission from Rome, but also in his detailed account of the whole Monothelite controversy in his *Chronica Maiora*, included at the end of his computistical work *De Temporum Ratione*.[6] The Monothelite controversy concerned whether one will or two, human and divine, operated in the person of the incarnate Christ, and it led to the arrest and exile of Pope Martin by the Byzantine Emperor. Alcuin, probably influenced by Bede's approach, saw the Adoptionist controversy in his day, which also concerned Christology, as another manifestation of Roman orthodoxy being assailed by heretical tendencies. His reaction was closely modelled on that of Bede, whose grasp of theology and history was very clearly revealed in his careful composition of this chronicle, with its well-informed focus on contemporary affairs towards its end. Alcuin inherited from the English church of his birth and upbringing therefore a keen vision of Rome's spiritual significance, and an earnest expectation of the role of the papacy in exercising its teaching authority as the guardian of apostolic orthodoxy, as well as in its encouragement of Christian evangelisation and mission. His attitude towards Rome and the papacy is evident in various specific contexts in his writings.

Alcuin and Rome

Alcuin travelled to Rome at least twice and perhaps more often: the first time was as a young companion of his master Aelberht in the 760's. In his York poem he recorded Aelberht's love of travel and pilgrimage, seeking out books, like Benedict Biscop before him, strong in his devotion to Rome, its holy places and monasteries.[7] Alcuin alluded to his time with him abroad in the epitaph he composed for him shortly after his return from another visit to Rome in 781.[8] It was on his way back from that visit to collect the *pallium* for his friend Eanbald, the new Archbishop of York, that he met Charlemagne once again in Parma, who summoned him to join his court.[9] Alcuin mentioned in two of his letters staying at the monastery of Murbach, as well as an earlier encounter with Peter of Pisa at a debate in Pavia with a Jew called Julius, both of which events must have occurred *en route* to or from Rome in his youth.[10]

Alcuin's interest in obtaining relics from the holy city probably dated from his first encounters with the major Christian shrines of the apostles and martyrs in Rome. His most striking allusion to Rome, however, was in his treatise *De ratione animae*, written towards the end of his life around the year 801 when he was Abbot of Tours.[11] Talking about the nature of memory, and following the example of Augustine in his *De Trinitate*, Alcuin asserted:

> for just as he who has seen Rome has it inscribed in his mind and knows its form; so when he hears the name of Rome recalled, he immediately turns his mind into his memory, where its form lies hidden, and recognising it, he draws it forth.

In a letter written to Offa of Mercia in either 792 or 793 about the proper way to appoint archbishops in England, Alcuin referred to the opinions of experts whom he had met in Rome.[12] In a letter of 798 to Charlemagne he referred to the variety in observance of the Lenten fast by Greeks, Romans and others that he had encountered while in the city where many exiled Greek communities and monasteries functioned.[13] Although Rome clearly made an abiding impression on Alcuin, his memories of travel in Italy were less happy, and he mentioned the risk of serious illness and physical danger there in several letters to his friends.[14]

What Rome meant to him emerges most clearly in his poetry. For example in his lament for the sack of Lindisfarne, he described Rome as 'the capital and wonder of the world, golden Rome, now only a barbarous ruin.'[15] He alluded to passing along streets lined with ruins to get to the basilica of St Paul-outside-the-walls in a poem for his friend and disciple, Candidus Wizo, who was going with Charlemagne to Rome in 800, *ad limina sancti Petri*.[16] He composed a poem for a new friend, Theophylact, probably the Bishop of Todi whom Alcuin had encountered as part of the papal legation to England in 786, or just possibly the principal librarian at the Lateran under Pope Hadrian I, in which he again described Rome as the capital of the world.[17] There remains a striking paean to the holy city which he wrote in 795 at the time of the accession of Pope Leo III:[18]

> *Hail, mighty Rome, splendour of the world, our glorious mother,*
> *And all those who born within you who flourish in this age.*
> *Also the great Pope Leo, head and honour of the world:*
> *You are the sceptre of justice, the light of your see,*
> *Flourishing forever by the gift of Christ.*
> *May the keeper of the keys of heaven and the noble teacher of the world*
> *Preserve you by the prayers offered for you everywhere;*
> *And may the saints protect you all by their holy prayers,*
> *Whom Rome still holds within the circuit of its mighty walls.*
> *O fathers and people, the glory of the Roman race,*
> *Farewell by the mercy of the Lord forever!*

His description was echoed in another poem that he wrote for Charlemagne as he set forth on his epic journey to Rome in 800, in which Alcuin again described Rome as the capital of the world, the See of St Peter the heavenly key-bearer, and a treasury of saints' relics.[19]

It is in a succession of poems composed in honour of the new Pope Leo III that Alcuin's theology of the papacy emerges clearly. They were perhaps composed before the limitations of the new Pope became apparent, and they probably project the expectations so amply fulfilled by his predecessor, Hadrian I, whom Alcuin like Charlemagne profoundly revered. In one poem Alcuin hailed Leo III among other things as the 'cultivator of justice', a term he used widely elsewhere, a 'lover of truth and piety.' [20] In another encomium he called him the pinnacle of the episcopate, the holy master of saints, the apostolic pastor and noble teacher, whose writ ran everywhere by charters signed in his holy name that were accompanied by written sermons. The pope was the golden light of the world, the salt of the earth and gate of salvation, whose prayers Alcuin sought for himself with a mention of his own name at the end of the poem. In the light of the scandals associated with the early part of Leo's reign, these accolades sound ironic to say the least, perhaps even deluded, and certainly rather ultramontane in their vision: an idealisation from afar. In another lengthy poem, written to the new pope in a similar vein, Alcuin mentioned the emissary, sent by his friend the Archbishop of York, Eanbald, who was a young man or *puer* whom he asked Leo III to receive kindly and to protect.[21] This poem is interesting also for its mention of the renovation of learning that was a common cause between the Carolingian world and the Roman See: 'may the teachings of divine law be renewed everywhere by you and yours, holy father, to make known the work of the ancient Fathers throughout the world, whose sayings sound forth from their holy pages.' Alcuin referred also the importance of Roman music for the life of the Church. He mentioned himself once again as the Pope's humble servant, in the last line of the poem.

One of the most remarkable and personal letters that Alcuin ever wrote was to Pope Hadrian I shortly before the Pope's death on Christmas day 795; indeed it is uncertain if it was actually sent before news of the Pope's demise reached the court of Charlemagne.[22] It was written at a difficult moment in Alcuin's life when events in his native Northumbria were coming to a head, which resulted in the murder of King Ethelred in April 796, and the consecration of Alcuin's friend and pupil, Eanbald, as Archbishop of York in August of that same year. The way now seemed barred for Alcuin to return home safely and to feel welcome and he had to come to terms with the finality of his exile on the continent and his new role as Abbot of Tours. Written towards the end of 795 therefore, the deeply penitential note of this letter may have had something to do with his gloom over the inevitability of his not becoming the next Archbishop of York.[23] It sounds as if Alcuin was passing through a deep depression as he sensed the approach of the last phase of his life and his increasing alienation from his homeland for reasons that remain largely unclear, but which caused him acute concern about the well-being of the Northumbrian Church to which he could make no direct contribution. So in the build-up to this period of personal crisis, it would seem, he turned to the pope himself for moral support, entrusting his cause to his friend Angilbert, who was going to Rome as Charlemagne's emissary and for whose *bona fides* Alcuin vouched at the end of his letter. Angilbert's embassy was deferred, however, due to the news that Hadrian had died. He went later to greet the new Pope, Leo III, on behalf of the King, bearing the gifts originally intended for Pope Hadrian, along with a letter from Charlemagne which Alcuin drafted, as well as one from Alcuin himself to Pope Leo.[24]

Alcuin's letter to Hadrian, however, is very revealing and important. The language of the letter is coloured by the teaching of Pope Leo I, known as Leo the Great. Alcuin saw Leo I as the great intercessor for Christian people worldwide, a spiritual advocate with God, whose help he felt he badly needed. The bond between them lay in their common baptism by which shepherd and flock were united in Christ: in support of this Alcuin alluded to the threefold commission of Christ to Peter after his resurrection.[25] Alcuin himself was weighed down by some unspecified personal sins and he asked for help as from a spiritual doctor. Could the Pope loose him from the chains of his guilt? He appealed to him in the words of the Roman centurion to Jesus on behalf of his sick servant in the gospel.[26] He also addressed the Pope in these remarkably florid words: 'O blessed tongue of your mouth, in which lies the medicine of eternal salvation, and by which the heavens may be opened to believers!' Alcuin concluded with a fervent short prayer to Christ on behalf of the Pope's well-being. This letter reveals his profound inner insecurity that emerges in some other letters; he was *amletico* in his inner heart-searching and anxieties, at times hamstrung it would seem in his sense of personal vulnerability, and his apprehension towards the rigours of divine judgement, which he felt was impending as he drew towards the end of his life.

The news of Pope Hadrian's death affected Charlemagne profoundly, as Einhard testifies in his *Life*: 'he wept as if he had lost a brother or a dearly beloved son.'[27] Some measure of the King's consternation and sense of bereavement may also be seen in the letters which Alcuin drafted for Charlemagne saluting Pope Leo III on his election, and to King Offa of Mercia requesting prayers for the deceased Pope, in whose memory the King was sending gifts to the English bishops 'to show our love and trust towards a friend most dear to us.' This letter was probably accompanied by a letter of Alcuin himself to the English bishops reiterating and supporting Charlemagne's request: 'for faithful friendship is tested most on behalf of a dead friend.'[28] Alcuin shared in the King's grief: for he clearly regarded the late Pope as a spiritual lode-star, having perhaps first been drawn to Hadrian's attention in the aftermath of the legatine visitation to England in 786. It seems that he felt some personal bond towards him and some members of his retinue whom he knew personally, like Theophylact of Todi; otherwise he could hardly have written as he did directly to the Pope. Hadrian may well have exerted a direct significant influence on Alcuin's spiritual life.

The single most striking physical relic of Alcuin's creation is in fact the beautiful memorial stone which Charlemagne commissioned in memory of Pope Hadrian, whose epitaph Alcuin composed, and which is now lodged high in the portico of St Peter's basilica in Rome, having been carefully removed from the old Constantinian basilica that Alcuin would have known.[29] Carved in fine black Mosan marble from near Dinant in Belgium, its lettering was inlaid with gold, closely and consciously modelled on antique Roman epigraphy, which it replicated to a flawless standard.[30] According to the York annals and also the Lorsch annals, it was placed there on the occasion of Charlemagne's coronation in St Peter's at Christmas 800 as his personal and royal memorial to the late Pope; probably Alcuin's own authority lies behind this information. It was also a memorial to Charlemagne himself as his name was inscribed twice, the second time in the characteristic style which appears also on his coinage:[31] this was a deliberate royal *imprimatur*. It was carved from stone hewn from the very heartlands of the Carolingian Kingdom, emulating the black marble so highly prized by the Romans and sought after from Charlemagne as a prestige commodity by Offa of Mercia.[32]

Wallach long ago demonstrated that this epitaph to Hadrian was indeed Alcuin's own work, with many connections to his other writing and poetry. The quality of the carving testifies to a skilled school of epigraphy at Tours, which Alcuin clearly fostered: 'its well-executed Roman square capital was fashioned after older Roman inscriptions, many of which were undoubtedly still extant at Tours during the time of Alcuin.[33] Moreover 'the *nomina sacra* of the inscription are identical with those occurring in manuscripts from the scriptorium of Tours;' while 'the extremely literary character of Hadrian's epitaph is obvious from the use made of Roman and Christian literary sources.'[34] These Wallach elucidated in great detail in his analysis of this elaborate verse and its sources within Alcuin's own writings and beyond.

The theology of the epitaph also parallels that of other letters of condolence that Alcuin wrote, some of which have been discussed already.[35] He asserted the separation of the body and soul at death and the immortality of the soul; this was evident in his own epitaph as well.[36] 'His vision of an incorporeally immortal soul is a remnant of ancient Greek thought that is contrary to the orthodox Christian point of view of a corporeal resurrection of the flesh from the dust of the grave.'[37] Alcuin it seems believed in both the immortality of the soul and the resurrection of the body; but in that order. For Alcuin, therefore, the death of someone was not a cause of lament for them; only for those remaining. This epitaph for Hadrian I is also important evidence for Alcuin's knowledge of existing *sylloges* of papal and other Roman inscriptions: for example in his partiality for the phrase *iustitiae cultor*, which has already been noted.[38] This phrase and others like it became popular Carolingian motifs as well as further proof of the existence of models of Roman epigraphy which their craftsmen could imitate.

The substance of the epitaph was a striking tribute to a great pope: it is a very beautiful and noble poetic tribute by Alcuin on behalf of Charlemagne, united as they clearly were in their personal respect and spiritual devotion to Hadrian:

> *Here the father of the Church, the glory of Rome, the noble patriarch*
> *Blessed Pope Hadrian has his rest.*
> *A man to whom God was his life, law his piety, Christ his glory:*
> *An apostolic pastor, prompt in all good works,*
> *Noble from his birth and family,*
> *But far nobler on account of his holy merits;*
> *Heart-felt and adorned in his devotion as a pastor,*
> *Always and everywhere generous in his gifts to the churches of God,*
> *He nurtured all who came to him along their pathway to the stars.*
> *Large-hearted towards the poor, second to none in piety,*
> *Vigilant always for his people by his holy prayers,*
> *His teaching, his good works; and in his restoration of your arches and walls,*
> *O noble Rome, capital city and honour of the whole world.*

This poem expressed personal remorse of Charlemagne, in whose name the epitaph was written: the King (and Alcuin too) addressed the late Pope as someone whose memory was that of the sweetest love.[39] Death for Hadrian would prove to be the gateway to life eternal. The poem concludes with a heartfelt prayer that at the day of judgement Hadrian would be welcomed into heaven as the faithful servant of his Lord: 'Your praise, holy father, will remain in this world forever.' This elegant memorial remains as a potent and visible expression of how Alcuin and Charlemagne both felt about a great pope and father-in-God. It is also a striking and beautiful epitome of the Carolingian *renovatio* of Christian Rome, evident to a certain extent in the holy city and more so beyond, which was pioneered by Hadrian I and continued by his two immediate successors, Leo III and Paschal I.[40]

Hadrian I

Pope Hadrian I, who reigned from 772 – 795,[41] played a decisive role in laying the foundations of the medieval papacy and also acting as god-father and role-model for the revival of Christian culture in Rome itself and in the Frankish domains under Charlemagne. He was a Roman aristocrat[42] and the choice of his name as pope was significant as he tried to assert the political and economic integrity of the papacy in the face of implacable enemies, notably the Lombard King Desiderius. He also secured the independence of the papacy from the vestiges of Byzantine rule by appropriating to himself many of its trappings, dating his documents by his pontifical year alone and minting coins without the imperial image on one side.[43] The circumstances in which he became Pope were fraught with danger, as his predecessor, Pope Stephen III, had proved abject, first by becoming dominated by his notary

Christopher, and then treated by the Lombard King with manifest scorn, whose agent Afiarta had Christopher and his accomplice Sergius brutally murdered in Rome.[44] Hadrian's first act was to amnesty the victims of this *putsch* and to return Afiarta to his master, Desiderius, having him arrested *en route* however at Ravenna where he was later executed. The story is told in vivid detail in the *Liber Pontificalis*, where the account of the momentous years 772-4 appears to be a contemporary witness.[45]

Charlemagne meanwhile repudiated the first wife of his youth, the Lombard princess imposed upon him by his mother Bertrada, while Desiderius continued to threaten Rome itself in the winter of 772-3. In response to secret overtures by Hadrian, Charlemagne decided to intervene personally against Desiderius and besieged Pavia from September 773 until its fall in June 774. It was during that siege that Charlemagne came on pilgrimage to Rome for Easter and concluded an agreement with Pope Hadrian that was to have long-term significance for European history: he confirmed the territorial promises made by his father Pippin III to Pope Stephen II in 754, which were the basis of the later papal state, although at this time they were more a statement of claims than of actual sovereignty. Charlemagne took very seriously his duties as a 'patrician of the Romans' but did not always acquiesce to Hadrian's political and territorial demands. Nonetheless their collaboration in dealing with the aftermath of iconoclasm and also Adoptionism in the years leading up to the synod of Frankfurt in 794 was striking and significant, as was their stance towards Byzantium.[46]

Under Hadrian, Rome began to reassume its grandeur as the capital of the Christian world in the West. Its walls were rebuilt and strengthened even though the inhabited area of the old city was a shadow of its former self. Four of the aqueducts were repaired, as were the embankments of the river Tiber. The economic development of the city and its relative security under Frankish suzerainty in Italy brought great wealth to the Church under Hadrian's energetic and reforming leadership: he transformed the productivity of the Church's own estates, the *domus cultae* outside the city, enabling the *diaconiae* within its limits to feed the poor and those in need. The *Liber Pontificalis* records a massive programme of rebuilding and refurbishment of the churches of Rome and their sumptuous decoration during Hadrian's primacy, during which time the importance of the city as a focus of pilgrimage and prestige continued to grow. The Rome of Christian antiquity, of Constantine and Theodosius, was being consciously recreated before the eyes of all who visited the holy city: in Rome and in Charlemagne's domains, notably at Fulda, building of the classic Christian basilican church was revived.

The style of this Christian *Romanitas* is still evident in some of the churches in Rome that remain from the period of Hadrian, for example in St Maria in Cosmedin, and especially in those of his successors, Leo III and Paschal I, who benefited from the wealth and the ideological programme that Hadrian initiated. Leo III built a splendid *triclinium* or banqueting hall at the Lateran palace in whose mosaics he drew an explicit parallel between Constantine and Charlemagne: on one side Christ is giving the keys of heaven to Pope Sylvester I and the *labarum* to Constantine; opposite to this, St Peter is giving the *pallium* to pope Leo III and the banner of Rome to Charlemagne as King. This mosaic was almost certainly completed before the imperial coronation of Charlemagne in 800 and so the whole project had its conception during the time of Hadrian.[47] In the Roman churches of St Cecilia in Trastevere and St Maria in Domnica, as well as in Pascal's family mausoleum of St Prassede, the full splendour of the papal vision of the Christian past may still be seen, with Pascal I himself portrayed as a living donor.[48] Frankish architects and craftsmen worked on both sides of the Alps during this period and Hadrian asked Charlemagne to provide timber for roof beams from the forests of Spoleto.[49] In all this development, 'the figure of Constantine formed a pivotal point in the whole philosophy of the Carolingian period. All Charlemagne's political ideas, his conception of a new empire and of his own status were based upon the image of the first Christian emperor.'[50] In this he was mightily encouraged by Hadrian I in Rome as well as by Alcuin closer to home.

This Christian imperial vision is very evident in the tone and language of some of the papal letters that were carefully preserved during the reign of Charlemagne in the *Codex Carolinus*.[51] This important archive of correspondence also shows how the Carolingian dynasty was gradually drawn into the orbit of the resurgent papacy during the reigns of Hadrian's predecessors, as they tried to shake off the Byzantine yoke and to deal with the Lombard and Saracen menaces to their position. Central to this was their appeal to the spiritual authority of St Peter as the heavenly key-bearer. In return for fidelity to his cause, the Frankish kings could expect earthly victory and enhanced prestige as a result of his intercession, as well as that of his temporal successors. Hadrian repeatedly alluded to the alleged gifts of land granted by Constantine to his predecessor Pope Sylvester; this was the context in which some Lateran advisers were concocting the infamous *Donation of Constantine*. Charlemagne was hailed by Hadrian as 'the new and most Christian emperor', another Constantine or Theodosius who would usher in times of plenty and stability for the Church. He was called to become the agent of St Peter himself. In a letter of 781, the Pope acclaimed him as a 'spiritual fellow-father', a second King David replete with the Spirit of God.[52] His destiny was to rule over the entire western world and to subdue the barbarians; all this exhortation was couched in the language of the Psalms. In 784 the Pope granted Charlemagne permission to remove marble from the imperial palaces at Ravenna for his new palace at Aachen, which was described by some of his courtiers as a new Rome, even a second Lateran. In another letter he assured the King that the ornate Cross that he had sent as a gift would stand forever in his memory on the altar in St Peter's.

Charlemagne attached great importance to his own pilgrimages to Rome and Einhard emphasised in his *Life* his devotion in particular to St Peter's basilica: 'Charlemagne cared more for the church of the holy apostle Peter in Rome than for any other sacred and venerable place.' His sole concern was that 'the city of Rome should regain its former proud position' with St Peter's basilica on the Vatican hill more richly adorned than any other church in Rome.[53] Charlemagne visited Rome on four occasions 'to fulfil his vows and to offer up his prayers': in 774 during the siege of Pavia to keep Easter in Rome; in 781 when he again spent Easter in Rome; during Lent and Easter in 787, when he broke off his devotions to subdue Benevento; and finally in 800 to re-establish Pope Leo III and to be crowned as Emperor in St Peter's by the Pope on Christmas day.[54] On each occasion he was met with great dignity, but could only enter the ancient city itself with papal permission to attend the stational papal liturgies appropriate to Holy Week and Easter in the great basilicas of St Maria Maggiore, St Paul-outside-the-walls and at the Lateran. At some point, perhaps in 781, Charlemagne commissioned the building of a suitable residence or *palatium* for himself and his successors beneath St Peter's in the neighbourhood of the *schola Francorum*, the enclosed area where Frankish pilgrims might lodge, whose creation was also attributed to his initiative.

On his earliest visit to Rome, Pope Hadrian gave to Charlemagne an important book of canon law called the *Dionysio-Hadriana*.[55] Its provisions underlay the *Admonitio Generalis* issued by Charlemagne in 789. No less significant was the sacramentary, the so-called *Hadrianum*, to which Hadrian made reference in a letter of 786/7, confirming that its authority was that of Gregory the Great and that it came in response to a message brought to Rome from the King by Paul the Deacon.[56] It was not in fact the Roman liturgy as practised in the time of Gregory the Great, nor was it current practice in Rome either: its origins lay in the middle of the seventh century. Because it was designed for papal use moreover it did not provide for the whole liturgical year. It fell to Benedict of Aniane to remedy its obvious deficiencies, and while Alcuin knew of it, he did not use it in his own liturgical compilations for the monastery at Tours. The importance of both the *Dionysio-Hadriana* and the *Hadrianum* however was their status as sources of Roman authority and prestige in matters of canon law and correct liturgical practice. The concern of the Carolingian reformers was to keep in step with Roman doctrine while adapting legal and liturgical practice to the traditions and needs of the Frankish Church.[57] Taken alongside the important letter that Hadrian wrote in response to the challenge of Spanish Adoptionism and his stern reaction to the Frankish condemnation of the second Council of Nicea and by implication of the *Libri Carolini*, these texts represent significant elements in the flow of ideas and books that took place between Rome and its northern satellite. They were potent symbols of papal authority as it was perceived and respected at that time in the person of Hadrian I.

An ivory panel portraying the Annunciation, the Nativity and the veneration of the Magi, probably made in Aachen around the year AD 800.

Chapter 9

Crisis and Coronation

Hadrian's was a hard act to follow: the *Liber Pontificalis* portrays his pontificate in glowing terms, as he lavished wealth on the Roman churches and as he acted decisively for the care of the poor and those flooded out of their homes when the Tiber rose. 'This blessed and distinguished pontiff completed all things needful, both in terms of alms for the poor and in the adorning of churches, finishing his race and expertly maintaining the orthodox faith.'[1] His successor, Leo III, was of a less lofty lineage, however, being a product of the Lateran curia rather than the Roman aristocracy; he probably came from southern Italy. He immediately sent word to Charlemagne of his election, sending him the keys to St Peter's tomb as well the banner of Rome. The switch of allegiance from Byzantium was now complete, if rather more servile in its attitude toward the 'patrician of the Romans' than Hadrian's would have been. During the early part of Leo's reign the *triclinium* at the Lateran was completed. For reasons that are unclear in their details, he riled the Roman aristocratic entourage of the late Pope, notably his nephew the chief notary, Paschalis, and the treasurer, Campulus. The encomium with which Leo's *Life* in the *Liber Pontificalis* begins is honeyed and unconvincing: the ensuing list of his benefactions cloaked the build-up of resentment that broke forth unexplained in the spring of 799. Paschalis and his allies ambushed the Pope on his way to a service and severely wounded him, trying to cut out his tongue and his eyes so as to render him unable to continue as a priest. At risk of his life he was held captive, but was rescued and spirited away to the relative safety of St Peter's, which was outside the city walls. The Frankish Duke of Spoleto then escorted him to his own city before sending the hapless pontiff over the Alps to meet Charlemagne, at the King's request, at Paderborn. 'He welcomed him reverently . . . as the vicar of St Peter and apostle: they greeted and embraced each other in tears.'[2] Clearly Charlemagne did not accept Leo's deposition, and as patron of the holy city he would now have to intervene, if need be by force, to rectify the situation. He sent emissaries to accompany the Pope back to Rome, and to investigate the charges against him of perjury, simony and adultery, which were taken seriously by the Franks. The conspirators were arrested and exiled and an uneasy peace was established.

Late in 800, and after spending part of the summer at Tours with Alcuin where the Queen died, Charlemagne finally set forth himself for Rome, arriving there at the end of November. As Einhard said, 'Charlemagne really came to Rome to restore the Church, which was in a very bad state indeed; but in the end he spent the winter there.'[3] At the beginning of December the King presided over a synod of Roman, Frankish and other senior clergy in which, at the end of the month on the eve of Christmas, the Pope swore to his own innocence. The synod had refused formally to sit in judgement on Leo and his enemies were exiled.[4] It was in this rather fraught political context that on Christmas Day Charlemagne received the title 'emperor' by the request of the synod and by acclamation of the Romans: clearly papal authority had collapsed. Yet the Pope crowned him as he knelt before the tomb of St Peter and did obeisance. Thereafter however, Leo served as a protégé of Charlemagne, dating his coins by his regnal years and enduring increasing Frankish interference in the affairs of the Roman church and its lands. Only towards the end of his reign, in 810, did he resist pressure from his Frankish overlord to insert the *Filioque* into the Nicene Creed. His violence towards his enemies after a failed conspiracy in 814, when Charlemagne had died, revealed his earlier subjugation but also his weak character. In other respects he continued the work of his great predecessor in terms of building and economic development; as did his successor Paschal I, who was as unpopular and who was actually denied burial in St Peter's. He was buried instead in his show-piece church of St Prassede, where he had constructed a lavishly decorated mausoleum to his mother, who is portrayed in mosaic there as *Theodora episcopa*.

No event from this period has captured the imagination of historians and others so potently as Charlemagne's imperial coronation by Pope Leo III on Christmas day 800 in St Peter's basilica. But it is easy to read too much into the event and to forget that it was precipitated by a serious crisis within the papacy and the Roman church. Charlemagne had to act to resolve it lest his own authority as the paramount Christian ruler in the West be undermined. Patronage was converted into protectorate therefore, for good or ill; and there is evidence in Einhard's *Life* that Charlemagne was uneasy about the way in which the Pope had acted on that famous occasion. Wise words of Grierson show why caution is needed in evaluating this event, however: 'The immediate importance of such texts as have survived becomes inflated out of all proportion to their real significance, and they have accorded to them a degree of reliability to which they are not entitled, and a precision which their authors never intended.'[5] He points out that the Byzantine chronicler Theophanes attached little importance to this event when recording a possible marriage alliance between Charlemagne and Irene, who ruled in Byzantium at that time. But by 813, the Byzantine Emperor was prepared to regard Charlemagne as an 'emperor' as well as a king. Charlemagne for his part accepted the imperial dignity as a means first of legitimising his authority in Rome itself, and also of asserting his overlordship, especially towards the Saxons who did not have a king as such.[6] But it is notable that on his death the title did not assist his successors in holding together his wide domains.[7] The memory of how it occurred grew in the telling, however, and would play a role in relations between the papacy and the Frankish and Ottonian dynasties for many years to come, as well casting its spell over a millennium of European history.

The gravity of the crisis that engulfed the papacy under Leo III may be glimpsed in the many letters that Alcuin wrote to Charlemagne and others as the scandalous events unfolded: there are in fact 23 letters of Alcuin that relate in some way to Leo III. They give a window into the thinking of those surrounding Charlemagne as he faced one of the most difficult challenges of his reign. They also reflect the problems of communication and of obtaining reliable news in those days. For the Frankish and English churchmen, so much rested on the authority of Rome as the fountain of orthodox belief and moral authority, for example in dealing with the reversal of iconoclasm and the challenge of Adoptionism, in promoting mission and in bringing due order to the episcopal leadership of the Church and to its liturgy. Under Hadrian I the moral authority of the papacy had become the cornerstone of the whole *renovatio* of Christianity, to which Alcuin and others gave their best energies, with Charlemagne's active support. The treatment of Pope Leo III, however provoked, was a scandal; all the more so as the Byzantine throne was without a male occupant. Where now was the effective centre of Christianity? Yet the political position of the papacy was hardly secure in an Italy plagued by rival war-lords, such as the rulers of Benevento, as well as Saracen raiders. Byzantine rule persisted in the south of the country and was at times a menace to the papacy as well as to the Franks; and Charlemagne, or rather his son Pippin, now ruled the Lombard Kingdom. The *Codex Carolinus* gives a vivid picture of the pressures exerted upon Hadrian I, who in turn made his own persistent claims on behalf of the papacy. Alcuin's letters are therefore a primary witness of the greatest importance, and in them his alliance with Charlemagne reached its apogee. They fall into five groups.

The first group was occasioned by the accession of the new Pope and the continuing business of the Church on both sides of the English Channel with which Alcuin was involved. The two letters of Charlemagne that accompanied the embassy of Angilbert of St Riquier to Rome in 796 were probably drafted by Alcuin.[8] The first commissioned Angilbert as the King's envoy, urging him to exhort the new pontiff to live honestly and canonically, to resist simony and heresy, and to prove a worthy intercessor for the Church and for the stability of Charlemagne's realms.[9] Did the tone of this letter reflect unease already among the senior Frankish clergy, as well as Alcuin himself, about the succession at St Peter's? The second letter was the formal greeting sent by the King to the Pope.[10] It is an interesting document inasmuch as in it the King rejoiced at the apparent unanimity which surrounded Leo's election and the profession of his fidelity to his Frankish patron. Charlemagne again expressed his grief at Hadrian's death, describing him as a 'most beloved father and most faithful friend.' The King made his expectations of the new Pope quite clear, renewing the covenant made by his father with the papacy and sustained between himself and the late Pope, reminding Leo of his own munificence towards St Peter's: the stability of the Church was now the King's prime concern.

Charlemagne commended Angilbert, who would be his confidential emissary and bearer of the gifts originally intended for Hadrian, as signs of his good will as 'the patrician of the Romans'. The defence of the 'most holy Roman church' was now their joint responsibility. Charlemagne portrayed his own role as a militant one against barbarians and infidels, while the Pope like Moses of old would raise his arms in prayer for the victory of all Christian people over their enemies, 'so that the name of our Lord Jesus Christ might shine throughout the world.' His warfare was a spiritual one but no less real or important for that. The Pope was to follow canon law to the letter as well as the traditions of the Fathers, and by his own example to shine as a light to the world. The tone of this letter was quite haughty and it sheds light perhaps on the reason why Hadrian kept Charlemagne at arm's length, despite their cordial friendship and mutual respect. Leo sounds already as if he is being treated as a protégé.

To these formal letters, Alcuin added one of his own to the new Pope, commending his friend Angilbert.[11] Its theology and tone are closely comparable to the poems that he also composed, which have already been discussed. He hailed Leo as the 'vicar of the Apostles, the heir of the Fathers, and a prince of the Church.' It is a strongly pastoral letter in its use of Scriptural imagery, in which Alcuin asked for papal absolution from his own sins. Alcuin also mentioned the collaboration of the Pope with the Archbishop of Canterbury in hearing the case of the English exile and priest, Odbert, in another letter which he drafted for the King and which was sent by Charlemagne to Offa of Mercia in 796, bringing to an end their diplomatic dispute and resolving a variety of issues.[12] The next year, 797, Alcuin wrote directly himself to the Pope in support of his friend, Eanbald II, the new Archbishop of York, asking Leo to grant him the *pallium* on the basis of the intentions of Gregory the Great, and alluding to his earlier letter by the hand of Angilbert, to which the Pope had responded favourably, in a letter now lost. In it Alcuin also refers to his request for prayers, seeking absolution as he had done from Hadrian, but in more personal terms. Had he in fact met Leo before he became Pope and was there some element of personal acquaintance? It might explain his concern as events unfolded.[13] These letters reflect Alcuin's seniority and reputation as a leading light in the Frankish and English churches. In 798, for example, he wrote to Charlemagne suggesting that a copy of the king's *libellus* against the Adoptionist Bishop, Felix of Urguel, should be sent to the Pope in Rome.[14]

There follow a rapid succession of letters by Alcuin addressed to his friend and ally, Arno, newly created the Archbishop of Salzburg, concerning the gathering storm as news of the plight of the Pope filtered over the Alps from

Rome to the Frankish church. In a letter written in the late spring of 798, Alcuin congratulated his friend on his receiving the *pallium* as Archbishop but deplored the crime that had been committed against the Pope in Rome in on 25 April of that year.[15] The Church seemed to be besieged by pagans without and false brethren within; and where the fountain of justice and moral order stood pollution had now occurred that would poison the whole body of the Church. This was a cancer that Alcuin viewed in the most apocalyptic terms. A shadow therefore looms over the other letters to Arno that remain from that fateful year, one of which was dated September 798. In one of them Alcuin sought news of Paulinus of Aquiliea and of his friend Candidus Wizo, both of whom were to play key roles in the impending crisis in Rome and its resolution. He wanted to know also how Arno had been received by the Pope and his impression of the situation in Rome, whither he had gone as one of Charlemagne's envoys while escorting the Pope back to his See.[16] Another letter written later in the autumn of that year addressed the same concerns, seeking news from Rome about the pope, and about the royal monastery of St Paul that was being built there.[17] Further recognition that all was not well for Pope Leo may be seen in a further letter in November, in which Alcuin responded with relief to news from Arno that the Pope was now safe from persecution and that his visit to Rome had not been in vain. He hoped that they would be able to meet up either at Tours or at Arno's northern monastery of St Amand after Easter.[18]

The third group of Alcuin's letters were to Charlemagne and they can only reflect the tip of their dialogue, written and verbal, about the fate of the Pope and the critical situation in Rome. They were written during 799 while the King was weighing up his own journey to the holy city. One of the most telling was written in June in response to a report from the King to Alcuin about the plight of the Pope.[19] Alcuin spoke eloquently of his spiritual concern about these crimes at the highest level of the Church, reminding the king that there were three pillars of Christendom. The first was the apostolic See of St Peter and its occupant, now under a scandalous threat. The second was the imperial ruler of 'second Rome' in Byzantium, which was however at present without a legitimate ruler, because the Empress Irene had murdered her own son, the Emperor Constantine in 797. The third pillar was Charlemagne himself, who was 'by divine grace' the ruler of all 'the Christian people,' whose dignity was intact and therefore at present pre-eminent over the other two. 'In you alone now reposes the entire welfare of the churches of Christ.' The king was called by God to be the punisher of crimes, even in Rome itself, 'where religion of the greatest devotion used once to shine, but now extreme acts of wickedness flood in.' The Romans, blind in their hearts, had attempted to blind their head, heedless of either the fear of God or of wisdom and charity, without which society would surely collapse. Alcuin went on to give a coded summary of the political situation in Italy, reflecting his excellent knowledge of what was at stake, but perhaps also his caution at trespassing directly on Charlemagne's own domain as ruler.

In another letter, written later in that summer, Alcuin acknowledged receipt while staying at Chelles with the Abbess Gisela, Charlemagne's sister, of the King's letters concerning Leo III, who was now his guest at Paderborn.[20] In it for the first time he enjoined the King to exercise his rule as guardian of the Christian *imperium*, its orthodoxy and its justice. It was now the King's responsibility to take advice as to how best to rectify the situation in Rome. Alcuin regretted that infirmity and age precluded his accompanying the King there, despite his desire to do so. He concluded with a poem upholding Charlemagne as the ruler of the day, 'presiding over the administration of sacred justice.'

There is also a letter very similar in tone written shortly after this one as part of their ongoing correspondence in which Alcuin expressed his relief to know that the Pope's health was sound, regarding it as a miracle, and asking about those of his pupils who were to go ahead of the King to Rome. He also congratulated Charlemagne on his victories over his enemies, the Huns and the Saracens.[21] Alcuin cited the classical tag about the role of the emperor to show mercy to those subject to him but to dethrone the proud, reminding the King how Augustine had given this a Christian interpretation in his *City of God*, a book to which Charlemagne was devoted.[22] How was the King going to secure the Pope in his own city, whom God had rescued from his enemies? How was justice to be done and proper retribution exacted? He reminded the King of how kings in the Bible marked their victories by generosity towards the Temple. He excused himself from becoming entangled with the Roman crisis directly, citing a line from Proverbs: 'it is better to sit in the corner of one's home than to engage with a contentious woman in a public place.'[23] He would therefore remain at his prayers in Tours. There is more than a hint here of ambivalence towards the imperial legacy of Rome, portrayed in the *Apocalypse* as the whore of Babylon, a feeling which Charlemagne himself may have shared, and an allusion to the perfidious reputation of the Roman clergy and aristocracy who had conspired against Leo. For however much the popes may have hoped for a second Constantine, Charlemagne and his advisers, including Alcuin, looked back to the warlike but devout kings of the Old Testament, for whom victory and piety were inextricably entwined.

A further group of letters comprise those written subsequently by Alcuin mainly once again to his friend Arno, Archbishop of Salzburg, who was much involved in resolving the crisis in Rome. Some insight into Alcuin's thinking and feelings during this critical summer, when for a time the King was his guest at Tours and in a state of bereavement over his Queen's death, may be gained from a letter he wrote to Arno in Salzburg.[24] He described Leo as a 'confessor for Christ' and expressed the desire to visit the Pope while he was at Paderborn, if the king would permit it but only if his health were up to the journey, which alas it was not. Alcuin knew the precise charges against Leo, however, of adultery and perjury and the problem of how the Pope might clear his name. Some were pressing for his retirement to a monastery without due process. But what due process could there be if the ancient principle were to be upheld that the apostolic see could not be judged by anyone, as it was the supreme moral authority of judgement itself?[25] 'How can the pastor who is the head of the churches of Christ remain immune in the Church if he can be unseated by ill-wishers?' Alcuin's injunction to Arno was to labour hard for the moral integrity of the Church and thereby underpin the apostolic See.

In so turbulent a world, there had to be one fixed point of doctrinal orthodoxy and moral authority to which appeal could be made in the face of heresy. This was the dilemma faced by Charlemagne and his advisers, and Alcuin felt it keenly.[26] Something of the gravity of the crisis may be detected in another letter to Arno in which Alcuin mentions a confidential report that Arno had sent him of the Frankish enquiries in Rome into the Pope's behaviour, which he had promptly burnt.[27] Only his close friend and disciple, Candidus Wizo, had read the document with him. The dilemma was clear: could the office of the pope be preserved without also upholding the position of Leo III, however unwise or corrupt he had been at or after his accession? So in another letter to Arno, who was back in Italy with the Pope and Charlemagne at the very end of 799, Alcuin exhorted him and his colleagues, Paulinus of Aquileia[28] and Peter Archbishop of Milan, to work for the peace of the Church. He wrote in a similar vein a year later to his friend Riculf, Archbishop of Mainz, who was in Rome trying to pacify the situation in the life of the church there after the restoration of the Pope and the coronation of Charlemagne.[29] The affairs of Italy continued to worry Alcuin as two more letters written in 801 to friends including Arno reveal.[30]

Two final letters remain which brought Alcuin some peace at last. One addressed Leo III directly, seeking his prayers and absolution, but also recalling to him the reality of divine judgement. He might be answerable to no earthly authority but he was certainly answerable, as Alcuin was himself, to God. Although at a crucial moment in 799 Alcuin had articulated the principle of the Pope being above any secular authority, this did not mean that the papacy was morally and spiritually unaccountable. He cautioned Leo explicitly against secular ambition and greed, or muffling his preaching and proclamation of the gospel. He signed off with a short poem commending him to Christ in terms of personal affection.[31] Finally in 802 he was able to write to Ethelheard Archbishop of Canterbury, congratulating him on the peaceful resolution of the vexed issue of the Lichfield Archbishopric created by Offa for personal and political reasons. The rights of Canterbury had been restored and the original intentions of Gregory the Great had been maintained.[32] Throughout this crisis over the papacy, however, Alcuin felt his age and was plagued from time to time by illness: he sensed that his influence over affairs was waning.

Alcuin was clearly part of a circle of clerical advisers who together coined the language of the Christian *imperium* over which Charlemagne alone could wield effective authority.[33] But in Alcuin's mind this constituted the *populus Christianus* who were spiritually dependent upon Rome. For half a century, the Holy See had been a Frankish protectorate. Now direct rule was needed to restore the moral authority of the papacy. There was an evident power vacuum, which the Byzantine Emperor could no longer fill; nor did the papacy desire it to do so: whether the use of the term 'emperor' in December 800 meant any more than immediate recognition of Charlemagne's political supremacy and overlordship, however, is now unclear. The King himself clearly resented the obsequious manner in which Leo crowned him, thereby claiming more power than the realities of the occasion warranted. In the words of Ganshof, 'he did not wish to seem as if he held his empire from the pope, and especially not from a pope who owed him so much.'[34] Although his new dignity was ratified at Aachen in 802 and his subjects swore oaths to him as a Christian emperor, the framework of Carolingian polity was little affected by this development because it was incongruous to it.

In the minds of Frankish churchmen it was a spiritual and symbolic aspiration that shored up the position of the papacy in temporal terms. Alcuin had played a part in its articulation but he was not alone in his influence. Nonetheless he had contributed to two potent myths that have bedevilled relations between the Roman See and European states until the present time. The more exotic of the two was the myth that popes could create emperors. The more sinister was the assertion that the pope could be judged by no human authority. But neither of these principles as such was really completely intended in the critical events leading up to the events of December 800; and it is important not to read back into a fraught situation more than was true at that moment to the unique conjunction of circumstances and interests that led Charlemagne to intervene in the ordering of the Roman Church and to secure the restoration of Pope Leo III.

Part Three
Legacy

Chapter 10
Abbot of Tours

The *Life of Alcuin* is an important source for the memory of Alcuin's time as Abbot of Tours. By the middle of the final decade of the eighth century, Alcuin was beginning to feel his age: if he was born around the time of the death of Bede in 735, he would have been sixty or thereabouts when Charlemagne insisted in 796 that he assume the abbacy of St Martin's at Tours.[1] According to the *Life of Alcuin*, he would have preferred to have retired to Fulda, to finish his days as a monk there by the tomb of his great compatriot, Boniface, following the *Rule of St Benedict*.[2] Sadly Alcuin felt unable to return to Northumbria because of its political instability and his possible vulnerability there for reasons that are not now clear. He intended also to delegate to his disciples the care of the several monasteries that Charlemagne had entrusted to him: these provided him with an income and also places to stay on his travels.[3] They included Ferrières, whose abbot Aldric later commissioned the writing of the *Life of Alcuin* in 821, and whose predecessor as abbot, Sigwulf, had been close to Alcuin and he was a principal witness to his memory. Alcuin received a monastery at Flavigny at some unknown date, also the monastery of St Loup de Troyes;[4] and in 796 he became Abbot of the small house at St Josse-sur-Mer, close to the important Channel port of Quentavic.[5] He may also have administered a small monastery at Berge.[6] But at no point before becoming abbot of Tours did he ever refer to himself as an 'abbot'.

Tours

Alcuin's appointment to the abbacy of Tours was highly significant, for it was an ancient and prestigious royal shrine, dedicated to St Martin, who lay buried there. According to Notker's *Life*, Charlemagne 'gave Alcuin the rule of the abbey of St Martin, near the city of Tours, so that, when he himself was away, Alcuin could reside there and continue to instruct all those who flocked to him there.'[7] It was an extremely wealthy foundation and had around two hundred monks and others. Its vast landholdings supported 20,000 serfs and retainers, a figure with which Elipandus of Toledo chafed Alcuin in one of his letters. Alcuin did not dispute this charge when he mentioned it in

An ivory pyx, probably from Aachen in the early ninth century, portraying
the healing of the demoniac by Christ in the gospels.

the prefatory letter to his friends that he attached to his final work against Elipandus.[8] Instead he defended his position as that of a trustee whose duty it was to make sure that such wealth was used for the benefit of the Church: 'For it is one thing to take possession of this world, another to be possessed by it.' Instead he declared his duty also to the King, who had entrusted him with this position as a resource for combating heresy in the Church, even as his spiritual father in York had predicted long ago. In fact, most of Alcuin's important works of theology along with many of his letters were composed while he was Abbot of Tours, a prodigious output that required significant resources for its generation, copying and circulation.[9] Tours was his base for his interventions in the Adoptionist controversy, whence he travelled extensively in the year 798. In some ways these multifarious duties and preoccupations away from the monastery probably weakened his effective rule as its abbot, at least in pastoral terms.

Alcuin was not a stranger to Tours, however, having had a friendship with his predecessor, Abbot Itherius, to whom Alcuin wrote during his final illness: 'I know that I shall not have such a friend again in your place after you have gone.'[10] These are interesting words inasmuch as they seem to indicate that he was not anticipating succeeding Itherius as Abbot when he wrote them. It may well be that it was at his behest that he composed his little treatise for the boys of St Martin *De confessione peccatorum* before he became their abbot.[11] But by becoming Abbot of Tours in 796 Alcuin became the titular and administrative head of a considerable domain, to which he had to give serious attention, in addition to his wider obligations. In eight years of his effective rule he established the strategy that would be followed by his successor as Abbot, Fredegisus, as a result of which Tours and its scriptorium became a power-house of creativity for the next half century.

This development required the steady planning and marshalling of considerable economic resources over time, to the reform of which Alcuin had to bend his mind, sometimes in the face of inevitable local opposition. These were the *onera saecula* of which he frequently complained in his letters.[12] For example, in 798, after returning from a long itinerary, he had immediately to set forth to visit the properties of the monastery in September because of the poor harvest which had affected supplies of wine and corn.[13] The next year he had to travel to the port of Quentavic to resolve some economic and other difficulties, perhaps related to traffic with England.[14] Charlemagne had appointed him as Abbot of Tours for several strong reasons, and he had high, and perhaps unreasonable, expectations of his reforming rule at Tours. Alcuin's was therefore no easy retirement, and it was only chronic ill-health that finally weakened his capacities as abbot and detached him from his day-to-day duties in the last couple of years before his death in 804.

Tours at the end of the eighth century was not unlike York in its economic role and development. It had been a Roman city of some importance, straddling the Loire at a crucial crossing-point, and the cathedral and the bishop's dwelling were located within the old fortress. The basilica and monastery of St Martin, already a venerable structure, was its own enclave some distance away, and between it various churches, cemeteries and dwellings had grown up which would later constitute the nodes of development in the medieval city of Tours.[15] It was an important port and a point of transit for goods from an extensive rural area that was still being re-colonised at this time.[16] Alcuin's development of the small monastery at Cormery, some miles outside the city to the south at a crossing on the river Inde, was part of this process and dependent upon it. Inevitably the growth of Tours itself as a town attracted a significant but poor population, coming in from the countryside, whose turbulence would cause Alcuin serious difficulties at the end of his life. Its wealth in the ninth century, and its position on a major river, rendered it vulnerable to Viking attacks, which in 853 destroyed much of the city including the basilica of St Martin.

Alcuin spent the summer of 796 at Aachen and only settled in his new home in the autumn of that year, perhaps reluctantly.[17] He now presided over an ancient shrine that was an important centre of pilgrimage with long traditions, closely associated with the Merovingian and Carolingian monarchies: St Martin was regarded as the patron of the Frankish monarchy. These pilgrims were catered for by the clergy of the basilica who provided the liturgical services along with essential pastoral support and hospitality. To their number were added at times large numbers of visitors from Britain, both Irish and English, coming to visit Alcuin himself, as well as to venerate the tomb of St Martin. An English priest called Aigulf got a poor reception and overheard some of the brethren complaining about the plague of visitors that their abbot was constantly attracting.[18] 'O God, liberate this monastery from these British: for as bees return from everywhere to their queen, so all these come to see him!' The Irish had been habitués of Tours long before Alcuin arrived, making significant contributions to the development of the scriptorium there in the earlier part of the eighth century. Although Alcuin dealt with the matter with his usual clemency, it probably reflected unease at his rule and the reforms that he was trying to implement.[19]

His own example as Abbot was morally formidable and demanding. The writer of the *Life of Alcuin* recalled Alcuin's diligence in reading and writing, teaching the young, his diligence also in his personal prayers and his commitment to the offices, his austerity and his night vigils. On one occasion at the very end of his life when he was blind it was believed that he had averted a fire in the basilica by praying with his arms stretched out cross-wise on the tomb of St Martin. In the mind of his biographer and those for whom he was writing who still remembered him, Alcuin proved himself the equal of the Fathers to whom he was so devoted. His commitment in assisting as a deacon at the daily celebrations of the mass by his close friend Sigwulf has already been considered and was unusual.[20] He was truly 'more monk than the monks',[21] and therein perhaps lay difficulties, as the community of St Martin's was a mixed one at that time, with no clear definition of its character, despite Alcuin's best efforts. Many of those that he was trying to educate were of peasant origins, as he once complained to Charlemagne in a letter from Tours in 799.[22] His foundation at Cormery proved a more congenial milieu. But his approachability was never in doubt, and many sick and poor folk found in him a true pastor and support, on one occasion at least inadvertently healing a blind man. The writer of the *Life of Alcuin* drew on many treasured memories, naming his sources where he could: he was evidently setting down in writing a well-established living tradition before its witnesses died out.

There is no tangible evidence left of how Alcuin actually organised, or re-organised, the monastery at Tours, or his other monasteries, apart from Cormery, in terms of charters and so forth: the archives were presumably destroyed in the Viking attacks in the middle of the ninth century or later.[23] But the output of the scriptorium at Tours during the fifty years after his death must reflect the impact of his effective administration of the community's resources, as well as that of his successor as Abbot, Fredegisus, for what would prove to be a major long-term project involving considerable expense. Each Bible alone required the skins of over two hundred sheep, and at least two full Bibles were copied for the next fifty years at Tours along with numerous other books.

Alcuin left an epitaph for one of the monks of Tours, called Paul.[24] He also left some verses that were set as inscriptions around the monastery: in the place where members of the *schola* gathered, for the dormitory, and also for the latrine.[25] Others accompanied the young waking up in the middle of the night, as they made their way into the choir in church.[26] The inscription composed for the scriptorium encapsulated many of Alcuin's characteristic preoccupations:

> *Here sit those who copy the words of the holy law,*
> *And also the sacred sayings of the holy fathers.*
> *These guard lest they sow frivolity among their words,*
> *Or commit folly because of the errors of their hands.*
>
> *They seek out with the utmost care correct versions of books,*
> *So that their pens may fly along the right paths.*
> *They distinguish proper grammar and sense with colons,*
> *Placing points each in their proper places:*
> *Lest the reader in church reads falsely,*
> *Or suddenly falls silent before his devout brethren.*
>
> *For it is a noble task to write out holy books,*
> *Nor does the scribe wish for any reward himself.*
> *It is better to copy out books than to till vines,*
> *For one serves the stomach, but the other the mind.*
> *The master can offer many volumes, old and new,*
> *To a person who can read the holy sayings of the fathers.[27]*

Of interest also are two poems in which he mentioned his own name in connection with works of restoration at monasteries under his hand. The first was for a shrine containing relics which he had commissioned.[28] The other was in celebration of the restoration of the vaults of an oratory in a monastery under his direction, perhaps Tours itself, and it has an autobiographical ring:

> *Alcuin the poet came as a pilgrim in this world*
> *To him who summoned him from noble Britain's land.*
> *Charles, the distinguished king of his own realm, received him,*
> *Out of his devotion to holy wisdom, but also for love of him.*
>
> *Alcuin ordered that the damaged roofs of these arches,*
> *Be completely restored, that you may now see, reader,*
> *Encompassing this entire space to make it a suitable place for holy relics:*
> *So that the repose of God's holy saints should be secure and honoured.*
>
> *Thus on earth their holy deeds may be venerated,*
> *Whom God has willed to reign forever in the heavens.*[29]

The cult of St Martin

To the many pilgrims who flocked at times to the shrine of St Martin, Alcuin as Abbot was the spiritual heir and successor of the saint. He composed special masses for the feast of the birth of St Martin and to mark the end of his octave. He also composed a much abbreviated *Life of St Martin* as well as a homily on his death, which were often transmitted together in many of the manuscripts, though they were originally quite distinct.[30] The cult of St Martin was long established, as was the definitive *Life* composed by his friend and disciple, Sulpicius Severus.[31] Alcuin's double composition was essentially pastoral in its intention and it was not on a par with his other hagiographies in terms of its content or development of thought, being composed at the end of his life in order to affirm afresh the tradition of which he was guardian as the Abbot, but in a simpler mode. Nonetheless it is a model of clarity and as such it provides a valuable glimpse into his more pastoral role as Abbot of Tours, communicating to ordinary people gathered in the venerable basilica to venerate the tomb of their saint.

His two homilies commemorating St Martin, for that is what they were, spoke also to the religious community over which he presided, setting up a mirror in which they might discern afresh their own vocation, individually and corporately. Alcuin portrayed their patron as:

> humble in his dress, joyful in speech, devout in his preaching,
> truthful in judgement, to be revered in his manner of life, vigilant
> in his prayers, assiduous in reading, constant in his demeanour,
> kindly in his affections, honourable in discharging his priestly
> ministry, and an indefatigable disseminator of the Word of God
> ... resplendent in all the virtues appropriate to a bishop.

In his sermon about the saint's passing, Alcuin emphasised his role as a peace-maker among his clergy, even at the very end of his life. This sermon was clearly intended to be preached in close proximity to the shrine of St Martin that lay behind the high altar of the basilica, with its immediate references to miracles that still occurred in Alcuin's time there, noting how Martin's epitaph commemorated three miracles of resurrection attributed to him. No less significant perhaps were the several inscriptions that Alcuin composed for use in other churches and monasteries for chapels and altars commemorating St Martin. These were intended for destinations as far apart as St Amand in northern France and Salzburg, the monastery of St Vedast and various churches in Poitiers, as well as others in places unknown.[32]

In the momentous year 800, Charlemagne himself came on pilgrimage with his Queen, Liudgard, to visit Alcuin at Tours in the summer before his fateful journey to Rome.[33] The *Life of Alcuin* recalled this visit with a strange story of how Charlemagne consulted Alcuin about which son should succeed him: Alcuin recommended Louis as the most pious and humble.[34] The visit was marred by the death of the Queen on 4th June, however, and her burial within the basilica of St Martin. Alcuin's letter of condolence to Charlemagne remains.[35] Just before this event, Charlemagne signed two charters at Alcuin's request on behalf of the small monastery that he was developing at Cormery near Tours.[36] This had been set up by Alcuin's predecessor, Itherius, in 792 as a community living under the *Rule of St Benedict*. In the first charter, Cormery was granted two ships toll-free, and in both charters the duty to observe the Benedictine rule was reiterated. The second charter confirmed the endowments of Cormery and its reliance upon the protection of its mother monastery at Tours. Alcuin's petition was described in the first charter as 'of our most beloved and venerable servant Alcuin' - *dilictissimi fidelis nostri Albini venerabilis*. In the second he was described as 'our beloved master' - *dilectus magister noster*. Meanwhile the King consulted closely with his friend about the major political crisis facing the Roman church and the other issues of the day. It was in many ways the apogee of Alcuin's abbacy at Tours.[37] The King's endowment placed Cormery on a secure foundation for the next half century.[38]

Conflict at Tours

Sadly, Alcuin's closing years as Abbot of Tours were dogged by increasing illness and finally blindness. It seems also that he began to lose his grip over the community at Tours, and his relationship with Charlemagne was marred momentarily by a serious scandal in 801 or 802 in which law and order broke down within the precincts of St Martin's, intruding into divine worship within the basilica. It is closely documented by a clutch of letters which probably indicate that more correspondence about the affair must have been lost.[39] What is significant about the letters that remain is the fact that they were not preserved together in any of the several collections of Alcuin's letters. They shed vivid light on the depth of his political involvement, however, and also on his knowledge of the law and customs of the Frankish church and society. They demonstrate the fact that the collections of his letters that do remain are highly selective and do not give a full picture of his involvement in secular affairs while connected to the court of Charlemagne.[40] They also indicate a dispute in which Alcuin as Abbot of Tours was reprimanded by Charlemagne after an official enquiry by a royal *missus*, in which church custom as he understood it collided with secular law, leading to a clarifying of Frankish practice in the interests of maintaining law and order. They also reveal the brittle nature of ordered society at that time, the perpetual fear of 'the poor', and the fact that a wealthy community such as St Martin's was set in the midst of a sea of poverty, relying for protection upon the aura of its saint, the resilience of its abbot, and the distant might and authority of the King.

In the first letter, Alcuin wrote to his close friends and allies at court, Candidus Wiso and Fredegisus, seeking their urgent intervention with the King on his behalf. He wrote a letter containing much of the same material and line of argument to one of the bishops, perhaps Archbishop Hildebold of Cologne.[41] The third letter was from Charlemagne himself to Alcuin and the monks of St Martin's at Tours: it reveals much about the community there, and indirectly about something of the problems that the ailing Alcuin was confronting.[42] The fourth letter was one of Alcuin's replies to the King in his own defence and that of his community, trying to put the record straight; while the fifth letter may relate to the fate of one of the younger monks involved: it was a letter of commendation to Arno of Salzburg, seeking refuge for him there.[43] It is from these letters that quite a detailed picture of what happened can be obtained.

The scandal arose because a fugitive cleric, condemned after due trial for various serious crimes by his Bishop, Theodulf of Orleans, escaped from captivity with a servant and fled to Tours to seek sanctuary at the shrine of St Martin, appealing from there directly to the King. Theodulf sent some men after him to arrest him which they did; but fearing an ambush while in Tours, they returned to Orleans without their prisoner, leaving him on the steps of the basilica. Clearly there was a background of tension and perhaps intermittent hostility and rivalry between Tours and Orleans and their church communities. It was at this point that the situation escalated: Theodulf, perhaps imprudently, sent an armed band to Tours to enforce his will, eliciting the support of Joseph, Bishop of Tours. Again, the question arises of whether there was some inevitable tension inherent in the situation in Tours itself between the cathedral community and the wealthy and prestigious basilica of St Martin, both in the same small city, which was being exploited or exacerbated in this instance.

The Bishop himself escorted eight of the armed men into the basilica on a Sunday morning. The fugitive fled to the shrine of the saint, behind the high altar, and prostrated himself there. When the armed men from Orleans climbed over the sanctuary rail, some of the monks charged forth and attacked them in defence of the sanctity of their shrine and in honour of their saint, and drove them off, though without bloodshed. The men from Orleans then seized the servant of the fugitive cleric outside the church as a hostage, who cried out for help and so provoked a riot. Word quickly got round the populace of Tours that its sanctuary was being attacked by armed forces from Orleans. The monks had to protect the intruders and drive the rabble out of the church.

None of the letters of Theodulf of Orleans remain but his rivalry with Alcuin is known from other sources, though perhaps it should not be overstated. He made his case forcibly to the King, and to judge from Alcuin's reply to Charlemagne he clearly knew the line that his episcopal neighbour was taking. Maintaining law and order was Charlemagne's first and principal concern, inevitably: hence Alcuin's letters to his close friends, in order to redress the situation and to convey a more accurate picture to the King. From Charlemagne's letter to Alcuin it is clear that the pivot of the issue was his duty to hand over a convicted cleric to the secular power as a result of the judgement of a bishop's court. Charlemagne himself had apparently issued an injunction to this end. Alcuin in his letters, however, was exercised by the need to protect those seeking sanctuary, and to uphold their right to appeal directly to the King. He also felt keenly the need for pastoral mercy towards someone who was already doing penance for his crimes. It is possible that the culprit had some connection with Tours before his condemnation, and if that were so it might account for the build up of tension on both sides; but hard cases make bad laws.

What is notable about Alcuin's letters to his friends, moreover, was his extensive knowledge of canon law and of the precedents relating to the right of sanctuary in church. He quoted a decree of a synod of Orleans in 511 against Theodulf's position and the decisions of earlier Merovingian councils.[44] He also revealed knowledge of the *Collectio Hibernensis* and the *Actus Sylvestri*, citing Roman law from the *Lex Romana Visigothorum* and the *Codex Theodosianus*. Underlying his line of argument in defence of the right to sanctuary and asylum were biblical precedents in the Old Testament.[45] Alcuin also pointed out to Charlemagne that in pagan times this had been an established custom, for example under the Romans: how much more should a Christian ruler respect and uphold this right and the precedents of the more recent Christian past?[46] It must be assumed that he did not hesitate to advance his arguments directly to the King as well.

The King's reply was a robust remonstrance to his old friend in his capacity as head of a troublesome religious community whose reputation Charlemagne did not entirely respect.[47] He also challenged the tone of the original letter to him from Alcuin that has now been lost: 'Alcuin had dared to accuse a bishop and to defend a criminal!'[48] A person duly condemned had no right to appeal over the head of his judge to the king, or to enter a church until his penance was complete. Instead it was Alcuin's plain duty to hand over the fugitive so that he could be tried afresh in a royal court. The king resented the fact that Alcuin had apparently defied his orders. He added to Alcuin's woes by castigating the community of St Martin for its mediocrity and mixed life: were they monks or canons, or what? Their wider reputation was evidently poor.

The implication was clear: that Alcuin was supposed to have remedied this internal confusion and its inherent disorder. This was probably the principal reason why he had been appointed by the King in the first place, but the matter would only be resolved under his successor, Fredegisus. Closer reading of the letter reveals that the King's remonstrance to the community was probably intended also to shore up Alcuin's authority as their ailing Abbot. Perhaps the rigour of his own life-style and his ceaseless writing, along with his many extra-mural commitments, had caused resentment and blunted his effectiveness. Or perhaps he was simply becoming too old for the task despite his own clear intentions. As a result Alcuin and Theodulf had found themselves at logger-heads, which the king considered intolerable. To remedy the situation, the community of St Martin had to answer to an enquiry presided over by a royal *missus* called Theotbert.

It was in response to this enquiry and the manner in which it was conducted that Alcuin wrote his letter to Charlemagne that still survives.[49] He defended the monks and their reputation as intercessors on behalf of the King and the realm. He said that he had no immediate knowledge of what had happened, nor had the monks' response been premeditated. Immediately he had learnt of the commotion, he had sent in one of his own retainers, Amalgarius, to the scene to rescue the emissaries from Orleans from the mob. Meanwhile the *missus* had dealt with some of the clergy very brutally during his nineteen day sojourn. Alcuin played down the role of the local bishop, however, but criticised Theodulf for sending so large an armed band. The reckless response of the populace was emphasised, with which Alcuin clearly had little sympathy or perhaps even much direct contact. The men of Orleans had repudiated Alcuin's gifts to them by way of compensation. He implied that the whole matter had been over-blown by Theodulf and urged the King to show mercy.

In fact it seems that the King ignored his advice as irrelevant to the maintenance of order, for in 803 he issued a capitulary *legibus addendum* to determine the rules governing the flight of criminals to churches for sanctuary.[50] The place of confession and penance was upheld, but not at the expense of royal justice. Clearly the scandals at Tours touched a matter of wider importance in relations between Church and state at this time, hence the direct involvement of the King and the resulting legislation. It also reflects the degree to which episcopal authority was being subsumed within the structure of Carolingian law and its enforcement.

Penance could play a supporting role in resolving local conflicts; but it could not supplant the due process of law. Alcuin's essentially pastoral approach fitted ill with the duties of a bishop within the Carolingian system in which Charlemagne took so keen a personal interest. Indeed this correspondence is the only glimpse there is of him in an administrative and official capacity. He was duty bound however to defend the community of which he was Abbot and trustee, its rights and privileges as he and they perceived them to be and Alcuin was no royal stooge. As a conflict of loyalties and obligations, it was a harbinger of greater conflicts to come in medieval Europe, in which any personal relations between ruler and subject were inevitably if temporarily set aside.

The death of Alcuin

The fire which nearly destroyed the basilica of St Martin in 803 was evidently the last straw for Alcuin who was already blind. It had started in the vestry when a candle set some vestments alight, and it quickly spread, causing panic and an urgent evacuation of stuff from the church in order to prevent the fire from spreading to the monastery hard by. They even started stripping the lead off the roof. Alcuin appeared on the scene, asking what was going on. His close friend Sigwulf nicknamed *Vetulus*,[51] urged him to get out of the building before the lead melted. Then as he turned to leave, his friend had second thoughts and begged him to pray at the tomb of St Martin instead. As Alcuin prostrated himself cross-wise on the ground the fire stopped, suddenly extinguished by a great flood of water, to everyone's amazement, giving great praise to St Martin, as well as thanks for the prayers of their holy abbot.

Alcuin prepared for his death by regular visits to the place that he had elected for his burial just outside the walls of the basilica, reciting the *Magnificat* along with the Advent antiphon *O Clavis David*,[52] followed by the Lord's Prayer and a sequence of favourite psalms of devotion, all from memory. During Lent 804 he would perambulate the various chapels of the basilica commemorating the saints there during the night vigils, lamenting his sins. He kept Easter but took to his bed on the night of the Ascension, so ill that he could hardly speak. Finally after three days he was able to chant again the antiphon *O Clavis David*, reciting the entire thing from memory. Then at the end of the night office of Pentecost, as the mass was being prepared, Alcuin died, on 19th May 804.[53]

That night a great column of light was seen over the basilica of St Martin, which was vouched for by Joseph, Bishop of Tours. His departure to heaven was also witnessed by a hermit in Italy, Alcuin appearing to him in a glorious dalmatic as a deacon ready to assist at the heavenly celebrations. He found out who it was by asking a monk of Tours sometimes afterwards, enquiring who had died at Pentecost in such holiness: 'He was called Alcuin, and he was the best master in all Francia' was the reply. Meanwhile his close friend, the priest Sigwulf, prepared Alcuin's body for burial. Afflicted by dire headaches and dizziness, perhaps caused by stress and bereavement, he took up the comb of his late friend in faith and with a prayer used it and was completely healed. Another brother called Eangist used it to cure his toothache. The Bishop of Tours overruled Alcuin's dying wishes, insisting instead on burying him within the basilica, near the shrine of St Martin, placing the epitaph that Alcuin himself had written above his tomb. Its closing words were 'Alcuin was my name, always the lover of wisdom.'[54]

Chapter 11

Alcuin and Monasticism

It is quite evident from the letters and other occasional writings of Alcuin that the nurturing of regular monastic life lay close to his heart.[1] Letters remain from him to at least nineteen monastic communities, sometimes several to the same community, scattered across the continent as well as in England and Ireland.[2] There are also letters to at least sixteen other monastic contacts and friends.[3] Alcuin's deliberate intentions in remodelling the hagiographies of Vaast and Riquier included the promotion of monasticism in close association with mission and this was reflected alongside his more personal commitment in recasting the hagiography and cult of Willibrord. To these hagiographies should be added the votive masses and hymns that he composed for those monastic saints.[4] These contributions to the cults of saints who had laid the foundations of mission and monastic life in the Frankish church should also be seen in the light of the numerous poetic inscriptions and epitaphs that he composed, often at the request of friends, to adorn and enrich various monastic communities; those for Tours have already been mentioned. There remain thirteen inscriptions composed for the abbey of St Amand where his friend Arno was abbot.[5] These were intended for altars to the Virgin Mary, St Michael, St Stephen, St Martin, St Andrew, St Peter, St Hilary and St Victor, as well as for the tomb and chapel of St Amand himself.[6] A similar portfolio of inscriptions remains that Alcuin composed for the monastery of St Vaast at the request of his friend, Rado, who was the Abbot.[7] Among these was one for the altar of St Benedict and his sister, Scholastica: 'The noble father Benedict may be venerated at this altar, who composed his devout Rule of life for monks.'[8] Alcuin composed no less than thirty-nine of these inscriptions for this single monastery. He also composed similar offerings for the monasteries at Poitiers and Nouaille, Fleury and Chelles; as well as twenty-four for St Peter's, Salzburg at the behest of his friend Arno, who by then was the Archbishop there.[9] Among these was one composed for an altar to St Paul, St Benedict and St Columba.[10] Alcuin also composed epitaphs for Venantius Fortunatus at Poitiers, for St Amand and St Vaast, as well as for more recent abbots such as Fulrad at St Denis and Gislebert at St Amand.[11] Close examination of the allusions in many of these inscriptions reveals the web of monastic association that was being built up across the monasteries at this time, with a strong sense

An inscribed silver Cross, perhaps a reliquary or a pendant from above an
Italian altar, from the late eighth or early ninth centuries, whose rich symbolism
emulates that of Lombard stone carving, portraying the symbols of the four
evangelists and the tree of life surrounded by peacocks and seven stars.

of a common history, often associated with missionary work, as well as a common devotional ethos. They reflect also a standard of Latin literacy capable of interpreting to monks and others by words what was also portrayed so richly and vividly in churches, manuscripts and works of art at this time.

Alcuin's letters also reveal that he was by no means alone in cultivating the resurgence of well-established and defined monastic life at this time. His influence in this area has to be seen in the context of the labours of others, some of whom were his friends and to whom he wrote: for example, Leidrad of Lyons and Amalarius of Metz, who had been for a time his pupils; likewise Arno of Salzburg and Riculf of Mainz, who were contemporaries and associates in the reform of the Church. The administrative competence of Adalhard of Corbie probably reflects Alcuin's example at Tours and his influence as well.[12]

Much of this monastic initiative bore fruit in the next generation, when other pupils of Alcuin's played a leading role in establishing increasing conformity in the observance of monastic life throughout the Frankish realm under Louis the Pious: Hrabanus Maur, who became Abbot of Fulda in 822 and Archbishop of Mainz in 847; Fredegisus who succeeded Alcuin as Abbot of Tours, nurturing the foundation at Cormery, and becoming chancellor under Louis; and Sigwulf, Alcuin's close friend, who became Abbot of Ferrières after his death. It was for this milieu that the *Life of Alcuin* was composed, a hagiography clearly steeped in a common memory, but that was already being moulded in its retrospective perceptions by the developments within monasticism promoted by Alcuin's close friend and protégé, Benedict of Aniane. Thus Alcuin was portrayed in a lineage that ran back through Hilary and Martin to Benedict, as well as heir to the insular monastic tradition that had nurtured him. Alcuin's desire to retire in 796 to Fulda was so that he might be able to observe uninterrupted the *Rule of St Benedict*, to which the foundation at Cormery was specifically committed by his predecessor, Itherius, as well as by himself with the support of Charlemagne. This commitment by Alcuin to the *Rule of St Benedict* was evident also in a letter of encouragement to the monks of Wearmouth-Jarrow, written in 793 after news of the sack of Lindisfarne had reached him, in which he enjoined them to remain faithful to the *Rule of St Benedict* that their founder, Benedict Biscop, had established.[13] What Alcuin felt about the significance of St Benedict may be captured in this poem:

> *Hail, Benedict, greatest shepherd of monks!*
> *Rule now by your prayers those whom you have created by your words.*
> *You lead your cohorts, which you generated in the Lord,*
> *Before the throne of the great Judge, O beloved father:*
> *There you may present them before the tribunal of the heavenly King.*
> *Aid us with your prayers always and everywhere,*
> *Enlarge the number of your flock, O beloved father:*
> *Then the glory of your sheep will grow, as will its shepherds,*
> *If by your merits you preserve us as your servants.*[14]

Benedict of Aniane

Alcuin's close friendship with Benedict of Aniane is testified to in both their *Lives* and their collaboration in the development of the liturgy. In the *Life of Alcuin*, there is the moving account of what may have proved a final meeting between them, in which Alcuin anticipated Benedict's imminent arrival at Tours; their personal dialogue about penitence has already been considered, and their collaboration in the development of the liturgy was equally close. The biographer of Alcuin recorded that Benedict was someone joined to him as the man of God closest to his heart, who often visited him at Tours seeking his advice and friendship.[15] In the prologue to the *Life of Alcuin* he commended Alcuin as exemplary for those following the life of canons and Benedict for those committed to monastic vows, both of them representing living and accessible links with the teaching and examples of the Fathers. The reference to their friendship in the *Life of Benedict* by Ardo is an important witness to Alcuin's reinvigoration of the community at Cormery:

> Alcuin, of the nation of the Angles, a deacon in rank, outstanding in wisdom, venerable by merit of his holiness, governing the monastery of the blessed confessor Martin who had been bishop of Tours, was held worthy of full honour at the court of the glorious emperor Charles. When Alcuin heard about and experienced the holiness of the man of God [i.e. Benedict], he linked himself to him in inviolable charity. From his letters addressed to Benedict, a booklet has been compiled. Once gifts had been offered, Alcuin resolutely demanded that some monks be given to him. The venerable father Benedict at once complied and Alcuin dispatched horses to fetch them. He situated them in a monastery named Cormery, which he had erected. There were, I think, twenty of them with a teacher set over them. By the good example of their way of life, a great multitude of monks was assembled.[16]

This development was related by Alcuin to Arno in a letter, written in 799.[17] The mention of the booklet of Alcuin's letters, compiled by Benedict and his disciples, is also significant, because it is now sadly lost. Had it survived it would probably have shed much valuable light on their collaboration in the nurturing of monastic life and collecting the patristic resources to sustain it, and perhaps also more about their active collaboration against Adoptionism. In fact, it is still possible to track their friendship through some of Alcuin's remaining letters. In two letters written well before Alcuin became abbot of Tours, he thanked Benedict in terms of strong friendship for a gift of herbs as medicine on one occasion;[18] and in another letter he asked him to deliver letters that he had sent to the court where Benedict was, one of which was for the King, and to copy one of them for common reading by their brethren, improving it if necessary.[19]

Later when Alcuin was at Tours, he wrote several letters to Benedict and others involved in active missionary work to combat Adoptionism.[20] His *Adversus Elipandum Toletanum,* written in 799, was accompanied by two letters addressed to Leidrad of Lyons, Nefridus of Narbonne and Benedict of Aniane.[21] In the same year, after the rebuttal of Felix of Urguel at the synod at Aachen, Alcuin wrote a general letter to the abbots and monks of Gothia in Septimania, on the borders of Spain, in which he referred to their reception of his earlier treatise *Liber contra Felicis haeresim*[22] by the hand of Benedict, and alerted them to his forthcoming work *Adversus Felicem*[23] which they would receive as soon as it had received Charlemagne's approval. This letter contained an important summary of what was at stake in the controversy with the Adoptionists, who were gaining a sizable following.[24] The next year, Alcuin sent a commendatory letter to Nefridus on behalf of Benedict, with whom he was parting with regret, and in which he spoke of the dangerous times in which they were living.[25] In a subsequent letter to them both, Alcuin encouraged them in their continued activities on behalf of the Church.[26] Benedict and Alcuin therefore had many friends in common, including Theodulf of Orleans, who wrote a poem for Benedict and his monks, and some of whom, like Leidrad and Nefridus, would continue active in collaboration with Benedict in the years after Alcuin's death in 804. Benedict himself died on 11th February 821.

Consideration of the thoroughness of Benedict's commitment to the *Rule of St Benedict,* after his initial dismissal of it, is one of the striking features of his *Life,* and also of the writings that he generated to guide and sustain monastic life in accordance with that *Rule.*[27] His life and work may usefully be compared as a monastic reformer with that of his contemporary in Byzantium, Theodore the Stoudite, though without the same propensity for controversy.[28] The character of Benedict's monastic compilations is very interesting inasmuch as it shadowed closely Alcuin's own approach to the Fathers, manifesting the same willingness to collate, edit and adapt in order to create the coherent application of a conscious tradition suitable for the needs of the Church, in this case the monasteries. It is most likely that Alcuin contributed much to further Benedict's initiatives in reforming and regularising monastic life, but the direct evidence has been lost.[29] Certainly the writer of the *Life of Alcuin* regarded Alcuin as a true monk in spirit, even if not bound by the formal vows that had been enjoined in Carolingian monasticism by the time that he was writing – *O vere monachum, monachi sine voto!*[30]

Benedict was of noble birth, a Visigoth from Septimania, who in 782 founded a monastery at Aniane in southern France. This became a power-house of reform by leading a strict monastic life in accordance with the *Rule of St Benedict.* Such was his own example and that of his monks that Aniane attracted recruits and endowments. In 792 it received a charter of immunity from Charlemagne, having become the head of a family of monastic communities over which Benedict exercised direct oversight.[31]

It was also enriched by a sumptuous church, a library and a school for monks, many of whom went elsewhere at the request of bishops like Leidrad and Theodulf, as well as of Alcuin himself.

It was on the basis of this major development that Benedict became under Louis the Pious, with whom he had worked closely while he ruled Aquitaine, the foremost monastic reformer as well as that King's close adviser. His labours culminated in the decrees of the synod of Aachen in 817, which commanded that all monks should live according to the *Rule of St Benedict* as interpreted by Benedict of Aniane. This set a momentous precedent for subsequent monastic history in Europe and marks the real beginning of Benedictine monasticism as a systematic and recognisable spiritual entity. Benedict's most notable work was his *Codex regularum monasticarum et canonicarum,* designed for daily reading to the monks and others living under rule in a community, and comprising a collation from the various monastic rules that shed light on the *Rule of St Benedict* itself and its meaning.[32]

No less significant was his *Munimenta Fidei,* a collection of patristic texts assembled at Aniane between 800 and 814, which contained among other things Benedict's own doctrinal writings. In this work he and his disciples proved to be true heirs of Alcuin, and this composite volume contained several of Alcuin's most important theological works. Benedict was also the architect of the various decrees that attempted to establish a uniform pattern of monastic life during the reign of Louis the Pious. He left an important legacy, model and memory, even if the upheavals in the later ninth century obliterated much that had been achieved tangibly in developing more systematic monastic life under the Carolingians in the first half of the ninth century.

The description of the church at Aniane, which was begun in 782, makes a paradoxical contrast with Benedict's earlier penchant for asceticism. Its cloisters were lined with marble columns and its splendour exuded a holiness of atmosphere that made an impact on all who entered it. Initially it was to be dedicated to Christ, but it was in the end dedicated by Benedict to the Holy Trinity. This was signalled by three small altars surrounding the main altar of the church: 'by the three altars the undivided Trinity is shown forth, and by the single altar the true Godhead in essence is declared.'[33] The altar itself was solid in front but concave behind, with a door concealing the relics. All the vessels in the building were in numbers of seven – elaborate candelabra, hanging lamps before the altar and a corona of lamps above the choir. There were other altars dedicated to St Michael, the apostles Peter and Paul, and to St Stephen. In the chapel of the Blessed Virgin Mary there were also altars to St Benedict and St Martin, while the cemetery chapel was dedicated to St John the Baptist. 'By these seven altars, by the seven candelabra, and by the seven lamps, the sevenfold grace of the Holy Spirit is understood.' The church therefore embodied and proclaimed the principal theological concerns of both Alcuin and Benedict: it was a shrine to Catholic monastic orthodoxy.

Angilbert of St Riquier

In this deliberate theological design, the monastic church at Aniane mirrored the no less significant monastic complex being created by Charlemagne's nephew, Angilbert, Abbot of St Riquier, with whom Alcuin had a close friendship, contributing a rewritten *Life of St Riquier* at the very end of his life in 800 or 801 to mark the renovation of his church and the promotion of the saint's cult.[34] The importance of this revised *Life* was highlighted by its prefatory letter to Charlemagne himself. Angilbert was often mentioned in Alcuin's correspondence, most notably in connection with his mission to Rome on behalf of Charlemagne in 796. Four letters remain from Alcuin to Angilbert, whom he nicknamed Homer, along with three poems.[35] What is significant is the way in which the vast rebuilding of St Riquier was a major exercise in theology expressed in stone, and as such it reflected the great wealth that Charlemagne and those around him could command. It indicated also the way in which the revival of monasticism was rooted in the desire to establish centres of firm and informed orthodox Christian worship and belief in the Trinity at the heart of the Carolingian church. It thus mirrored the literary, educational and liturgical efforts of Alcuin and others in combating heresy and other distortions such as the veneration of images.

In 781, Charlemagne appointed Angilbert as *primicerius* of the palace chapel at Pavia where his infant son, Pippin, was titular King of Italy.[36] Angilbert's friendship with Alcuin dated from this time, for it was at Pavia that Charlemagne met Alcuin and first invited him to join his court in 782. Angilbert fell in love with Charlemagne's daughter, Bertha, by whom he had two sons; but in 789 he was appointed to be the lay-Abbot of St Riquier and commenced its extensive rebuilding. In 792 he took Felix of Urguel from the synod of Regensburg to Rome, taking with him also the synopsis of the *Libri Carolini* for Pope Hadrian I. In 794 he took the decision of the synod of Frankfurt once again to Rome, and returned there in 796 on the King's behalf, whose intimate counsellor he now was, bearing gifts from the Avar hoard for Pope Leo III. In 800, the refurbished monastery at St Riquier was dedicated at Easter with great solemnity in the presence of Charlemagne, Alcuin and others, and later in that year Angilbert accompanied Charlemagne to Rome. He was a poet on a par with Alcuin, and an educated and articulate exponent of Carolingian theology, transforming St Riquier into a living embodiment of belief in the Trinity and the Incarnation. Later he witnessed Charlemagne's will in 811, and died shortly after him in 814. His was a distinguished and significant career that sheds much indirect light on that of his close friend, Alcuin, as well. Whatever its theological conception, Angilbert's architectural ensemble at St Riquier reflected much glory on Charlemagne and his family.

To mark the rededication of the renewed monastery of St Riquier in 800, Angilbert composed a book in two parts, that detailed the theology lying behind its planning and construction, and the liturgy conducted therein.

'The image of the Trinity was quite literally the structural integrator of Angilbert's programme, the image into which both the physical house and the liturgy were built. There were, for example, three churches in a triangular cloister.'[37] The whole complex was intended to be an epitome of the City of God, where the true worship of the Trinity and the Incarnate Christ might be carried out by day and by night to the glory of God and the well-being of Charlemagne's realm. It was very much a royal project as a potent religious symbol and as a bulwark against heresy.

The church dedicated to St Mary, described by Angilbert as *Dei Genetrix*,[38] was itself a reproach to Adoptionism: it was used on Maundy Thursday to commemorate the giving of the Eucharist, and at Pentecost to mark the descent of the Holy Spirit.[39] For Angilbert, as for Benedict and Alcuin, the number seven also had a profound mystical and theological significance, representing the sevenfold gifts of the Spirit which flowed from Christ as the Wisdom of God.[40] The parallels with the monastic church at Aniane are striking. No less interesting was Angilbert's insistence on lay participation in the liturgy at major festivals.[41] The whole complex was dedicated to Christ the Saviour.[42] 'St Riquier was thus of the greatest importance to Charlemagne and to the theologians who informed his policy. It was, at its root, through the creative vision of Angilbert, an expression of Carolingian culture in its formation.'[43]

Monastic education

Such theology in art and stone, accompanied by elaborate liturgy, could only be understood and participated in by an educated monastic community which was led by a learned elite and that was able to communicate its meaning and relevance to a sympathetic and informed laity, upon whose generosity monasticism ever depended. Royal patronage could assist the process of endowment, but wealth alone could not generate or sustain monastic life. It was Alcuin's genius to implant, with Benedict of Aniane and others, a definite educational role within the reformed monasticism that was being developed at this time. The union of Benedictine monasticism and education may seem obvious and normal within the long hindsight of Western history up until today; but it was in fact an innovation and on a scale not originally envisaged by the *Rule of St Benedict*, beyond the obvious need for simple liturgical literacy in a monastic community.

The word *schola* meant originally a common room or dormitory. In the *Rule of St Benedict* it denoted the whole community at the work of prayer – the *opus Dei*. 'It was only in the Carolingian world that a *schola* became an institutionalised "location of learning."'[44] But there was a tension inherent in the situation if the pursuit of learning in a monastery cut across more ascetical withdrawal in the service of God or distracted from the inevitable practical round of duties necessary to sustain the common life. How could the love of learning and the desire for God be creatively combined?[45] This created difficulties in the generation immediately after Alcuin when the pursuit of grammar and dialectic by Irish *scolastici* and others could provoke Benedict of Aniane to repudiate their trespass upon the doctrine of the Trinity.[46] In his own writing exhorting monastic life, contained throughout his letters to monasteries and monastics, Alcuin showed the way by example and argument. In this he was of course heir to the insular tradition, rooted in Ireland and Anglo-Saxon England, where monastic life and education were already combined: in Bede, Aldhelm, Willibrord and Boniface and others, including Alcuin himself, it had found its powerful expression and provision of articulate resources.

It was in the *Admonitio Generalis* of 789[47] and the *Epistola de litteris colendis*[48] that the application of this experience and vision to Carolingian monasteries was first adumbrated formally, probably under the guidance of Alcuin. One of the intentions was undoubtedly to make the monastic way of life attractive to the free or noble person and not just to those of peasant background.[49] The main programme of basic education comprised learning the psalms, their *notae* and the liturgical chants; also calendar calculation [*computus*] and grammar, supported by suitably corrected texts. The *Epistola de litteris colendis* sought to commend the higher learning of the gifted few as a worthy part of life according to monastic rule. In the mind of Alcuin, such learning completed monastic life even if it was a relative innovation: it too was an ascetic endeavour, governed by its own disciplines and sheer hard work. It also required a dedicated work-force of skilled artisans, scribes, artists to prepare and copy the manuscripts. The scriptorium thus became of central importance as a theatre of learned monastic discipline and endeavour. Alcuin's view was that 'on one side, there was saintly simplicity; on the other, sacred learning.'[50] For Alcuin the foundation text of Christian learning was Matthew 12.36, words of Jesus which he summarised thus in the *Epistola de litteris colendis*: 'either by your words will you be justified or by your words you will be condemned.' Accurate use of language was the gateway to divine truth as revealed in the Bible; it was also the vital instrument of mission.

Alcuin set forth his vision of monastic education most clearly in a short treatise, construed in the form of a dialogue, the *Disputatio de vera philosophia*.[51] In many of the manuscripts it served as a preface to his *Ars grammatica*, though its application was to all branches of learning.[52] Its intellectual importance lay in its use of Boethius' *De Consolatione Philosophiae*, a text that Alcuin virtually rediscovered and introduced into the mainstream of Christian learning once again.[53] What is notable from a theological angle is the way in which Alcuin here, as in his letters, held fast to the ideal of 'true philosophy' as he envisaged it: the spiritual pursuit of truth supported by disciplined learning, argument and prayer, rooted in patristic tradition.

The very phrase 'true philosophy' seems to be Alcuin's, whatever its Christian antecedents. In the *Disputatio de vera philosophia* this is placed in the context of monastic formation and education. It entailed discerning the ephemeral nature of worldly things as distractions from the true orientation of thought and desire. Moderation alone was appropriate to human well-being:[54] divine wisdom was the true source of human happiness. A mind engaged in *lectio divina* sought systematically the moral, natural and theological meaning of the text of the Bible. Thus led by wisdom, the human mind enters upon the ladder of divine ascent, towards the vision of God in contemplation. Following Augustine's exegesis of Proverbs 9.1, Alcuin declared that the seven liberal arts – grammar, rhetoric, dialectic, arithmetic, geometry, music, and astrology (i.e. astronomy) – were in fact steps to this contemplative knowledge of reality, which was the true end of human life. They represented antique columns, baptised by the seven-fold gifts of the Holy Spirit and now supporting the structure of the Church, as was actually exemplified in many renovated churches at that time in Rome and elsewhere.[55]

Christ, who was the creator of the Church, was the incarnate Wisdom of God, a line of thought that Alcuin derived from Gregory the Great and also Bede, as well as from St Paul. In the context of Adoptionism, this was an important assertion of the inherent union of divine and human in Christ. Drawing on his own experience and writings, 'Alcuin firmly placed correct understanding of the Incarnation at the centre of a liberal arts education in his exegesis of Proverbs 9.1. He also made the ability to defend the Incarnation against heretics one of the main goals of education.'[56] Their mastery equipped a monastic teacher in opposing heresy by logical disputation, while also clarifying and articulating orthodox Christian doctrine. Persuasion not coercion was the right approach to heretics. It may be therefore that Alcuin only completed the *Disputatio de vera philsophia* after his defeat of Felix of Urguel at the synod of Aachen in 799 by the very methods that he was commending.[57]

Alcuin also defended the use of the seven liberal arts, and especially that of dialectic, in his letter of commendation to Charlemagne which prefaced his treatise *De fide sanctae et individuae Trinitatis*.[58] Their disciplined practice over a lifetime not only opened the pages of Scripture, but it also weaned a person off material things and false values, paving the way for mystical union with God. This line of argument can be found in several of Alcuin's letters to former pupils and others.[59] In his letter to Charlemagne about his progress at establishing such an educational programme at Tours, he portrayed the environment that he was seeking to create as a *hortus conclusus*, condign to spiritual theology and redolent of the Song of Songs, a replica of the one he had himself experienced in York, from whence he sought permission to retrieve some of his books. In his commitment to monastic education therefore, 'Alcuin was not merely a compliant instrument of court policy, but an independent advocate of his own, monastically inspired religious and cultural programme.'[60] Use of the liberal arts could no longer be suspect or optional because of their pagan origins: for baptised into the service of Christ they drew forth from the treasuries of Scripture things old and new.[61] It was in this spirit that Alcuin composed the educational treatises that would serve the cause of monastic education for many centuries after his death.

A simplified summary of monastic formation from the milieu of Alcuin may be found in the long anonymous poem *Haec praecepta legat devotus*, which may well come from his pen, though this is by no means certain.[62] Its authorship by Alcuin rests upon the testimonies of Hrabanus Maur, who was his pupil, and later of Lupus, Abbot of Ferrières, a monastery within the Alcuinian connection.[63] It comprises a series of 200 single line proverbs, prefaced by a five line poem, pertaining to the Christian life in general and monastic life in community in particular, culled from various sources, that were evidently part of the lingua franca of the oral tradition of monasticism within which Alcuin and others were working.[64] Such sayings would have been easily committed to memory and made the focus of monastic teaching, meditation and discussion. Their principal source was a corpus of proverbial moral sayings attributed to a late antique writer, the *Disticha* of Cato. But these were incorporated within a wider ambit of sayings, many of which have close connections with the thought and teaching of Alcuin, addressing a more popular level of thought and monastic practice.

They commended the love of Christ and the repudiation of material wealth, 'for it is best for the mind to be vested in the love of Christ.' 'Do not love yourself, nor the world, but only Christ.' They touched on the qualities of relationships needed within a community, avoidance of envy and gossip and the cultivation of true friendship: 'for it is most difficult to find a true friend.' Learning too was commended: 'A good mind excels all other treasures.' They addressed also the qualities of rule and teaching: 'a devout and kindly ruler is the joy of his people.' 'The teacher will be truly great who in his deeds fulfils what he teaches.' 'A wise king will defend his people better, whereas a weak ruler will disperse his entire population.' Finally, 'the root of wisdom is to fear the Lord with the mind.' They demonstrate again how important the sapiential writing in the Bible was as the foundation of monastic community life, because it was essentially practical, easily memorised and then ruminated upon.[65] In the mind of Alcuin, Proverbs, Ecclesiastes and the Song of Songs provided a progressive path into divine wisdom, instructing the devout reader first in moral, then in natural, and finally in contemplative philosophy.[66] Alcuin wrote commentaries on all these three books of the Bible as part of his provision for monastic education.

The spiritual orientation of Alcuin's educational philosophy and its anchorage within the life of monastic and other religious communities is therefore the central consideration when considering in detail the content of the education that he prescribed and for whose development he wrote so extensively. For him, regular monastic life was also a bridge between the clergy and laity, between the highly educated and the ordinary Christian. He related to many educated laity directly, and much that he wrote was intended for them as well: herein lay his genius as an educator. The long use that was made of so many of his core educational writings is testimony to their relevance, accessibility and vitality.

The Halton Moor cup that was found in Lancashire: a striking piece of early
Carolingian art, fashioned out of gold and silver, and patterned with chasing
animals and leaf scrolls.

Chapter 12

Letters, Friends, and Manuscripts

The most remarkable legacy of Alcuin is undoubtedly to be found in the various collections of his letters, some of which were made in his own lifetime: for it is through these that fullest access may be had to his thought and beliefs, as well as to his personality, and his attitude towards friendship in particular. It is remarkable that his powers of communication and affection can still come across so eloquently after more than twelve hundred years, making his letters the most important window into the mind of a person in the early medieval period between those of Gregory the Great and Anselm. The unique character and abiding value of Alcuin's letters were clearly recognised by more than a handful of his contemporaries, who secured their careful collection and copying, certainly as exemplars, but also as memorials to someone whose stature towered over his contemporaries, inspiring deep loyalty, emulation, and appreciation. They were also a vital component of his mission to provide the laity with a moral theology that would enable them to lead a Christian life. The story of the collecting of Alcuin's letters provides therefore a valuable insight into his immediate legacy in the early ninth century, as well as later in England in the tenth century. Their historical importance for anchoring many important aspects of the last fifteen years of Alcuin's life and work has been amply demonstrated throughout this study.

The letter collections

There are at least 283 letters remaining that may safely be attributed to Alcuin; but none may be dated before the early 780s, and few if any were written while he was based in York and before he went to the continent. There are around fifteen letters that probably date from before the end of 793.[1] The rate of letters now remaining peaks between the years 798-801, leaving a few from Alcuin's declining years: 'Even for the best-documented years we clearly have only a small part of what once existed.'[2] The *Life of Benedict of Aniane*, for example, mentions a collection of Alcuin's letters made by him but which is now lost. There may have been many more letters dealing with the Adoptionist crisis, for example; and very few business letters remain from his hand, a gap reflected also in the paucity of charters from that period in which Alcuin is named as a beneficiary or witness. Prominent among his later letters are those addressed to Arno, Archbishop of Salzburg, who was evidently a close friend and ally. Yet none of Arno's replies to Alcuin now remain; nor from others of his correspondents, for example Paulinus of Aquilea. This is partly because copies of letters sent out and those received were not filed together at that time. Nonetheless 'transcriptions of nearly eighty different letters, more than a quarter of the total extant, are to be found in three manuscripts written during Alcuin's lifetime.'[3]

The number of Alcuin's letters remaining that were addressed to Arno reflects also the fact that he was the first actively to collect Alcuin's letters for his own interest and use. Arno remained Abbot of St Amand in northern France while serving as Bishop and, after 798, as Archbishop of Salzburg; and it was at St Amand that the first collection of Alcuin's letters was compiled and copied, probably in 799, in a manuscript that soon went to Salzburg and that is now in Vienna.[4] There are twenty of Alcuin's letters in this earliest known collection, which rank in importance alongside the inventories commissioned by Arno for assessing the resources of his see, as well as other books such as the earliest remaining Salzburg formulary-book.

Shortly before Alcuin's death in 804, Arno commissioned a major codex of 134 leaves containing a further 60 of Alcuin's letters along with his *Disputatio Pippini cum Albino,* and the earliest collection of more than thirty of his poems.[5] This volume was the work of a whole team of scribes, reflecting Arno's organising capacity as a bishop. Most of these letters were addressed to people not necessarily connected to the church of Salzburg and 'the majority belong to Alcuin's pre-Tours years.' In some places his original wording has been altered or edited 'to make them more intelligible and usable as didactic texts or letter-exemplars at Salzburg.'[6]

While Arno was collecting some of Alcuin's letters in Salzburg, written to others as well as to himself, the monastery at Tours was also making a different collection, probably shortly after Alcuin's death.[7] This early ninth century manuscript now contains seventy letters from Alcuin but probably contained more, perhaps as many as ninety-four to judge from a possible copy made from it later in the ninth century at Rheims.[8] Behind these and other early collections lay a now lost 'basic Tours collection' of letters retained from as early as 796.[9] Its contents may be reflected in a shorter collection of Alcuin's letters made at the monastery of St Gallen in the 820s when that community committed itself to a relationship of confraternity with the monastery at Tours.[10] Later in the century a comparable copy was made at the monastery of St Vaast in Arras from a common exemplar.[11] A third version, now lost, was behind an important eleventh century English collection of Alcuin's letters.[12] None of the letters in the fundamental Tours collection date from after the summer of 799, however, and its core may well have been a 'formula letter-book' created by Alcuin himself for his pupils' use shortly after he came to Tours as abbot in 796.[13]

In all these collections derived from Tours there are singular gaps: for example, they contain no letters to Arno of Salzburg, nor the letter written by Alcuin before he became abbot to the pupils at Tours concerning the confession of sins.[14] None of Alcuin's letters dealing with the Adoptionist controversy were preserved in the collections emanating from Tours. Nonetheless some of these were collected elsewhere and appear, for example, in a text dealing with the doctrine of the Trinity associated with Hincmar of Rheims.[15] On another occasion an unknown teacher compiled a short handbook, perhaps around the year 824, from some of Alcuin's computistical writings, including six letters drawn from the fuller Tours collection.[16] Another tribute to Alcuin's memory is found in a small collection of his letters associated with the monastery of St Emmeram in Regensburg.[17]

Two important manuscripts, written at St Denis near Paris around the year 820, may have some link with Alcuin's friend, Adalhard Abbot of Corbie, as they contain letters to him not found elsewhere, as well as letters to female members of the royal family with whom Alcuin enjoyed close ties of friendship.[18] Very few of the letters in this important collection are found in the other collections and they range over a long period of Alcuin's life, embracing numerous contacts and including three 'letter-poems'. It is just possible that this tradition reflects a more personal collection made initially by Alcuin himself.[19] There is no doubt that he was not averse to utilising phrases and expressions in a way which probably indicates that he kept copies of letters drafted as formulary sources for his own purposes.[20]

A manuscript commissioned by a senior cleric in England early in the tenth century and now in the library of Lambeth Palace is another major witness to the likely content of the basic Tours collection of Alcuin's letters.[21] It is striking for its display capitals which mark the opening lines. Most of it follows closely the Troyes manuscript but the last six letters are unique to this English manuscript. It bears witness to the availability of an important collection of Alcuin's letters in England just before the beginning of the revitalisation of monastic life under Dunstan at Glastonbury.[22] Portions of three letters of Alcuin to Charlemagne have also been identified in two fragmentary leaves now in the Newberry Library in Chicago.[23] Both these manuscripts are examples of early English square minuscule, which was developed during the reign of Alfred the Great as an English attempt at standardisation comparable to Caroline minuscule, but which could be used for copying Anglo-Saxon as well as Latin texts.[24]

These two manuscripts are important in the context of other works of Alcuin known to have been available in England in the first part of the tenth century, notably his *De Virtutibus et Vitiis*, his *De Dialectica*, and his *De Orthographia*.[25] It has also been pointed out the degree to which Alfred's vision of Christian kingship and the need to revive learning embodied the teaching of Alcuin.[26] The King's concern to translate Boethius' *De*

Consolatione Philosophiae and Gregory's *Pastoral Care* may be an indirect tribute to the memory of Alcuin, mediated perhaps through the influence of Grimbald from St Bertin's monastery, who came to England at the King's invitation. It may well be, therefore, that a significant part of Alcuin's legacy is to be found reflected in the confidence and clarity with which the tenth century reformers articulated the duties of Christian monarchy, and restored Benedictine monastic life and learning in England.

The sense that Alcuin may indeed be the *eminence grise* behind the work of Dunstan and his collaborators and their disciples may be corroborated by the fact that two of the most important manuscript witnesses to his letter collection were copied in England early in the eleventh century, though the first of them was probably collated much earlier. The first and most striking is the collection of material associated with both Alcuin and Dunstan, which is a manuscript now in the British library, but which was possibly copied at Christ Church, Canterbury after the death of Dunstan in 988, probably in or around the year 1000: it is MS BL Cotton Tiberius A. xv.[27] It contains 117 letters by Alcuin and it seems to have been composed in stages in various parts of England throughout the tenth century as the most comprehensive collection of his letters ever made until the printed editions of the early modern period. The second manuscript is no less interesting being a collection of Alcuinian and other ecclesiastical material made by Wulfstan, Bishop of Worcester and Archbishop of York, who was a protégé of Dunstan and who continued his policy in both church and state: it is MS BL Cotton Vespasian A xiv pt. iii.

The source for much of the distinctive material in the Tiberius manuscript seems to derive from a lost continental copy, whose provenance was Tours and which was evidently available in England during the second half of the tenth century, as part of a letter of Alcuin within it was quoted extensively by Abbot Aelfweard of Glastonbury to Archbishop Sigeric of Canterbury.[28] An earlier letter in it to Dunstan also quotes from one of Alcuin's letters.[29] Both these manuscript collections give priority to Alcuin's correspondence with England, mainly for its topical relevance, but also as a way of appropriating the Christian history of the country, which was a major cultural preoccupation of the tenth century reform movement.

It is possible that the northern element in the Tiberius manuscript was originally collated at York during Alcuin's lifetime, with its origin as a register composed there to some extent before he finally left Northumbria for the continent.[30] The use of material from this northern tradition at Canterbury is first attested in a quotation from Alcuin included in a letter written by one of Dunstan's immediate successors as Archbishop of Canterbury to Bishop Wulfsige of Sherborne and now contained in the Sherborne Pontifical.[31] It has close affinities with the letter of Abbot Aelfweard of Glastonbury and these examples may therefore indicate that at least part of the larger collection of Alcuin's letters was available at Glastonbury before the time of Dunstan's death, perhaps even collated during his time as Abbot.[32] It seems that it was the interests of his successors at Canterbury that determined the final composition of the Tiberius manuscript; but it may well have been Dunstan's authority, example and memory that lay behind the whole initiative.

The collection made for Wulfstan Archbishop of York was no less practical in its intent and it bears the impress of his mind as well the mark of his handwriting in various places.[33] It was intended for personal use and reference and it is therefore much smaller than the Tiberius archive. There remains uncertainty as to whether Wulfstan found the Alcuin material in the archives of York or of Worcester. It seems that there was a common source for both manuscripts, however, which were probably independently produced to some extent. The Vespasian manuscript is in fact a composite document, full of material helpful to an archbishop of York at that time. It concludes with a striking letter of protest from Wulfstan to the Pope, citing a unique letter of Alcuin, and protesting about the fees charged to archbishops when they made their pilgrimage to Rome to collect the *pallium* as well as the other attendant costs of so lengthy and dangerous a journey.[34] Wulfstan pointed out that in the beginning popes had simply sent the *pallium* to England.

Wulfstan clearly found in Alcuin a kindred spirit when advising the English and Danish kings, Ethelred the Unready and Cnut, and reacting sharply and moralistically to the renewed Viking threat in his day. Hence their common appeals to the warnings of Gildas as they found them in the opening pages of Bede's *History*.[35] By examining why Wulfstan chose what he did from the writings of Alcuin, a useful insight may be obtained into his thinking as a bishop and statesman, as well an enhanced appreciation of Alcuin's great skill in applying Christian theology to public life and private behaviour. Part of a stern letter by Alcuin to Ethelheard the Archbishop of Canterbury was underlined by Wulfstan and then incorporated into his famous and minatory *Sermo Lupi ad Anglos*.[36]

Parts of this Vespasian manuscript are in Wulfstan's own handwriting, and one of its themes was the vexed issue of church wealth, its proper use and due protection. Alcuin's letters were reinforced by others associated with Dunstan and other more contemporary ecclesiastical figures: 'To Wulfstan, the Alcuin letters' relevance stood undiminished two centuries later.'[37] It seems that Wulfstan drew some of his resources from Canterbury, however, following the lead set by Dunstan's immediate successors there. For these successors to the great reformers saw themselves as heirs to a strong canonical tradition of which they were trustees and protagonists; and the trenchant writings of Alcuin gave guidance and expression to their legitimate concerns at a time of considerable upheaval in England in the early eleventh century.

The last medieval glimpse of the relevance of some of Alcuin's letters for understanding the traditions of the Anglo-Saxon church may be found in the use made of them by William of Malmesbury in his historical writings, the *Gesta Regum* and the *Gesta Pontificum:* he completed his work in compiling them by 1125.[38] He drew on a collection that was very close to the Tiberius manuscript, though the precise relationship remains disputed. Much later, the Tudor historian John Leland extracted sixty-five letters of Alcuin and Dunstan from what he described as 'an old codex.'[39] Leland's citations are similar to William's amended ones, for William did not hesitate to adjust his sources, as he did in his book the *Antiquity of Glastonbury*. William tended to quote lengthy extracts from Alcuin's texts, sometimes edited and adjusted by him, in an illustrative rather than analytic way.[40] He clearly regarded him as a significant primary historical authority on a par with Bede's *History*.

Like Wulfstan before him, William deployed Alcuin's letters for their relevance to topical issues, notably the appropriate relations between the primates of York and Canterbury, which were often fraught in the twelfth century. William of Malmesbury clearly saw Bede, Alcuin, and Dunstan standing in an unbroken tradition that had shaped the English church over many centuries before the Norman Conquest in 1066.

Indeed there can be little doubt that the vision and probably the writings of Alcuin, and especially his letters with their political directness and theological practicality, lay directly and indirectly behind the programme of political and ecclesiastical reforms that marks the tenth century in England.[41] For example, both the *Regularis Concordia* and the *Coronation Order*, to single out two of the most distinguished and abiding records of that reform movement, embodied clearly and confidently the Christian polity adumbrated by Alcuin and Benedict of Aniane in their day as guidance and corrective to Charlemagne and his successors. What had been relevant to the Carolingian Church and its monasteries now applied to the bishops and rulers of England, as did Wulfstan's legislation and his treatise of political theory, the *Institutes of Polity*, in the next generation.

The debt of the tenth century reformers to Alcuin's legacy may be discerned also in the Latin versions of some of his writings that underpin their translation and inclusion within Anglo-Saxon theological texts from this period. For example there is a sizeable portion of the letter that Alcuin wrote to his friend Rado, Abbot of St Vaast, to accompany his revised version of that saint's life, included as a chapter in an Anglo-Saxon translation and adaptation of the *Rule of Chrodegang of Metz*.[42] Aelfric translated Alcuin's answers to questions about the meaning of the book of Genesis for his disciple Sigwulf and incorporated material from them in some of his homilies. His *Colloquy* clearly emulated the dialogue teaching style of Alcuin and others before him.[43] He also utilised Alcuin's treatise *De virtutibus et vitiis*, which was preserved in several Latin texts from this period which underlay other distinctive translations into English for use in homilies.[44] The extent to which Alcuin's legacy of teaching enriched vernacular Christianity and education in England in the tenth and eleventh centuries has yet to be established.

Disciples and manuscripts

Both biographers of Charlemagne paid tribute to Alcuin's considerable influence and great learning. There remain eighteen letters of Alcuin to Candidus, who was also a close colleague and companion of Arno of Salzburg, accompanying him twice to Rome in the momentous years between 798 and 800, and so becoming privy to the scandal surrounding Pope Leo III. Candidus was of English origin and a pupil of Bishop Higbald of Lindisfarne, who joined Alcuin at Aachen in 793. His *Dicta Candidi* complemented the *Dicta Albini* and they both remain as testimony to the lively debates fostered by Alcuin among his disciples.[45] The sermons attributed to Candidus are no less interesting as examples of communicating orthodox belief about the Incarnation and the Trinity in a creedal form to a general audience, along with suitable moral exhortations. They also confirm a link between their author and a church in Maastricht that for a time was part of Alcuin's patrimony.[46] Alcuin composed a poem for him on the eve of one of these visits.[47] He also dedicated his commentary on *Ecclesiastes* to him along with two of their other friends, one of whom was Fredegisus.[48] Candidus is mentioned in the *Life of Alcuin* and also most probably in the *Liber Vitae* of St Peter's, Salzburg.[49]

Fredegisus was Alcuin's immediate successor as Abbot of Tours and later became chancellor under Louis the Pious. It was under his leadership that many of the practical reforms initiated by Alcuin were established, notably the work of the Tours scriptorium. He too played an active role as a frequent intermediary between Alcuin, Charlemagne and Arno of Salzburg.[50] Another protégé of Alcuin's was the Irishman, Joseph the Scot, who was a poet and the author, at Alcuin's request, of an abbreviation of Jerome's commentary on Isaiah.[51] While Alcuin was detained in England at the end of 790, he asked Joseph to keep his ear to the ground at the court of Charlemagne on his behalf.[52] In 787/8 the King sent him with others as an emissary to Benevento in Italy where they narrowly escaped being killed. Joseph represents in the circle of Alcuin an unknown number of his Irish associates and protégés, some of whom found their way to Tours while he was Abbot there, much to the chagrin of some of the Frankish monks.[53]

The disciple closest in spirit and learning to Alcuin was undoubtedly Hrabanus Maur. Alcuin regarded him with real devotion and gave him the nickname *Maurus* after one of the disciples of St Benedict. He addressed him as such in a charming poem written probably in 799, describing him as a true disciple of St Benedict.[54] Indeed he was as a monk of Fulda, who had been sent by his Abbot, Baugulf, to study with Alcuin at Tours: in due time he himself became Abbot of Fulda between 822 and 842, before becoming Archbishop of Mainz in 847. Under his leadership, Fulda became a major centre of learning, and two of his most notable pupils were Lupus of Ferrières and Walahfrid Strabo.[55]

In a letter written towards the end of his life, Alcuin thanked Hrabanus for his letters, which revealed his love of wisdom and learning: 'for nothing is more laudable in a person than the adornment of wisdom and the affection of charity.'[56] He urged him to pursue the study of the Bible by day and night, 'seeking out how Christ was predicted in the prophets and shown forth in the gospels: and when you have found him, do not lose him, but lead him into the dwelling-place of your heart, and possess him there as the ruler of your life.'[57] Alcuin was eager that Hrabanus should love Christ 'as his redeemer, ruler and the benefactor of all good things.' He was to be charitable to those in need, and to take active pastoral care of the young in his care, guiding their morals: for 'they should so learn in adolescence that they may come to possess what they should later teach in their older years.'

In this letter, Alcuin was not able to respond to Hrabanus' request for a copy of Bede's commentary on the Catholic Epistles as it was still on loan to Gisela, Abbess of Chelles; but he would retrieve it from her for him.[58] Hrabanus had also asked for a book entitled *De benedictione patriarcharum* which was probably that now appended to Alcuin's *Quaestiones in Genesim*,[59] but which had apparently been composed in conjunction with Hrabanus and Beornrad of Echternach, who had become Archbishop of Sens. Alcuin then clarified for Hrabanus the (false) etymology of the Greek and Latin word *epistola*: 'have this interpretation until you should find a truer or better one!'[60]

This is a very interesting letter that reveals the strength of relationship between Alcuin and a mature pupil with whom he clearly had a strong affinity. In another letter of the same period, Alcuin wrote again to Hrabanus, who had now returned to his life as a monk at Fulda, describing him once more as a pupil of St Benedict.[61] He asked him to complete a book that he had promised for Alcuin, which was almost certainly his *De laudibus sanctae Crucis*, which in one of its manuscripts enfolds explicitly Alcuin's memory.

Hrabanus amply repaid the devotion and teaching of his master Alcuin and became one of the foremost biblical scholars and poets of his day. It is from his commentary on Ephesians, for example, that much of Alcuin's own work has been deduced, as Hrabanus was assiduous in marking his writings according to their sources, including Alcuin.[62] His own mark was 'M' in honour of Alcuin's sobriquet for him. Elsewhere he cited some of the monastic precepts that were associated with his old master,[63] or drew selectively from his poetry.[64]

'Of all Alcuin's students, it is Hrabanus Maurus who emerges as the one who followed his master's footsteps most closely, both as an encyclopaedist and as a teacher, as Alcuin had been, steeped in Alcuin's ideals. . . . In a touching poem which sometimes preceded his virtuoso *Liber sanctae Crucis*, Hrabanus put words into Alcuin's mouth, making his master intercede in prayer to St Martin on his behalf.'[65]

In the Vatican manuscript containing this poem, there is an accompanying picture of Hrabanus Maur and Alcuin presenting their work to St Martin.[66] Furthermore it is only in the *Martyrologium* of Hrabanus Maur that there is any explicit evidence of liturgical commemoration of Alcuin in the first half of the ninth century upon the anniversary of his death on 19th May, although the concluding stories in the *Life of Alcuin* point in the direction of a limited cult at his tomb in Tours for a while. In the *Annals of Fulda* Alcuin was remembered as outstanding for his holiness and doctrine. He had wished to join that community, where Boniface was buried, before he was made Abbot of Tours in 796 when he was aged around sixty, but it was not to be.

There is a great deal of Alcuin's thought and phraseology in the poetry of Hrabanus Maur, most often in that intended for others in the Alcuin circle and used quite selectively. In one such poem he drew on Alcuin's consolatory poem in response to the sack of Lindisfarne[67] to console a contemporary monk, Hatto, who had also studied under Alcuin with Hrabanus, and whom he nicknamed Bosonus, a friend mentioned in the letters of Jerome.[68] In his commentaries Hrabanus's debt to Alcuin is manifest, both in terms of selective though not always complete citations from his writings, alongside others from the Fathers; and also in terms of his skilful adaptations and development of Alcuin's thought, as in his poetry.[69] 'The conflict between biblical Latin and the language of the classics lost its significance for these Carolingian scholars, whose end was precisely to master the classics to the extent that they could advance their comprehension of the Bible.'[70] This confidence and competence in biblical study may be glimpsed further in the work of those trained under Hrabanus at Fulda. One such was a monk called Ercanbertus, and in his commentary on John's gospel may be glimpsed the process whereby teaching in a monastery at this time was received and noted down, and also the way in which the work of Alcuin was being appropriated by the generation after those whom he had taught.[71] Of these the most notable was Hincmar of Rheims, which probably accounts for the fact that the earlier of the two manuscripts containing the *Life of Alcuin* was preserved at Rheims.[72]

The most striking physical testimony to the legacy of Alcuin is the many manuscripts of his works that remain from the Frankish monastic libraries of the ninth century.[73] Ganz has identified 25 manuscripts of Alcuin's *De virtutibus et vitiis*, 30 of his *De fide*, many of which also contain his *De ratione animae*, which is preserved on its own in only three ninth century manuscripts. There are 20 manuscripts of his *Disputatio de rhetorica et de virtutibus*, 22 of his *De dialectica*, 16 of his *Ars grammatica*, and 16 of his *Interrogationes et responsiones in Genesim*. While there are in fact 20 ninth century manuscripts that contain collections of some of his letters, there are only 8 that contain his commentary on the Song of Songs and 10 containing his commentary on St John's gospel. Alcuin's hagiographies survive in only a few manuscripts, while his Adoptionist writings hang by a thread.

The predominance of the south-eastern German monasteries in generating these manuscripts is striking, though this may be in part a result of the destructive inroads of the Vikings in northern Francia in the second part of the ninth century. 'For much of the ninth century, and longer in some places, Alcuin was a recognisable scholar-personality, whose works were in demand precisely because they were Alcuin's and known to be, and because they were, in every sense, accessible introductions to their subjects. In the tenth and eleventh centuries, they were part of the general Carolingian heritage in the libraries of the older religious communities in the territory of the former Empire and were introduced spasmodically into those of more recent foundations.'[74] It was only in the eleventh and twelfth centuries that so many of his theological writings were, with the notable exception of the *De Fide*, eclipsed or subsumed into works often attributed to others.

It is at the monastery of St Gallen that the single most striking collection of his works still remains, most of which were copied in beautiful Caroline minuscule very soon after his death in the first part of the ninth century. There are in fact 38 manuscripts which can now be examined online.[75] The links between Tours and St Gallen were close and one of the earliest Tours Bibles is preserved there:[76] it is dated to the early years of the abbacy of Fredegisus. Alcuin's influence has also been traced, though without great certainty, in the illumination of certain manuscripts associated with Tours and elsewhere in his lifetime.[77] The range and quality of the ninth century library at St Gallen gives a vivid glimpse of the scope of learning and education available there in the generations immediately after the death of Alcuin, being a tangible monument to his memory, stimulus and legacy.

Conclusion

Memory

Alcuin and the historians

The revival of interest in Alcuin, mainly in Catholic circles, after the Reformation and up to the First World War is an interesting story. Some of Alcuin's writings were among the first books to be printed in Europe.[1] His *De Dialectica* was printed as early 1480, albeit as a work of Augustine's; his *De Fide* was printed in 1493. His *De Fide* was also included in the *Bibliotheca sanctorum patrum*, edited by Marguerin de la Bigne and printed in Paris in an appendix to this work in 1579, along with his *Quaestiones in Genesim* and his *De virtutibus et vitiis*.[2] The first comprehensive printed edition of Alcuin's works was published in France in 1617 by André Duchesne, using exclusively manuscripts available in French libraries.[3] John Leland, the Tudor antiquarian, made copies of some of Alcuin's letters from monastic manuscripts in England, but these were not published until 1714/5 by Thomas Hearne. The first printed collection of any of Alcuin's letters was in 1601 and 1605 at Ingolstadt by the Jesuit, Heinrich Canisius.[4] The person who deserves most credit for putting Alcuin on the map, however, was Frobenius Forster, the Abbot St Emmeram in Regensburg, whose monumental efforts appeared in a two volume *opera omnia* in 1777.[5] Forster's edition underlies that of Migne in his *Patrologia Latina*, volumes 100 and 101.[6]

Canisius, who died in 1610, worked closely with the monastery of St Gallen, which holds a unique collection of early Alcuin texts.[7] His *Antiquae Lectiones* constituted a significant effort to place these texts on a reliable footing, with due cognisance of their manuscripts, and careful reproductions of some of the diagrams associated with the texts, for example those inserted between Alcuin's *De Dialectica* and *De Grammatica*. Important and revealing correspondence remains between Canisius and the librarian at St Gallen of the day, Metzler.[8] This German initiative was however quite independent of and parallel to that of André Duchesne in France at around the same time, which did not draw upon the manuscripts preserved at St Gallen.

Forster's edition was in a different class to that of Canisius or Duchesne, and it represents some of the finest work to emerge from the south German Enlightenment that was rooted in the Benedictine monasteries. Forster presided as Abbot of St Emmeram for 34 years and commanded considerable resources, financial, intellectual and archival. In many ways he mirrored the work and capacity of Alcuin himself, while matching the scholarly initiatives of the Maurist fathers in France at that time, including Martène and Mabillon. He corresponded with 42 libraries across Europe in the pursuit of accurate manuscripts and information. Forster's principal contact at St Gallen was Pius Kolb, the librarian there for fourteen years. Some of their correspondence remains from the years 1755/6 and 1760/1, which charts Forster's growing interest in and respect for Alcuin and his writings, and his diligent desire to understand more fully, and to document accurately, Alcuin's influence during the reign of Charlemagne.[9] St Gallen thus made a decisive contribution to the preparation of Forster's *magnum opus* containing Alcuin's works, which was published in 1777 and stretched to 1800 pages. Its structure and contents are largely apparent in Migne's edition, which makes its obligation to Forster quite explicit. Compared with some of the sources upon which Migne had to rely elsewhere, Forster's edition was relatively solid ground; and it has served scholars of Alcuin well over the last two hundred years, even if the need for adequate modern critical editions of Alcuin's many writings remains. Migne's work was in some respects a labour of *haute vulgarisation* for the benefit of the wider Catholic Church rather than primarily a narrowly scholarly enterprise;[10] but his volumes of Alcuin's writings have served both purposes well.

In the nineteenth century there was a steady revival of interest in Alcuin within the context of Carolingian history and its bearing upon the self-understanding of France and a newly reunited Germany. Ernst Dümmler played a key role in producing a new edition of Alcuin's poetry in 1881 as part of the *Monumenta Germaniae Historiae*, matching this with his outstanding edition of Alcuin's letters in 1895, and contributing meanwhile to some major studies of material relevant to Alcuin and his period, published by him and others in 1873, 1891 and 1893, notably the *Monumenta Alcuiniana*.[11] In 1887, Arndt published the *Life of Alcuin*, also in the series *Monumenta Germaniae Historiae*.[12] In the supplement to the bibliography of this book, it is possible to trace the development of Alcuinian studies throughout the nineteenth century, beginning with the pioneering and perceptive work of Lorentz.[13] Dümmler's work has to be seen therefore as an element within a wider process of historiography, along with the important work of Sickel in Vienna.[14] Leadership throughout the period before 1914 thus came mainly from German, Austrian and French scholars.

The English were slow to recognise the significance of their great forebear. William Stubbs was one of the first to begin to remedy this myopia in his presentation of the manuscripts contained in his *Memorials of St Dunstan* that was published as part of the Rolls series in 1857; but he did not follow up his intuition, concentrating more on the post-Conquest period of English history. Initial interest in the English-speaking world of scholarship was rather in Alcuin's role in fostering education at Charlemagne's court; although by the end of the nineteenth century his stature as a liturgist was recognised in Anglo-Catholic circles by the founding of the Alcuin Club in 1897, with the explicit intention of restoring Catholic elements of worship faithful to the tradition of the *Book of Common Prayer*.[15] This was at the time when Pope Leo XIII declared Bede to be a Doctor of the Catholic Church in 1899. The historical significance of both Bede and Alcuin was therefore as proxies in the conflict between Anglicans and Roman Catholics over the Catholic spiritual inheritance in England. The first really serious attempt in English at an appreciation of Alcuin's life and work and its abiding significance was accomplished by Andrew West in 1892, who was a professor at Princeton in America.[16] This was followed shortly afterwards by Gaskoin's fine study that was published in 1904.[17] Further interest in Alcuin was evident in Brown's book, published in 1908.[18]

It would seem that the tragedy of the First World War interrupted the continued convergence and collaboration of English and continental scholarship, and that after 1918 each country, Germany, France and England went their separate ways, with intermittent collaboration across national and confessional boundaries, some of which may be noted in relation to specialist studies bearing upon various aspects of Alcuin's legacy. The work of liturgical and palaeographical scholars between the wars on the continent, many of them Catholic monks, must be noted in this regard particularly.

The two studies relating to Alcuin that exerted most influence initially upon English-speaking scholarship in the second half of the twentieth century were Levison's masterpiece, *England and the Continent in the eighth century*, that was written during the Second World War while he was taking refuge in Durham, and published in 1946; and the perceptive study published by Kleinclausz in 1948.[19] Thereafter the field was led by Ganshof in France, whose writings about Charlemagne's kingship and other topics relating to Alcuin were translated into English; and Wallach in America, whose work pioneered new modes of appreciation and evaluation of Alcuin's intellectual contribution. The rapid growth of universities on the continent and in the English-speaking world has facilitated the proliferation of specialist studies that have provided the foundation and substance for this study of Alcuin. In due time, they will engender production of the critical editions of his writings that alone will enable full justice to be done to his achievement and legacy.

Envoi

The range and quality of the specialist scholarship that underpins this book demonstrates nonetheless that it is now possible to gain a rich and balanced picture of Alcuin's beliefs and labours, and to form some accurate assessment of his influence and significance within his own generation, as well as for those who came after him. The myths that Alcuin was the prime mover in the 'palace school' of Charlemagne, or the sole reformer of Catholic liturgy at that time, or the architect of Charlemagne's 'imperial' coronation in 800 have long been destroyed and demonstrated to be far less interesting and true than the detailed picture that may now be discerned of Alcuin's multifarious activities and lasting legacy. The even quality and lucidity of his writings is the other salient feature to emerge from so many of the specialist studies, commanding their high quality and vitality as scholarship over a long period. Singular among these must be Alcuin's letters that offer such a unique, if selective, vantage-point from which to survey the context in which he operated and the manner of his relationships with others. They are a remarkable and precious archive by any standards, and engaging too in their style and aspirations. There is a quality to Alcuin's own writing which gives to the study of his life and work its inherent coherence, unity and relevance.

Even allowing for his exceptional ability and opportunities, and the circumstances that favoured the preservation on the continent of so much of his writing, Alcuin stands as a monument to the depth and vigour of Christianity in England in the generation after the death of Bede. The catastrophic loss of material from the eighth century in Northumbria, largely as a result of the Viking raids, prevents a full evaluation now of the world which Alcuin describes so eloquently in his poem about the church of York. Nonetheless the various aspects of his formation that may still be discerned, intellectual, moral, political and spiritual, all point to a strong church tradition of worship and education that was also actively engaged in missionary work on the continent. Alcuin and his family were closely associated with this enterprise. He was also fortunate to grow up and flourish in relatively stable political and economic circumstances; and his work on the continent under the patronage of Charlemagne continued in this favourable environment, which Alcuin knew all along was a fragile and vulnerable social creation.

By the time that Charlemagne 'head-hunted' him, Alcuin was evidently a person of stature within the Northumbrian church. The documentation that indicates his role in the life of the church and society in York and beyond during the first part of his life remains tantalisingly oblique: but his involvement in the legatine visitation of 786 was clearly a turning-point and probably drew him to the attention of Charlemagne's ecclesiastical advisers. It may also have marked the consolidation of his contacts in Rome as well. The confident tone of his subsequent letters to rulers and bishops in England reflects his standing among them as well as his moral authority. He could not have held his own with Charlemagne as he did had he not been already formed within a lively interchange at the highest level between churchmen, kings and aristocrats in English society. Likewise his formidable intellectual output in the last fifteen years of his life, largely on the continent, must reflect and embody his long experience as an active and effective teacher at York. The new resources that Alcuin encountered on the continent built on a deep foundation of learning already laid in England, as he himself portrays in his York poem. He had to hold his own among a group of very able scholars attracted to the court of Charlemagne, with some of whom he collaborated closely in critical matters.

Alcuin's relationship with Charlemagne, who was at the height of his powers, is the single most remarkable feature of this story. Its candour and resilience reflect well on both men. Alcuin's ability to transcend flattery and to cajole the thinking of the King is singular, as is his moral courage in challenging from time to time aspects of royal policy, for example towards the Saxons and other conquered people. Like Boniface before him, Alcuin was a fearless critic of the worst features of clerical behaviour, prodding bishops on both sides of the Channel and reminding them eloquently of their duties. At a time when the moral stature of the papacy was suddenly thrown into doubt by the accession of Pope Leo III after so distinguished a predecessor as Hadrian I, Alcuin and his close associates had to step into a moral and theological vacuum whose political ramifications rightly concerned Charlemagne too. Yet in this crisis, Alcuin was no mere opportunist, sensing the critical nature of the situation and indicating to the King a role that was more than simply one of political intervention and expediency. Alcuin's articulation of the role of a Christian ruler as the defender of the Faith was a notable one, even if he was not alone in his vision.

Alcuin was a team-player in the sense that when confronting the major moral and theological challenges that arose together at the end of the eighth century he worked closely with others, notably Paulinus of Aquilea, Arno of Salzburg and Benedict of Aniane. The Western Church faced a unique conjunction of defining issues in the 790s: errant Christology in Spain; the overthrow of anointed kings in England; the resurgence of the veneration of images in the Eastern Church; and the intermittent challenges posed by a Byzantine regime, whose stature was no longer respected and whose power in the western Mediterranean was waning fast. In addition to this, the 'enemies' of Christendom prowled around the frontiers of Charlemagne's domains: Vikings to the north, Huns and Avars to the south-east; Islamic rulers in Spain and 'Saracen' pirates in the Mediterranean; always there were the incorrigible Saxons, and further east of them the Slavs to be subdued. Charlemagne was kept constantly on the move as a war-leader for the whole period of his long reign. Yet Alcuin challenged him and debated with him the deeper significance of his rule, reminding him that he was accountable to God for the authority that he wielded.

Alcuin's role as a theologian has not been fully appreciated: yet in so many ways he advanced the work of Bede; and both of them looked back to Gregory the Great as the prism through which they might appropriate and apply the legacy of the Fathers, notably Augustine. Alcuin could certainly be ranked as a 'Doctor of the Church' alongside Bede for his work in defining western Christology and understanding of the Trinity, including the deeper reasons for the use of the *Filioque*. The fact that his *De Fide*[20] was copied and used so steadily throughout the Middle Ages and then printed is a manifest tribute to that legacy. Liturgically he left his mark in this central area of Christian worship and belief by the fact that his writings composed a large part of the office for Trinity Sunday in the western medieval church and its monasteries; and by his insistence, along with Paulinus of Aquilea, that the Nicene Creed be solemnly recited during the mass after the gospel. His contribution to the veneration of saints was also significant, in his poetry and in prayers and letters, most notably in his promotion of the feast of All Saints.

Alcuin's influence in terms of the cultivation of prayer among clergy and laity for at least two hundred years, his completion of the liturgical provision for the celebration of the mass, his hymns and some of his poems, were no less significant. These contributions must rank alongside his more immediate influence upon the conduct of Christian mission and the suitable catechetical preparation of converts for baptism. His outspoken opposition to forcible conversion was striking and fearless, and it was clearly respected by his friends, who preserved his letters on this subject.

Alcuin's capacity as a theologian who was capable of addressing the needs of the laity was no less significant: the popularity of his *De Virtutibus et vitiis*[21] and its widespread copying throughout the Middle Ages reflects his great pastoral skill and powers of communication, and also his important influence upon the Carolingian understanding and practice of penitence. No less importance was the impetus that Alcuin gave to the study and accurate copying of the Bible, gearing the scriptorium at Tours to this end. His own exegetical work complemented and completed that of Bede and Gregory the Great before him.

Alcuin was hailed in his day as a great teacher, and this is apparent in all that he wrote as well as in many of his letters to his friends and disciples. Herein lay his genius, whose out-workings were the numerous educational treatises that he composed at the end of his life while Abbot of Tours in order to distil his long experience, and which remained of value for many years after his death. The fact that so much other writing remains that was for a long time attributed to him, even if it was composed by others who followed his lead, is itself a tribute to his prowess as an enabler of thought and as an example. No less significant was Alcuin's own commitment to the spirit of monastic life and his encouragement of its reformation by his younger friend, Benedict of Aniane. His own experience as Abbot of Tours was not without its difficulties however; but his personal commitment as 'more a monk than any professed monk' was never in doubt, as his biographer makes abundantly clear in his *Life* of Alcuin.

In his wider ministry, Alcuin was pre-eminently a person who applied Christian theology to the realities of life, at the level of public policy, in the ordering of schools, churches and monasteries, as well as in the area of private morality and devotion. Yet there was an inner fastness of spiritual life that under-pinned all that he did and that becomes apparent in some of his letters, in his poems and also in his prayers. He was indeed a poet of prayer and a person of deep mystical sensibility. His love for his friends and pupils matched his love for Christ, which was marked by a deep sense of compunction, vulnerability and penitence. His was a restless heart, seeking and sensing through the affections of his friends the advent of Christ himself. The devotion that they felt towards him, the creative impact of his memory, and his own personal holiness are very apparent; and his death at Tours was marked by signs of sanctity even if no formal cult of Alcuin as a saint was long established there or elsewhere.

Alcuin's role was therefore truly of fundamental importance to Western Europe and its Church: but like all good foundations it can easily be lost sight of and taken for granted. Yet his legacy may be discerned behind the resurgence of monastic life in the tenth century, and the singular political and ecclesiastical developments in England during the time of Dunstan. Those who preserved his letters in particular, in England as well as on the continent, performed the greatest service: for it is in them that Alcuin's voice may still be heard in all its clarity, conviction and love.

Notes

Notes to Chapter 1
York

1. DAB 34.
2. Ibid.138-9.
3. See Alberi, M., *The patristic and Anglo-Latin origins of Alcuin's concept of urbanity* JML (1993) 95-112.
4. ALC 45.42; c.f. Allott, S., (tr.) *Alcuin of York* (York, 1974) 2-3.
5. ALC 11.59 is a poem written at this time in a similar spirit to the brethren of York, inspired by Virgil, and commemorating the return of the cuckoo in spring.
6. *O omnium dilectissimi patres et fratres, memores mei estote: ego vester ero, sive in vita, sive in morte.*
7. ALC 87; see Godman, P., *Alcuin – The bishops, kings & saints of York* (Oxford, 1982) xliii. The dream is discussed in Dutton, P. E., *The politics of dreaming in the Carolingian empire* (University of Nebraska Press, Lincoln & London, 1994) 44.
8. Godman 131, lines 1602-5. This is an early example of Alcuin's penchant for nicknames, which may have originated within the practice of the community at York.
9. Ibid. lines 1652-3.
10. HE IV.xiv: this had occurred to a child in the monastery at Selsey, founded in Sussex by Wilfrid, and it fell upon the anniversary of the death of king Oswald of Northumbria.
11. Chapter xxii in Campbell, A., (tr.) *Aethelwulf's 'De Abbatibus'* (Oxford, 1967) 55f. There is a similar story in the earliest life of St Dunstan in Stubbs, W., *The Memorials of St Dunstan* (Rolls series, London, 1857, Kraus reprint, 1965)15f.
12. ALC 2.
13. DAB 26-31.
14. Ibid. 29.
15. ALC 2 - *'Vita Alcuini'* cap.1.v.
16. See for example Godman's list of references to Virgil in the York poem in 152-3; c.f. also Roccaro, C., *Rinnegamento e divieto della 'lectio' virgiliana nella 'Vita Alcuini'* in *Studi di filogia classica in onore di Giusto Monaco* 4 Palermo (1991) 1519-33.
17. ALC 92.
18. Wilgils was commemorated by Willibrord in his personal calendar on 30th January; he was also commemorated as the father of Willibrord their founder in the Echternach monastery's martyrology: Wilson, H. A., *The Calendar of St Willibrord* HBS (1918) 20.
19. DAB 146-153.
20. See Deug-Su, I., *L'opera agiografica di Alcuino* (Spoleto, 1983).
21. ALC 45.9; discussed in DAB 164 n.104.
22. Ibid.165.
23. Godman op.cit. line 1651: *Euboricae ad portum commercia iure reduxi.*

24. Ibid. lines 35-6.

25. EHD 160 p.788-9; Bede mentions Frisian merchants engaged in slave-trading in London HE IV.xxii(xx): this was one of the sources of wealth of Ethelbert king of Kent, who controlled London and Essex and the context to the mission sent by Gregory the Great in 597.

26. HE V.xi; see Levison, W., *England & the continent in the eighth century* (Oxford, 1946) 51.

27. ALC 11.59 – see note 5 above.

28. HE II.xiv.

29. HE I.xxix – in his letter to Augustine in Canterbury, Gregory clearly expected the two centres of the renewed church in Britain to be in their historic locations of London and York. A bishop from York attended the council of Arles in the time of Constantine the Great.

30. Levison op.cit.18-22, for the significance of the *pallium*.

31. DAB 162-3.

32. Godman op.cit. line 24 – words used by Bede to describe London in HE II.3.

33. Ibid. lines 208-9.

34. Levison op.cit.35 for the significance of church dedications to St Peter.

35. James, E., *Alcuin and York in the eighth century* in P. L. Butzer & D. Lohrmann (eds.) *Science in western and eastern civilisation in Carolingian times* (Basel, 1993) 23-39; DAB 154 n.78 for a survey of some of the more recent archaeological investigations.

36. DAB 159 with notes.

37. Godman op.cit. line 19; & DAB 154 n.77.

38. Wilson, D. M., (ed.) *The Archaeology of Anglo-Saxon England* (Cambridge, 1981) 117.

39. Colgrave, B., (tr.) *The Life of Bishop Wilfrid by Eddius Stephanus* (Cambridge, 1985) chapter xvi p.32-5; see Dales, D. J., *Light to the Isles – mission & theology in Celtic & Anglo-Saxon Britain*, (Cambridge, 1997) chapter vii; & Mayr-Harting, H., *The coming of Christianity to Anglo-Saxon England* (3rd ed. London, 1991) chapter 9. For the cult of St Cuthbert see G. Bonner, D. Rollason, C. Stancliffe, (eds.) *St Cuthbert, his cult and his community to 1200* (Ipswich, 1989).

40. EHD 1 p.174. The continuation of Bede's HE [EHD 5 p.285] notes a severe drought in that year; according to Simeon of Durham, the great fire of York occurred on April 23 – EHD 3 p.265. See Plummer's note in *Two of the Saxon Chronicles* vol ii (Oxford, 1899) 42.

41. EHD 4 p.281.

42. Godman op.cit.xlvii-lx; see also Stapleton, P. J., *'Kontrastimitation' and typology in Alcuin's York poem* Viator 43[1] (2012) 67-78 for an examination of the subtle way in which Alcuin cast the role of St Oswald, for example, in the bigger horizon of Christian and ancient history. See also Clemoes, P., *The cult of St Oswald on the continent* (Jarrow, 1983).

43. Ibid. lines 847-875 – *lectio nunc fieret, sed nunc oratio sacra.1q.*

44. Ibid. lines 1087-8; c.f. St John 7. 37-8.

45. Alcuin's descriptions compare closely with the language describing papal refurbishments in Rome during this period in the *Liber Pontificalis:* Davis, R., (tr.) *The Lives of the eighth century Popes [Liber pontificalis]* (Liverpool, 1992/2007).

46. Godman op.cit. lines 1213-1248.

47. See Coates, S., *The bishop as benefactor & civic patron: Alcuin, York & episcopal authority in Anglo-Saxon England* Speculum (1996) 529-558.

48. Godman op.cit. lines 1277-9 *Tempora tunc huius fuerant felicia gentis, quam rex et praesul concordi iure regebant: hic iura ecclesiae, rex ille negotia regni.*

49. Ibid. lines 1484-1506.

50. See the descriptions of craftsmanship in Campbell, A., (tr.) *Aethelwulf's 'De Abbatibus'* (Oxford, 1967), cap xiv, 34-8.

51. Godman op.cit. lines 1507-1520.

52. DAB 326.

53. DAB 322-4 where the association with the cult of St Stephen, a third century pope [into whose newly created monastery church Pope Paul I (757-67) translated the relics of St Sophia, an unknown martyr] is discussed in some detail. The manuscript is Berlin Phillips 1869 – see DAB 207 n.234.

54. There was a similar dedication to Hagia Sophia in Benevento in Italy in the eighth century – DAB 321 n.221.

55. Morris, R. K., *Alcuin, York and the 'Alma Sophia'* in L. A. S. Butler & R. K. Morris, (eds.) *The Anglo-Saxon Church* CBA 60 (London,1986) 80-89; C. Norton makes the case for its location underneath the present Chapter house of the cathedral, accounting for its unusual alignment in Norton, C., *The Anglo-Saxon cathedral at York and the topography of the Anglian city* Journal of the British Archaeological Association 151 (1998) 1-42; but this presupposes a circular structure: in the absence of any firm archaeological evidence its location remains speculative.

56. For example, see Alberi, M., *The 'Mystery of the Incarnation' and Wisdom's house (Prov.9.1) in Alcuin's 'Disputatio de Vera Philosophia'* JTS NS 48/2 (1997) 505-516. Note the portable altar found in the eleventh century in the tomb of bishop Acca at Hexham dedicated to *Almae Trinitati – Agiae Sophiae – Sanctae Mariae* discussed by Morris op.cit. 83. One of Alcuin's several votive masses was dedicated *De Sapientia*: its concluding prayer closed with the words – *et praepara agiae sophiae dignam in cordibus nostris habitationem.* cf Deshusses, J., *Les Messes d'Alcuin*, AL 14 (1972) 1-41, where this is prayer 10; also in PL CI 451B [=ALC 68].

57. See Rabe, S. A., *Faith, art and politics at Saint-Riquier: the symbolic vision of Angilbert* (Philadelphia, 1995).

58. Hiscox, N., *The Aachen chapel: a model of salvation* in Butzer, P., & D. Lohrmann, (eds.) *Science in Western and Eastern civilization in Carolingian times* (Basel, 1993) 115-126.

59. Wallace-Hadrill, J. M., *Early Germanic kingship in England & on the Continent* (Oxford, 1971) 151.

60. This process is examined in Chaney, W. A., *The cult of kingship in Anglo-Saxon England – the transition from paganism to Christianity* (Manchester, 1970).

61. The context of Northumbrian law is discussed in Wormald, P., *The Making of English Law – king Alfred to the twelfth century*, vol 1 (Oxford, 1999), 106-8.

62. Wallace-Hadrill, J. M., op.cit.53f.

63. Ibid. 56, sometimes referred to as ps-Cyprian; c.f. ALC 45.17 where it is cited by Alcuin.

64. Whitelock, D., *Gildas, Alcuin and Wulfstan* MLR 38 (1943) 125f; c.f. Grosjean, P., *Le 'De Exidio' chez Bede et chez Alcuin* Analecta Bollandia 75 (1957) 222-6; see also ALC 45.17 & ALC 45.129 – both of which were letters sent by Alcuin to the church of Canterbury.

65. HE I.xxii

66. Godman op.cit. lines 70-73.

67. Wallace-Hadrill, J. M., op.cit. 59-60; c.f. Colgrave, B., *Two lives of St Cuthbert* (Cambridge,1940/1985); & Colgrave, B., *Felix's Life of St Guthlac* (Cambridge, 1956/1985).

68. Godman op.cit.xlvii-lx
69. Wallace-Hadrill, J. M., op. cit. chapter iv
70. Ibid. 78-9; c.f. the preface of HE for the role of Abbot Albinus of Canterbury.
71. Colgrave, B., (tr.) *The earliest life of Gregory the Great* (Cambridge, 1985)
72. Godman op.cit. lines 115-126.
73. Ibid. lines 216-221.
74. Ibid. lines 235f; c.f. Orchard, N., *The English and German masses in honour of St Oswald of Northumbria* AL 37 (1995) 347-358; also Stapleton, P. J., art.cit; & Clemoes, P., art.cit.
75. Ibid. lines 507-74.
76. Ibid. lines 570-572.
77. Ibid. line 1282 c.f. introduction xlixf, and especially lix.
78. Godman op.cit. lix n.1; cf ALC 45.16 [EHD 193]. This contains the key statement: *'We are fellow citizens in a two-fold relationship; sons of one city in Christ – the Church, and natives of one country.'*
79. ALC 45.16 [EHD 193] Part of this letter was quoted by William of Malmesbury in the twelfth century in his *De Gesta Regum.*
80. Stenton, F. M., *Anglo-Saxon England* (3rd ed. Oxford, 1971) 88-95.
81. HE iv.26 c.f.Yorke, B., *'Rex doctissimus': Bede and king Aldfrith of Northumbria* (Jarrow, 2009).
82. Godman op.cit. lines 843-846.
83. Lapidge, M., & Herren, M., *Aldhelm – the prose works* (Ipswich, 1979): text with an introduction to Aldhelm's *Epistola ad Acircium* 31-47.
84. Bede *Historia Abbatum* chapters 9 & 15, in Plummer, C., *Baedae Opera Historica* (Oxford, 1896) 373 & 383-4; & D. H. Farmer, *The Age of Bede* (London, 1983) 194 & 201.
85. Bede wrote his *De Temporibus* in 703 just before the death of Aldfrith; c.f. Wallis, F., *Bede – the reckoning of time* (Liverpool, 1999) lxiv-vi.
86. HE v.15 & 21.
87. Stenton op.cit.89. To these might be added king Ceolwulf, to whom Bede dedicated his *History,* though he was not a successful ruler politically; he retired to Lindisfarne in 737.

Notes to Chapter 2
Emissary

1. See Levison, W., *England & the Continent in the eighth century* (Oxford, 1946); & Dales, D. J., *Light to the Isles – mission & theology in Celtic & Anglo-Saxon Britain,* (Cambridge, 1997).
2. See Lapidge, M., *Aedilwulf & the school of York* in *Anglo-Latin literature 600-899* (London, 1996) 384.
3. Paris, BNF lat.528 f.132r-v; ALC 11.4 with an extensive bibliography; note also Simisi, L., *La 'Cartula' di Alcuino, viaggio virtuale attraverso la Frisia e l'Austrasia* in Gottschalk, D., (ed) *Testi cosmografici, geografici ed odeoporici del medioevo germanico* (Louvain, 2005) 239-59.
4. See Godman, P., *Poets & Emperors* (Oxford, 1987) 44-5.
5. Ibid.p.45; but challenged by DAB p.318 who regarded the poem as an overture of Alcuin to those whom he had only recently met.

6. Godman, P., *Alcuin – the bishops, kings & saints of York* (Oxford, 1982), line 846

7. *Ecclesiae specimen, sophiae splendor habetur.*

8. EHD 183 – H&S iii 390-4.

9. H&S iii 398-9.

10. EHD 185 & 188.

11. EHD 187 & 190 – H&S iii 434 & 439-40; also H&S iii 400-1.

12. EHD 186; c.f. Story, J., *Carolingian connections: Anglo-Saxon England and Carolingian Francia, c.750-870* (Ashgate, 2003) 51-3; & Levison, W., *England & the Continent in the eighth century* (Oxford, 1946) 280f – appendix vii: on the correspondence of Boniface & Lullus.

13. HE I. xxxii.

14. EHD 187 – H&S iii 434.

15. EHD 160 p.788; c.f. the history of Simeon of Durham drawing on early Northumbrian annals - EHD 3 s.a. 767, p.268; & H&S iii 433 for the extract from Anskar's *Life of Willehad.*

16. EHD 160.

17. EHD 3 s.a. 773, p.269.

18. EHD 3; c.f. Story, J., op.cit. 95-104.

19. EHD 3 s.a. 792, p.272.

20. It is high up inside the portico of St Peter's, at the left-hand end facing the basilica.

21. The names of Charlemagne and his treasurer Megenfrid, a close friend of Alcuin's, were included in the Durham *Liber Vitae:* c.f. Story, J., op.cit. 103.

22. See Story, J., op.cit. 130f; this was initially the observation of William Stubbs.

23. Frankish annals also reflect interest in and memory of English affairs and history, their collation being associated with Fulda and Salzburg; c.f. Story, J., *The Frankish annals of Lindisfarne & Kent* ASE 34 (2005) 59-110.

24. See Story, J., *Cathwulf, Kingship & the royal abbey of St Denis* Speculum 74 (1999) 3-21.

25. Paris, BNF, MS lat.2777 fols.56v-58r.

26. Cubitt, C., *Anglo-Saxon church councils, c.650-850* (Leicester, 1995) 171, n.62; c.f. Wallach, L., *Alcuin & Charlemagne: studies in Carolingian history & literature* Cornell Studies in Classical Philology 32 (Ithaca, 1959/1968) 5-28.

27. Story, J., art.cit.5.

28. ALC 45.18; c.f. Wallace-Hadrill, J. M., *The Via Regia of the Carolingian age* in B. Smalley (ed.) *Trends in medieval political thought* (Oxford, 1965) 22-41 [also in *Early medieval history* (Oxford, 1975) 181-200, on page 190].

29. Story, J., art. cit. 11; see also Alberi, M., *'Like the army of God's camp': political theology and apocalyptic warfare at Charlemagne's court* Viator 41[2] 2010, 1-20.

30. Story, J., art.cit.5, n.12 – Cathwulf signs off with the admonition *Lege et intellige diligenter.*

31. See Garrison, M., *The English and the Irish and the court of Charlemagne* in Butzer, P., Kerner, M., & Oberschelp,W., (eds.) *Karl der Grosse und sein Nachwirken, 1200 Jahre Kultur und Wissenschaft in Europa / Charlemagne and his heritage: 1200 years of civilization and science in Europe* (Turnhout, 1997) 97-124.

32. According to Notker the Stammerer in his *Life of Charlemagne* cap I.1 in Thorpe, L., *Two Lives of Charlemagne – Einhard & Notker the Stammerer* (London, 1969) 93-4; c.f. Garrison, M., *Letters to a king and biblical exegesis: the examples of Cathwulf and Clemens Peregrinus* EME 7 (1998) 305-328.

33. See Cubitt, C., op.cit. chapter 6; & Story, J., *Carolingian connections: Anglo-Saxon England and Carolingian Francia, c.750-870* (Ashgate, 2003) chapter 3; there is an important discussion in Wormald, P., *The Making of English Law – king Alfred to the twelfth century*, vol 1 (Oxford, 1999) 107.
34. EHD 3 s.a. 786 p.271 – this is Whitelock's translation.
35. EHD 191 – H&S iii 447-62. The decrees of the legates were known in the tenth century to archbishops Oda of Canterbury and Wulfstan of York who used them in their legislation.
36. HE IV 5 & 17/15: the second synod was called to deal with the heresy of Eutyches; Abbot John came from St Peter's in Rome at Theodore's request to teach Roman chant, but also as a papal emissary to report on the orthodoxy of the English church to Pope Agatho: John died at Tours *en route* to Rome - HE IV.18/16.
37. H&S iii 368.
38. EHD 191 p.839 – the term *theodisce* [ancestor of *deutsch*] was used to describe the vernacular.
39. ALC 45.9; c.f. Story, C., op.cit. 63-4; & also Cubitt, C., op.cit. 168, for consideration of the close relationship between the language of the legatine canons and Alcuin's own letters.
40. See Levison, W., *England & the Continent in the eighth century* (Oxford, 1946)127-8.
41. EHD 191.
42. H&S iii 445.
43. H&S iii 362-376.
44. I.e. 9 am or thereabouts: hours were measured by the length of the day throughout the year.
45. I.e. Muslims.
46. Decree 10: H&S iii 452 – this was widely ignored, however, in the subsequent development and administration of Anglo-Saxon law where there was no real distinction made between ecclesiastical and national legislation.
47. Words of Prudentius are cited: *tinxit et innocuam maculis sordentibus humum* from his *Enchiridion* 5.3, where the last word however is *Adam*; the sins of mankind are a blot on the landscape of God's pristine creation.
48. There is an interesting allusion to this in connection with the singing of psalms; H&S iii p.372. The emphasis on the spiritual purpose of psalms to induce compunction is very close to the teaching of Alcuin about the use of the psalms in private prayer and public worship.
49. Decrees 26 & 27: H&S iii 371-4.
50. *sed etiam pro regibus ac ducibus, totiusque populi Christiani incolumitate*: ibid. 375.
51. *ita quoque reges et principes admonuimus, ut obediant ex corde cum magna humilitate suis episcopis, quia illis claves coeli dati sunt . . :* ibid. 452.
52. *igitur si angeli sacerdotes appellantur, a secularibus judicari non possunt*: ibid: Alcuin applied this principle to the plight of Pope Leo III in 798-9.
53. *Ubi lucrum, ibi damnum: lucrum in arca, damnum in conscientia*: ibid. 457.
54. The eighth decree: ibid. 451.
55. Story, J., op.cit.68 and for what follows.
56. See Scheibe, F. C., *Alcuin und die Admonitio Generalis* DA 14 (1958) 221-9; & Scheibe, F. C., *Alcuin und die Briefe Karls des Grossen* DA 15 (1959) 181-193.
57. Story, J., op.cit.83.
58. Alcuin's influence in these decrees is carefully examined by J. Story op.cit.61-4; and in detail by C. Cubitt op.cit. chapter 6. Bullough however takes a more

sceptical view in DAB 346-56, while Wormald was inclined to the view that the decrees of these synods influenced Alcuin, and not the other way round: c.f. op.cit.106-7. This summarises his more detailed consideration of the Mercian dimension of this legislation in Wormald, P., *In search of King Offa's 'law-code'* in I.N.Wood & N. Lund (eds.) *People and places in northern Europe 500-1600. Essays in honour of Peter Sawyer* (Ipswich, 1991) 25-45.

59. See Hartmann, W., *Alkuin und die Gesetzgebung Karls des Grossen* AGG 33-50.
60. ALC 45.18.
61. See also Chelini, J., *Le vocabulaire politique et social dans la correspondence d'Alcuin* Faculté des Lettres (Aix en Provence, 1959).
62. ALC 37 & ALC 45.131.
63. C. Cubitt op.cit.184.
64. They were known in the tenth century and used by Oda of Canterbury; cf. Schoebe, G., *The chapters of archbishop Oda [942-6] and the canons of the legatine council of 786* Bulletin of the institute of historical research, 35 (1962) 75-83.
65. C. Cubitt op.cit.189-90.
66. Wormald, P., *The Making of English Law – king Alfred to the twelfth century*, vol 1 (Blackwells, Oxford) 1999, 107.
67. ALC 11.21: this poem could, however, be dedicated to Theophylact the librarian of Pope Hadrian I; in it Alcuin commends himself to the prayers of his [new?] friend and of the Pope in Rome. If so this may have been *before* the legatine synod, perhaps after his visit to Rome in 780/1: c.f. DAB 356-7, who suggests, however, that this may have been the same person. As Bishop of Todi, Theophylact was the papal emissary to a synod held in Chalcedon in 788 and was also present at the synod of Frankfurt in 794.

Notes to Chapter 3
Letters to England

1. EHD 3 s.a. 793 p.273.
2. ALC 45.16; EHD p.193.
3. ASC s.a.793 – EHD 1 p.181 & Simeon of Durham s.a.793, mentioning lightning, dragons, & whirlwinds; Alcuin mentioned bloody rain falling on the cathedral in York during Lent.
4. ALC 45.30: this letter precedes ALC 45.16 in the London manuscripts of Alcuin's letters, compiled in the later tenth century.
5. ALC 45.18 was also written to King Ethelred and named members of his court who were known to Alcuin, cautioning them against discord or predatory attacks on the Church.
6. See Veyrard-Cosme, C., *Reflexion politique et pratique du pouvoir dans l'oeuvre d'Alcuin* in D. Boutet et al. (eds.) *Penser et pouvoir au Moyen Âge [viii – xv siècle]. Études offertes à Francoise Autrand* (Paris, 1999) 401-25: '*Chez Alcuin, théorie et pratique du pouvoir semblent intrinsequement liés. La correspondence est dictée par un impérieux devoir de parler et d'exhorter.'* p.421.
7. ALC 45.17: this letter drew on an anonymous Irish tract from the seventh century *De duodecim abusivis saeculi* sometimes referred to as pseudo-Cyprian. The poem is translated in Dales, D. J., *A mind intent on God – an Alcuin anthology* (Norwich, 2004) 93-4.

8. Bede quoted Gildas extensively and with evident approval in HE I.22. See Whitelock, D., *Gildas, Alcuin and Wulfstan* MLR 38 (1943) 125f.

9. Godman, P., *Alcuin – the bishops, kings & saints of York* (Oxford, 1982), lines 70-77.

10. See Veyard-Cosme, C., art.cit.406, for a detailed examination of the language used by Alcuin to express his vision.

11. See Chelini, J., *Le vocabulaire politique et social dans la correspondence d'Alcuin* Faculté des lettres (Aix en Provence, 1959): The Old Testament was *'la forte unité de sa langue et de sa pensée politique et sociale.'* p.100. This is reflected also in much Carolingian legislation at this time.

12. See ALC 45.314; discussed in Levison, W., *England & the Continent in the eighth century* (Oxford, 1946) 244-6.

13. ALC 45.17: this poem is appended in some manuscripts to this letter; see H&S iii 474-8, translated in Dales, D. J., op.cit. 93-4 [abbreviated here].

14. ALC 45.19: there is a group of letters directed to this monastery by Alcuin: ALC 45.67, 282, 284 & 286, all of which reveal his long-standing friendship with the community and with those who led it.

15. See the discussion in Veyrard-Cosme, C., *Le paganisme dans l'oeuvre d'Alcuin* in L Mary et al. (eds.) *Impiés et paiens entre Antiquité et Moyen Âge: Textes, images et monuments de l'Antiquité au haut Moyen Âge* (Paris, 2002) 323-51.

16. ALC 45.20; EHD 194; c.f. the poem ALC11.9: Bullough regarded both these works as constituting an *opus geminatum.*

17. Once again Alcuin uses 'British' and 'English' as synonyms with regard to the Church.

18. See Veyrard-Cosme, C., *Reflexion politique et pratique du pouvoir dans l'oeuvre d'Alcuin* in D. Boutet et al. (eds.) *Pensée et pouvoir au Moyen Âge [viii – xv siècle]. Études offertes à Francoise Autrand* (Paris, 1999), 409: *'Pour servir le Christ, l'éveque, "miles Christi," s'engage dans une lutte spirituelle.'*

19. Translated in Godman, P., (tr.) *Poetry of the Carolingian Renaissance* (London, 1985), 127-139.

20. Lines 85-6.

21. Line 217.

22. ALC 45.21 was a letter very similar in tone, also addressed to Higbald.

23. ALC 45.22.

24. Veyrard-Cosme, C., op.cit.412.

25. This is evident from the discussion of these themes in Cristiani, M., *"Ars artium" La psicologia di Gregorio Magno* in M. Mazza & C. Giuffrida (eds.) *Le transformazioni della cultura nella tarda Antichità* (Rome, 1985) vol I 309-331.

26. 'In the perspective of eternity.'

27. ALC 45.42.

28. *Regularis vitae vos ordinet disciplina ...*

29. ALC 45.44.

30. Job 8.9.

31. ALC 45.45: elsewhere Alcuin warned his pupils of the health hazards of journeys to Italy.

32. ALC 45.48.

33. *Et est haeresis pessima, simonaica videlicet ... qui vendit episcopatum, aurum accipiet, sed et regnum Dei perdet.*

34. ALC 45.114; c.f. Simeon of Durham's annal in EHD 3 s.a.796, p.274

35. *Esto forma salutis omnium.*

36. See EHD 3 s.a. 797, p.274: Eanbald received this *pallium* from Rome in time to confirm his position as archbishop on 8ᵗʰ September 797.

37. ALC 45.115: this letter was copied and sent to Paulinus of Aquileia where parts of it were included verbatim in his *Libellus Exhortationis*, composed in either 796 or 797; c.f. ALC 45.123.

38. EHD 3 s.a. 801, p.276.

39. ALC 45.226.

40. ALC 45.232 - EHD 207

41. Alcuin was perhaps alluding here to the recent flight of Archbishop Ethelheard of Canterbury from Kent.

42. ALC 45.233 - EHD 208; ALC 45.295 may be a letter to a former pupil close to this circle.

43. ALC 45.209.

44. ALC 11.23: translated in Godman, P., (tr.) *Poetry of the Carolingian Renaissance* (London, 1985) 124-7.

45. Godman considers that it described Alcuin's departure from Aachen in 796 and his friendship with Angilbert, in Godman, P., *Alcuin's poetic style & the authenticity of 'O mea cella'* Studi Medievali. iii. 20 (1979) 555-583; whereas Newlands makes a strong case for York as the principal, if idealised, location, in Newlands, C., *Alcuin's poem of exile 'O mea cella'* Mediaevalia II (1985) 19-45. See also Orchard, A., *Wish you were here: Alcuin's courtly poetry & the boys back home*, in S. Rees-Jones et al (ed.) *Courts & regions in medieval Europe* (York, 2000) 21-44.

46. Godman, P., art.cit.579 & 582.

47. See Pucci, J., *Alcuin's cell poem: a Virgilian reappraisal* Latomus 48 (1990) 839-49.

48. Newlands, C., art.cit. 24 .

49. ALC 45.121 - EHD 201.

50. In this letter, Alcuin quoted from the Song of Songs 4.12 & 5.1; he also cited Isaiah 55.1.

51. Lines 13-4, possibly referring to Aelberht, Archbishop of York and Alcuin's mentor.

52. Lines 25-6.

Notes to Chapter 4
Alcuin and Offa

1. See Levison, W., *England & the continent in the eighth century* (Oxford, 1946); Story, J., *Carolingian connections: Anglo-Saxon England and Carolingian Francia, c.750-870* (Ashgate, 2003) chapters 5 & 6; also Wallace-Hadrill, J. M., *Early Germanic kingship in England & on the Continent* (Oxford, 1971); and particularly Wallace-Hadrill, J. M., *Charlemagne and England* in *Karl der Grosse I – Personlichkeit und Geschichte* (Dusseldorf) 683-698 [also in *Early medieval history* (Oxford, 1975) 155-180].

2. See references in Story, J., *Carolingian connections: Anglo-Saxon England and Carolingian Francia, c.750-870* (Ashgate, 2003) 180 n.44.

3. Chapters 5-6.

4. ALC 45.62.

5. ALC 45.61.

6. Proverbs 10.1.

7. ALC 45.36,102, 300 and perhaps 103 as well.

8. ALC 45.36; ALC 45.103 is a briefer and more cryptic message in response to the tragedy, reflecting perhaps Alcuin's personal loyalty to the murdered king.

9. Revelation 14.4.

10. ALC 45.300.

11. Yorke, B., *Nunneries and the Anglo-Saxon royal houses* (London & New York, 2003) 52 & 107-8.

12. There are 18 biblical references in this short letter.

13. ALC 45.79.

14. There are 16 biblical references in all.

15. ALC 45.105 to which ALC 45.106 may be a companion, though its recipient is unnamed; it is very different in tone and more generalised. It is unlikely that ALC 45.315 was written to Aetheltrudis, however: cf. Mattei-Cerasoli, D. L., *Una lettera inedita di Alcuno* Benedictina 1:2 (1947-8) 227-230. As another window into the depth of lay piety this letter, even if it is not by Alcuin, is a significant and interesting text.

16. ALC 45.82

17. *Offae regi et genti Anglorum nunquam infidelis fui.*

18. The Latinised form of the Anglo-Saxon name *Unwona.*

19. ALC 45.124; c.f. ALC 45.285 and also ALC 45.301 to the East Anglian bishops of Elmham and Dunwich and ALC 45.70 to abbot Wulfhard who became bishop of Hereford.

20. Alcuin described himself as 'Father Alcuin' in this letter.

21. ALC 45.122 - EHD 202.

22. H&S iii 486-7; discussed in Wallace-Hadrill, J. M., art. cit. 691f., who confirms the likely date as between 793-6.

23. EHD 196; c.f. H&S iii 487-8.

24. ALC 45.87 & 85; see the acute and detailed analysis of their style in Scheibe, F. C., *Alcuin und die Briefe Karls des Grossen* DA 15 (1959) 181-193.

25. ALC 45.64 - EHD 195.

26. See the discussion of these letters to Mercia in DAB 442-5.

27. ALC 45.63.

28. ALC 45.314; see the text and discussion in Levison, W., op. cit. 244-6.

29. ALC 45.101 - EHD 197.

30. Isaiah 1.4.

31. See the picture of political turbulence recorded in the Northumbrian annals associated with Simeon of Durham: EHD 3 s.a. 796-799.

32. Proverbs 20. 28.

33. See ALC 45.100.

34. ALC 45.100 - EHD 197; discussed by Scheibe in art.cit. 183f.

35. Referred to in the Northumbrian annals associated with Simeon of Durham: EHD 3 s.a.795.

36. ALC 45.104.

37. *praedicate veraciter, corrigite viriliter, exhortamini suaviter.*

38. EHD 3.

39. Discussed very fully in Story, J., op.cit. chapter 4: Alcuin seems to have been a principal though not the sole source of information about Frankish and foreign affairs that were included in the Northumbrian annals for the closing decade of the eighth century.

40. Quentavic was near Boulogne by Etaples.

41. EHD 20; the annal reports an archive of letters from Offa to Gervold, now lost.

42. See Story, J., op.cit. 184f.

43. ALC 45.7; EHD 192.

44. ALC 45.9; ALC 45.82 to Beornwine in Mercia may hint at the difficult position in which Alcuin found himself at this stage, suspected perhaps of disloyalty by some in the Mercian court.

45. See ALC 45. 230 & 232.

46. Discussed in Story, J., op.cit 197-9: this rumour may date from the years before the legatine visitation in 786.

47. C.f. EHD 21 – extracts from the *Annals of the Frankish kingdom* s.a. 808 & 809. See Wallace-Hadrill, J. M., art.cit 696-7.

48. In Story, J., op.cit. 164-7, where she considers whether the kings of Northumbria were in some way bound to Charlemagne and his interests by some form of *fidelitas*. Pope Leo III seemed to think so according to his letter supporting Charlemagne's action. The attempt to create this bond of obligation by way of marriage alliance may lie behind the quarrel between Offa and Charlemagne: Offa was not amenable to any form of domination, being of a similar temperament and ambition to his continental rival.

49. Gregory the Great may have regarded Kent as within the Frankish zone of influence; as perhaps the Byzantine court did at that time also.

50. Hence perhaps Offa's purported doubts about Alcuin's loyalty at times: see Wallace-Hadrill, J. M., art.cit. 688-9.

51. ALC 45.108.

52. EHD 3 s.a. 790, p.271.

53. Proverbs 16.12; 20.28; 25.5.

54. ALC 45.109 - EHD 200.

55. EHD 3 s.a. 796, p.274.

56. EHD 3 passim.

57. EHD 3 s.a. 799, p.275.

58. ALC 45.122 - EHD 202.

59. ALC 45.129.

60. ALC 45.128: citing John 10. 11 & 13; c.f. also ALC 45.130 – possibly written to Ethelheard.

61. A view confirmed by the letter [EHD 204] of king Cenwulf to Pope Leo III, who told the Pope that Offa had indeed acted out of enmity towards Archbishop Jaenberht and the people of Kent. Cenwulf wanted the archbishopric moved to London according to Gregory's original plan, but in his reply Pope Leo III refused to overturn the traditional primacy of Canterbury [EHD 205]. See EHD 209, the letter in which Pope Leo confirmed this position in 802 and EHD 210, the decree of the synod of Clovesho in 803 abolishing the archbishopric of Lichfield.

62. ALC 45.255; c.f. ALC 45.256, which may also have been written to Ethelheard by Alcuin, and, if so, in a more personal vein.

63. ALC 45.230: In this letter he cautioned the archbishop to ensure that his retinue did not appear sumptuously dressed in the presence of Charlemagne on their journey back to England from Rome.

64. See EHD 210.

65. ALC 45.231 - EHD 206.

66. As reported in the northern annals EHD 3 s.a. 799, p.275.

67. ALC 45. 290 & 291; see also ALC 45.288, 292,[293],311.

Notes to Chapter 5
Charlemagne

1. There is a perceptive overview of their relationship in Schieffer, R., *Alkuin und Karl de Grosse* AGG 15-32. The best introduction to Einhard is in Leonardi, C., *I racconti di Eginardo* in *Medioevo Latino – La cultura dell'Europa Cristiana* (Florence, 2004) 249-274.
2. Thorpe, L., *Two Lives of Charlemagne – Einhard & Notker the Stammerer* (London, 1969).
3. Einhard's *Life* cap 25.
4. Cap. 25: *Virum undecumque doctissimum:* the role of the deacon as teacher is striking here.
5. St Gallen *Life* cap 1.
6. Ibid. cap 2.
7. Grimald died in 872 so he would have been a very young pupil of Alcuin's.
8. St Gallen *Life* cap 9.
9. The rise of the Carolingians and the reign of Charlemagne are best approached through the following studies, written or translated into in English: Levison, W., *England & the Continent in the eighth century* (Oxford, 1946); Barbero, A., *Charlemagne – father of a continent* (tr.) A. Cameron (University of California Press, 2004); Becher, M., *Charlemagne* (Yale, 2003); McKitterick, R., *Charlemagne – the formation of a European identity* (Cambridge, 2008); Story, J., (ed.) *Charlemagne – empire & society* (Manchester, 2005).
10. The steady investment in education and literacy and the early nurturing of native clergy were two other critical factors in the growth of the early Anglo-Saxon church and its missionary activities to the continent.
11. The wonderful Tassilo chalice at Kremsmunster in Austria remains as a spectacular monument to his patronage involving Anglo-Saxon craftsmanship.
12. Einhard's Life cap 16.
13. It survives to this day, but heavily restored, at the side of the western façade of St John Lateran.
14. The classic discussion is in Pirenne, H., *Mohammed & Charlemagne* (New York, 1954).

Notes to Chapter 6
Alcuin and Charlemagne

1. The best overview of the significance of this exchange is provided by Springsfeld, K., *Alkuins Einfluss auf die Komputistik zur Zeit Karls des Grossen* (Stuttgart, 2002); also Springsfeld, K., *Karl der Grosse, Alkuin und die Zeitrechnung* in Berichte zur Wissenschaftsgeschichte 27 (Wiesbaden, 2004) 53-66. See also Hein, W., *Die Mathematik im Mitterlalter: von Abakus bis Zahlenspiel* (Darmstadt, 2010).
2. ALC 45.149.
3. ALC 45.155.
4. ALC 45.197 & 198. Note Bullough's reservations, however, about ALC 45.197 in DAB 35.n.77. It is certainly unusual as it is cast in the form a prayer to Christ and contains a soliloquy of consolation by him to those recently bereaved.
5. ALC 45.50, 90, 96, 102, perhaps 149-50 & certainly 190.

6. ALC 45.197.
7. Matthew 11.28.
8. ALC 45.198; c.f. ALC 45.185.
9. John 11. 25-6.
10. *'David amate.'*
11. ALC 45. 41. Bullough challenged Dummler's dating of this letter because of the way Alcuin addressed the king as *rector et doctor.* DAB 380 n. 152; but surely not as late as 799 – c.f. DAB 433 n. 3, because of its content.
12. See Veyrard-Cosme, C., *Réflexion politique et pratique du pouvoir dans l'oeuvre d'Alcuin* in D. Boutet et al. (eds.) *Pensée et pouvoir au Moyen Âge [viii – xv siècle]. Études offertes à Francoise Autrand* (Paris, 1999) 401-25; also Deug-Su I., *Cultura e ideologia nella prima età Carolingia* (Rome, 1983) 111; Steinen, W. von den, *Karl und die Dichter* in Bischoff, B., (ed.) *Karl der Grosse – Lebenswerk und Hachleben: vol II – Das Geistige Leben* (Dusseldorf, 1966) 63-94, notably 78-9; also Wallace-Hadrill, J. M., *The Via Regia of the Carolingian age* in. B. Smalley (ed.) *Trends in medieval political thought* (Oxford, 1965) 22-41; also in *Early Medieval History* (Oxford, 1975) 181-200: see 196f.
13. ALC 45.121; part of this is translated in EHD 201.
14. ALC 45.231.
15. See Chelini, J., *Alcuin, Charlemagne & St Martin de Tours* Revue d'Histoire de l'Église de France 47 (1961) 19-50.
16. ALC 45.238 & 240.
17. ALC 45. 238 – the closing poem.
18. Thorpe, L., *Two Lives of Charlemagne – Einhard & Notker the Stammerer* (London, 1969) Einhard's 'Life' cap 24-5, p.78-9.
19. See Gandino, G., *Il 'palatium' e l'immagine della casa del padre: l'evoluzione di un modello nel mondo franco* Studi Medievali 50 (2009) 75-104.
20. Ibid. St Gallen *'Life'* cap 8.
21. ALC 28. In a letter ALC 45. 258 to Arno of Salzburg, written in 802, Alcuin made reference to this his most recent treatise. It was one of his most popular and copied writings throughout the Middle Ages. No less revealing are the dedicatory letters that he wrote to the king prefacing his treatise against Felix of Urguel ALC 6; and also his *Dialogus de Rhetorica et Virtutibus* ALC 39. This was cast in the form of a dialogue between Charlemagne and Alcuin, as was also the *De Dialectica* ALC 26. That Alcuin was able to use this conceit with any credibility as a mode of dialogue must reflect his widely known and respected intellectual relationship with the King, as well as the King's receptivity and intellectual acuity.
22. ALC 45. 163: the words were *aeternum, sempiternum, perpetuum, immortale, saeculum, aevum & tempus.*
23. ALC 45. 136; see Lauwers, M., *Le glaive et la parole. Charlemagne, Alcuin et le modèle du 'rex praedicator': notes d'écclesiologie carolingienne* AY 221-244.
24. ALC 45.308.
25. *'To Charles the king, by the gift of Christ the king of kings, august emperor, best, highest and forever'.*
26. ALC 45.307; see Chazelle, C. M., *To whom did Christ pay the price? The soteriology of Alcuin's epistola 307* PMR 14 (1989) 53-62.
27. The phrase is Phelan's: see Phelan, O. M., *Catechising the wild: the continuity & innovation of missionary catechesis under the Carolingians* JEH 61 (2010) 455-474, passim.

28. See Godman, P., *Poets & Emperors* (Oxford, 1987).

29. ALC 11.6; see Chazelle, C. M., *The Crucified God in the Carolingian Era* (Cambridge, 2001) 15-7 with a photograph of the unique manuscript: Bern, Burgerbibl.212 f.123; Godman, P., (tr.) *Poetry of the Carolingian Renaissance* (London, 1985) 138-143, which has the text and translation and also a diagram of the original; see also Meyer, H.-B., *'Crux, decus es mundi' - Alkuins Kreuz- und Osterfrommigkeit*, in B. Fischer & J. Wagner (eds.) *Paschatis sollemnia: Studien zu Osterfeier und Osterfrommigkeit*, (Basel, 1959) 96-107.

30. Godman. P., op.cit.19-20. Alcuin's pupil, Joseph the Scot, and also Theodulf also composed acrostic poems; as did Dunstan and Abbo of Fleury in the tenth century: see Lapidge, M., *St Dunstan's Latin poetry* Anglia xcviii (1980) 101-6 & Gwara, S., *Three acrostic poems of Abbo of Fleury* JML (1992) 203-25.

31. ALC 11.7; see Godman, P., *Poets & Emperors* (Oxford, 1987), 56-59, with a diagram of the text on page 57; there is a photograph in Chazelle, C. M., op.cit.22.

32. ALC 11.13; c.f. ALC 11.37a & 11.37b where the common friendship with Angilbert is a significant element in two other poems by Alcuin intended for Charlemagne.

33. ALC 11.26; see Godman, P., (tr.) *Poetry of the Carolingian Renaissance* (London, 1985) 10-1 & translation 118-20.

34. Exodus 31.2-11; 35.30-35 & 38.22-3; c.f. Holder, A. G., (tr.) *Bede – on the Tabernacle* (Liverpool, 1994): Einhard was himself and active builder and patron of churches.

35. ALC 11.27; c.f. ALC 11.38 – a poem for the king and his daughter; see also ALC 11.40 - a lament for his absence over winter from court, written perhaps in 798/9.

36. ALC 11.42; see Scott, P. D., *Alcuin as poet: rhetoric & belief in his Latin verse* University of Toronto Quarterly 33 (1964) 233-257.

37. ALC 11.45; see discussion of this important poem in Godman, P., *Poets & Emperors* (Oxford, 1987) 74-6: Alcuin's appropriation of Virgil was significant: there are significant parallels to its use in this poem in a letter written by Alcuin at around the same time in 799 to Charlemagne - ALC 45.178; c.f. ALC 45.177 also which closes in a poetic paean praising the king.

38. ALC 45.178; this is Godman's comment in op.cit. p.76; see Holtz, L., *Alcuin et la reception de Virgile au temps de Charlemagne* in (ed.) H Scheffers *Einhard: Studien zu Leben und Werk* (Darmstadt, 1997) 67-80.

39. ALC 11 [125.4] This poem mimics the style of Alcuin so closely that some have considered it to be by him and directed on behalf of the king to Paul the Deacon or Peter of Pisa.

40. Ibid. cap 18.

41. Scharer, A., *Charlemagne's daughters* in Baxter, S., Karkov, C., Nelson, J. L., & Pelteret, D., (eds.) *Early medieval studies in memory of Patrick Wormald* (Ashgate, 2009) chapter 18, p.269-282.

42. See Rabe, S. A., *Faith, art and politics at Saint-Riquier: the symbolic vision of Angilbert* (Philadelphia, 1995).

43. Garrison, M., *The social world of Alcuin: nicknames at York and at the Carolingian court* in GL p.59-80.

44. See ALC 11.13 – a poem for Charlemagne in response to a visit from Angilbert.

45. ALC 11.14.

46. ALC 11.27; see note 35 above.

47. ALC 11.37a & 37b: there is debate over the structure and integrity of this poem, which taken together addressed Angilbert first and then through him his uncle the king.
48. ALC 11.38.
49. ALC 11.12; c.f. ALC 11.39, which was written to another daughter of Charlemagne, either Bertha, or perhaps Gisela herself.
50. ALC 11.41 – *Tu mihi dulcis amor semper soror inclyta salve.*
51. ALC 45.29.
52. ALC 45.119.
53. ALC 45.188 – a copy was sent to Paulinus of Aquilea who included some lines from it in his *Libellus exhortationis,* composed according to Bullough in 797 or 798.
54. ALC 45.217 – see Hammer, C. I., *Christmas Day 800: Charles the younger, Alcuin and the Frankish royal succession* EHR 127 (2012) 1-23, for a full consideration of Alcuin's role as mentor to Charles and his place within the royal family and in planning for the succession to Charlemagne.
55. See Angenendt, A., *Karl der Grosse als 'rex et sacerdos'* in FK 255-278.
56. See the discussion in Scheck, H., *Reform and resistance: the formation of female subjectivity in early medieval ecclesiastical culture* (New York, 2008).
57. ALC 45.72.
58. ALC 11.67: Alcuin had written to her earlier in 793 a long letter of spiritual direction: ALC 45.15. In it he laid great emphasis on the role of reading in nurturing prayer, because through books 'our Lord God speaks to you.'
59. ALC 45.154.
60. Fredegisus was to encourage the royal princesses, Gisela and Rotrudis in their studies in a letter written by Alcuin to him at Christmas 801: ALC 45.262.
61. Alcuin wrote again to Gisela and Rotrudis in April 801 with news [via Candidus Wizo] of Charlemagne in Rome, ALC 45.216, sending to them a work by Bede for copying – probably his *In epistulas canonicas expositio.*
62. ALC 45.228.
63. It is interesting to contrast the tone of this letter with two others written by Alcuin to women which are much more formal: ALC 45.279 [which Bischoff thought was actually directed to Gisela and Rotrudis] in which Alcuin commended reading the *Dialogues* of Gregory the Great; and one whose Alcuinian origin is less certain: ALC 45 [315], edited in Mattei-Cerasoli, D. L., *Una lettera inedita di Alcuno* Benedictina 1:2 (1947-8) 227-230.
64. ALC 51; Alcuin's treatise *De animae ratione* : ALC 17, was composed at the very end of his life for Gundrada, sister of Adalhard of Corbie and a cousin to Charlemagne, at her request.

Notes to Chapter 7
Statesman

1. King, P. D., (ed.) *Charlemagne – translated sources* (Lancaster 1987) 230: capitulary 56; c.f. H&S iii 481-2.
2. Wallach, L., *Charlemagne and Alcuin - Diplomatic studies in Carolingian epistolography* Traditio 9 (1953) 127-154; on pages 141-2 Wallach challenged the assertion that Alcuin in some way represented the church in Britain; he represented the king, who had recalled him from England.

3. See the symposium edited by Berndt, R., (ed.) *Das Frankfurter Konzil von 794: Kristallisationspunkt karolingischer Kultur* (2 volumes – Mainz, 1997); its context and significance is well discussed in Hartmann, W., *Die Synoden der Karolingerzeit im Frankenreich und in Italien* (Paderborn, Munich & Vienna, 1989); see also Meyer, H.-B., *Alkuin zwischen Antike und Mittelalter* Zeitschrift fur Katholische Theologie 81 (1959) 405-60 where reservations about Alcuin's limited role are made on p.455f.

4. ALC 4 with an extensive bibliography; the seminal discussion and analysis was by Scheibe, F. C., *Alcuin und die Admonitio Generalis* DA 14 (1958) 221-9; see also DAB 379-84; the text is translated in P. D. King, op.cit.209-20.

5. II Kings 22-3.

6. The *Collectio Dionyso-Hadriana*.

7. An exception may be cap 82 which contains a very interesting credal summary similar to the *Quicunque Vult*. It was one of a corpus of credal material promoted throughout the Carolingian church for teaching purposes – see Kelly, J. N. D., *The Athanasian Creed* (London, 1964) 41-4.

8. ALC 45 [316]; see Wallach, L., *Charlemagne's 'De Litteris Colendis' and Alcuin* Speculum 26 (1951) 288-305 & Martin, T., *Bemerkungen zur Epistola de litteris colendis* Archiv fur Diplomatik 31 (Cologne/Vienna, 1985) 227-272. The sole surviving manuscript is now in the Bodleian Library in Oxford: Laud. misc.126; but it is barely entirely legible. It is fortunate that it was spotted and collated by Lehmann with the Metz manuscript before is destruction during the Second World War. Bullough thought that the last clause of the letter concerning monks involving themselves in secular courts was a draft element intended for the *Admonitio Generalis*: DAB p.379 n 151; see his discussion of *De Litteris Colendis* on pages 384-6; but see Wallach, L., art.cit. 298. The translated text is in P. D. King op.cit. 232-3. See also Glatthaar, M., *Zur datierung der Epistola Generalis Karls des Grossen* DA 66[2] (2010) 455-78.

9. Notably in cap. 72 & 73 of the *Admonitio Generalis*.

10. Wallach dated it between 794 and 796: art.cit. 302; but Martin confirms the likely earlier date: art.cit. 249-50. His text of both manuscripts in parallel is to be preferred.

11. DAB 365-6; cf the mention of Angilram by Alcuin in ALC 45.90.

12. Note the explicit citation of the *Rule of St Benedict* in the capitularies of the synod of Frankfurt, cap 13: King. P. D., op.cit. 226.

13. Wallach, L., art.cit. 294.

14. King, P. D., op.cit. 232; this favored axiom of Alcuin's was supported by reference to Matthew 12.37.

15. For an example of the problem of incorrect Latin in the eighth century see Levison, W., *England & the Continent in the eighth century* (Oxford, 1946), appendix X: 'Venus a man', 302f.

16. King, P. D., op.cit. 217.

17. Mark 12. 29-30.

18. The *Admonitio Generalis* was accompanied by a double edict of commission issued from Aachen on 23 March 789 which sheds further light on the detailed conditions being addressed. The text is translated in King, P. D., op.cit. 220-2.

19. EHD 3 s.a. 792, p.272.

20. The treatises are ALC 5, 6 & 64. See Cavadini, J. C., *The last Christology of the West – Adoptionism in Spain & Gaul, 785-820* (Philadelphia, 1993); also the extensive discussion by Bullough in DAB 419-431.

21. Cap 82. Paulinus of Aquilea drafted a very full hybrid version of the Nicene Creed which was endorsed by the Frankish bishops and circulated: DAB 425f; c.f. Cavadini, J. C., *Elipandus and his critics at the council of Frankfort* FK 787-808.

22. This was not what Nicea II had decreed, however.

23. DAB 420 n 280: Codex Carolinus 95 & also 421 note 283.

24. ALC 45 [313] & [317]; see Wallach, L., *Charlemagne and Alcuin - Diplomatic studies in Carolingian epistolography* Traditio 9 (1953) 127-154; [re-edited in Wallach, L., *Alcuin & Charlemagne: studies in Carolingian history & literature* Cornell Studies in Classical Philology 32 (Ithaca, 1959/1968) 147-58.] These letters were paralleled by the *Libellus Sacrosyllabus* of the Italian bishops, led by Paulinus of Aquilea.

25. ALC 45. [313].

26. Wallach, L., art.cit. 132 & also 145-6; c.f. Levison, W., *England & the Continent in the eighth century* (Oxford, 1946) 237.

27. British support could be assumed by Charlemagne after Alcuin's return in 794 with confirmation that the English church had repudiated the decrees of Nicaea II as they had been received, and transmitted by Alcuin on the king's behalf for their consideration.

28. Wallach, L. art.cit.136.

29. ALC 45.[317]; discussed in Wallach, L., art.cit.136f.

30. ALC 45.137 & 208.

31. Wallach drew attention also to parallels in editing and theological approach between these two letters and some of the later parts of the *Libri Carolini* that he believed may have been adjusted by Alcuin around the same time; art cit.143f. Particularly striking are the common references to a synodal theory that would give to Frankfurt a 'universal' significance because of its fidelity to orthodoxy as defined by the ecumenical councils: ibid.148.

32. It makes no mention however of the presence of British bishops.

33. John 8.36.

34. Scheibe, F-C., *Alcuin und die Briefe Karls des Grossen* DA 15 (1959) 181-193.

35. ALC 45.85 - EHD 196.

36. ALC 45.100 - EHD 197.

37. Scheibe, F-C., art.cit. 188.

38. ALC 45.101 – EHD 198; see Scheibe, F-C., art.cit. 190.

39. ALC 45. 93.

40. ALC 45.92; see DAB 455f.

41. See Wallach, L., *Alcuin's epitaph for Hadrian I* American Journal of Philology 72 (1951) 128-144; see discussion in Deug-Su I., *Cultura e ideologia nella prima eta Carolingia* (Rome, 1983) 86f: note the comment on 110, however: *La tendenza di Alcuino ad assolutizzare nella cristianita la 'potestas' carolingia non e sostanzialmente diversa da quella osservata nelle lettere papali.*

42. The long-term implications of this aggression for subsequent medieval European history are well outlined in Christiansen, E., *The Northern Crusades* (London, 1997); the word 'Slav' means 'slave'.

43. See McCormick, M., *The liturgy of war in the early middle ages: crisis, litanies & the Carolingian monarchy* Viator 15 (1984) 1-23.

44. McCormick, M., *Eternal victory: triumphal rulership in late antiquity, Byzantium and the early medieval West* (Cambridge, 1986) 349. See also Alberi, M., *'Like the army of God's camp': political theology and apocalyptic warfare at Charlemagne's court* Viator 41[2] 2010, 1-20.

45. Edward Gibbon observed long ago that 'so intimate is the connection between the throne and the altar that the banners of the Church have seldom been seen on the side of the people.'

46. Mayr-Harting, H., *Charlemagne, the Saxons & the imperial coronation of 800* EHR 111 (1996) 1113-1133.

47. McKitterick, R., *Charlemagne – the formation of a European identity* (Cambridge, 2008) 253-5.

48. Hen, Y., *Charlemagne's Jihad* Viator 37 (2006) 33-51.

49. King, P.D., op.cit. 205-8.

50. ALC 45.6.

51. Hen, Y., art.cit.40.

52. King, P. D., op.cit. 230-2; c.f. Reuter, T., *Charlemagne and the world beyond the Rhine*, in Story, J., (ed.) *Charlemagne – empire & society* (Manchester, 2005) 183-94.

53. Hen, Y., art.cit. 42f. c.f. Mayr-Harting, H., art.cit.1128-9 & also Mayr-Harting, H., *Alcuin, Charlemagne and the problem of sanctions* in Baxter, S., Karkov, C., Nelson, J. L., & Pelteret, D., (eds.) *Early medieval studies in memory of Patrick Wormald* (Ashgate, 2009) chapter 14 p.207-218.

54. Markus, R.A., *Gregory the Great & his world* (Cambridge, 1997); c.f. HE I.30. This approach contrasted sharply with St Augustine's defence of coercion against the Donatists and others: see *'St Augustine's attitude to religious coercion'* in Brown, P. A., *Religion & society in the age of Augustine* (London, 1972) 260-78.

55. ALC 92.

56. Arno of Salzburg was himself actively engaged in missionary work among the Avars.

57. See Dumont, B., *Alcuin et les missions* AY 417-430; also Falkowski, W., *'Barbaricum' comme devoir et défi du souverain chrétien* AY 407-416; also Dales, D. J., *Light to the Isles – missionary theology in Celtic & Anglo-Saxon Britain* (Cambridge, 1997) chapter 9.

58. The paradox of social pressure and conformity however was evident at the very beginning of the mission to Kent, when king Ethelred 'compelled no-one to accept Christianity, though nonetheless he showed greater affection for believers since they were his fellow citizens in the kingdom of heaven. But he had learned from his teachers and guides in the way of salvation that the service of Christ was voluntary and ought not to be compulsory. It was not long, however, before he granted these teachers a place to settle in, suitable to their rank, in Canterbury, his chief city, and gave them possessions of various kinds for their needs.' HE I.26.

59. ALC 45.110: see the most recent overview in Phelan, O. M., *Catechising the wild: the continuity & innovation of missionary catechesis under the Carolingians* JEH 61 (2010) 455-474.

60. C.f. letters ALC 45.111,112,113.

61. It provided the basis for a later treatise on catechism by someone in the *familia* of Arno of Salzburg early in the ninth century.

62. Alcuin built his case on clear biblical foundations: I Cor 3.1-2; I Cor 14.40; Matthew 9.17; Matthew 28.19-20; Romans 10.10.

63. ALC 45.111.

64. There are 16 biblical references as foundations for his argument.

65. In a letter ALC 45.211, written to the king in 800/801, Alcuin lamented Megenfrid's death.

66. ALC 112 & 113; he also sent him a copy of his letter to Charlemagne - ALC 45.110.

67. The biblical references in this letter are: Matthew 4.19; John 21.10-11; Matthew 28.19; Hebrews 11.6; Matthew 19.26; John 6.44; John 14.6; John 3.5; III John 1.8; I Cor.3.2; Matthew 9.17; John 8.

68. See Bouhot, J-P., *Alcuin et le 'De catechizandis rudibus' de St Augustine* Recherches Augustiniennes 15 (1980) 176-240.

69. An unspoken implication here might be that Charlemagne's aggression towards Spain may have contributed to the fomenting of heresy within the Spanish Church and especially in the border areas.

70. *Cooperatur homo Spiritui sancto in salute hominis. . . . Sacerdos corpus aqua abluit, Spiritus sanctus animan fide justificat.* Cf ALC 45.107 which is another letter to Arno about preaching to the Avars.

71. *O felix et beata vita, ubi semper quod amatur videtur et quod videtur nunquam fastidit! Ubi Deus omnibus aeternus amor, aeterna laus, gloria et beatitudo.*

72 ALC 45.118; c.f. ALC 45.119 – which is a letter in a similar vein to Pippin, King of Italy.

73 See Christiansen, E., op.cit.; also Fletcher, R., *The Conversion of Europe* (London, 1997), chapters 7 & 8; see Bullough, D. A., *Was there a Carolingian anti-war movement?* EME 12 (2003) 365-76.

Notes to Chapter 8
Rome

1. See Louth, A., *Greek East and Latin West – the Church AD 681-1071* (New York, 2007) chapter 3; also Smith, J. H. M., *Europe after Rome* (Oxford, 2005) chapter 8.

2. The best overview is provided by Herbers, K., *Der Beitrag der Papste zur geistigen Grundlegung Europas im Zeitalter Alkuins* AGG 51-72.

3. See Carragain, E. O., *The City of Rome & the world of Bede* (Jarrow, 1994); & also Levison, W., *England & the Continent in the eighth century* (Oxford, 1946) chapter 2.

4. See Llewellyn, P., *Dark Age Rome* (London, 1971), especially chapter 6.

5. HE IV.17-18 [15-16] where the teaching work of John, the precentor of St Peter's in Rome is recorded, who was sent by Pope Agatho at the request of Benedict Biscop. He came as the Pope's commissary to report on the Monothelite controversy and to report back upon the orthodoxy of the English church. He died and was buried at Tours where his tomb lay in Alcuin's time.

6. Wallis, F., *Bede – the reckoning of time* (Liverpool, 1999) 229f; much of Bede's information was drawn from a contemporary version of the *Liber Pontificalis*.

7. Godman, P., *Alcuin – the bishops, kings & saints of York* (Oxford, 1982) lines 1454-9; c.f. DAB 242-7.

8. ALC 46[1]2; c.f. discussion of this epitaph in Lapidge, M., *Knowledge of the poems [of Venantius Fortunatus] in the earlier [Anglo-Saxon] period* – appendix to R. W. Hunt, *Manuscript evidence for knowledge of the poems of Venantius Fortunatus in late Anglo-Saxon England* ASE 8 (1979) 287-295; also Lapidge, M,. *Aedilwulf & the school of York* in *Anglo-Latin literature 600-899* (London, 1996) 381-98.

9. See the discussion about the precise chronology of this visit to Rome in DAB 333-5.

10. ALC 45.271 & 172.

11. ALC 17: it was written at her request to Gundrada, a sister of Adalhard Abbot of Corbie and a cousin of Charlemagne's and was one of the most copied of Alcuin's works.

12. ALC 45[314] – in Levison, W., op.cit.246.

13. ALC 45.143.

14. For example ALC 45.173 to Arno of Salzburg; c.f. also ALC 45.281 where Alcuin cautions one of his pupils, perhaps Candidus Wizo, about the fact that *Italia infirma est patria, et escas generat noxias.* Its wine induced fever! See Jullien, M-H., *Alcuin et l'Italie* AY 393-406.

15. ALC 11.9: see translation in Godman, P., (tr.) *Poetry of the Carolingian Renaissance* (London, 1985) line 36-7, p.129.

16. ALC 11.44: in this poem Alcuin asked him to obtain some Roman relics from Pope Leo III.

17. ALC 11.21; Theophylact of Todi was present also at the synod of Frankfurt in 794.

18. ALC 11.25.

19. ALC 11.45; c.f. ALC 45.28 in which Alcuin made mention of his quest for relics to Paulinus of Aquilea.

20. ALC 11.15.

21. ALC 11.43.

22. ALC 45.27; the significance of this letter is discussed in a very speculative way in DAB 116f.

23. DAB 454; if that is indeed what Alcuin actually wanted or expected, which is unclear.

24. ALC 45.93 & 94.

25. John 21.15f.

26. Matthew 8.8.

27. Thorpe, L., *Two Lives of Charlemagne – Einhard & Notker the Stammerer* (London, 1969) cap 19, p.75.

28. ALC 45.93, 100 & 104.

29. ALC 46[8]: its execution was mentioned in the York annals EHD 3 s.a.794 p.273: a very likely sign that Alcuin's authority lay behind the Frankish history contained within them for this period, as its description is very precise: 'a tablet recording his good deeds in letters of gold and written in verse.'.

30. See Story, J., et al., *Charlemagne's black marble: the origins of the epitaph of Pope Hadrian I* Papers of the British School at Rome vol.73 (2005) 157-90: minute geological examination has confirmed the precise location of the quarry.

31. See Wallach, L., *Alcuin's epitaph of Hadrian I* American Journal of Philology 72 (1951) 128-144; also Scholz, S., *Karl der Grosse und das Epitaphium Hadriani: ein Beitrag zum Gebetsgedenken der Karolinger* in Berndt, R., (ed.) *Das Frankfurter Konzil von 794: Kristallisationspunkt karolingischer Kultur* (Mainz, 1997) 373-394; also discussed in DAB 459-61.

32. ALC 45.100: EHD 197.

33. Wallach, L., art.cit.128.

34. Ibid. p.129 & 140-1.

35. For example, the letter that Alcuin wrote to Charlemagne on the death of his queen in 800: ALC 45.197.

36. ALC 46 [2] 123.

37. Wallach, L., art.cit.140.

38. Ibid. p.141.

39. *Tu mihi dulcis amor, te modo plango, pater. Tu memor esto mei, sequitur te mens mea semper*

. . .

40. The best overview is provided in Krautheimer, R, *Rome: profile of a city* (Princeton, 1980), chapter five, where he indicates the ways in which the Carolingian vision of *Romanitas* differed quite significantly from the conscious revival of late Christian Roman antiquity pursued by Hadrian and his successors. For Pascal I see Goodson, C. J., *The Rome of Pope Paschal I: papal power, urban renovation, church rebuilding and relic translation: 817-824* (Cambridge, 2012).

41. See Hartmann, F., *Hadrian I (772-795)* Papste und Papsttum 34 (Stuttgart, 2006).

42. Hadrian I was brought up by his powerful uncle, Theodotus, who was portrayed as a living donor in the church of St Maria Antiqua beneath the Palatine hill on the edge of the Forum in Rome.

43. Bullough, D. A., *Empire and emperordom* EME 12 (2003) 377-387.

44. See Kelly, J. N. D., *The Oxford Dictionary of Popes* (Oxford, 1986) 95f.

45. Davis, R., (tr.) *The Lives of the eighth century Popes* (Liverpool, 1992/2007) 106f where the significance of the *Life* of Hadrian is discussed in detail.

46. See Noble, T. F. X., *The Republic of St Peter: the birth of the papal state, 680-825* (Philadelphia, 1984); also Llewellyn, P., *Dark Age Rome* (London, 1971).

47. Krautheimer, R., *Studies in early Christian, medieval & renaissance architecture* (New York, 1969) 237, & 254 n. 205: the modern version of the Lateran *triclinium* mosaic is a copy of the original mosaic made between 1736 & 1744; in it Charlemagne is described as *rex*.

48. Krautheimer, R, *Rome: profile of a city* (Princeton, 1980), chapter 5; according to the *Liber Pontificalis*, Paschal was a divisive and unpopular figure. See Goodson, C. J., op.cit.

49. Krautheimer, R., *Studies in early Christian, medieval & renaissance architecture* (New York, 1969) 224: The monastery and church of Quattro Coronati in Rome is an interesting example of Carolingian architectural influences at work in the middle of the ninth century, for example in the entrance tower to the complex on the Celian hill above the road going up to the Lateran from the Coliseum above San Clemente.

50. Ibid 235-6.

51. PL 98: it contains a total of 98 letters, of which those from Pope Hadrian number 49.

52. PL 98. col.392a – the phrase in Latin is *spiritalis compater*.

53. Thorpe, L., *Two Lives of Charlemagne – Einhard & Notker the Stammerer* (London, 1969) 80-1.

54. Schieffer, R., *Charlemagne and Rome* in Smith, J. H. M., (ed.) *Early medieval Rome & the Christian West: essays in honour of Donald A. Bullough* The Medieval Mediterranean 28 (Leiden, 2000) 279-295.

55. Hartmann, F., op.cit.267-272; the date and occasion are confirmed by a later note inserted by a Wurzburg monk, authenticating the codex as that given by Pope Hadrian to the king as ruler of the Franks and Lombards and patrician of Rome when he was in the city of Rome.

56. Hen, Y., *The royal patronage of liturgy in Frankish Gaul – to the death of Charles the Bald (877)* HBS (London, 2001) 74f.

57. Ibid. p.85-6.

Notes to Chapter 9
Crisis and Coronation

1. Davis, R., (tr.) *The Lives of the eighth century Popes* (Liverpool, 1992/2007) 168.
2. Ibid. p.184; the occasion was marked by a famous poem *Karolus magnus et Leo Papa* attributed to Einhard: there is a translated extract in Godman, P., (tr.) *Poetry of the Carolingian Renaissance* (London, 1985) 197f.
3. *Life of Charlemagne*, cap.28.
4. See Wallach, L., *The genuine and the forged oath of Leo III* Traditio 11 (1955) 39f; & *The Roman synod of December 800 and the alleged trial of Leo III* HTR 49 (1956) 123-144.
5. Grierson, P., *The Carolingian empire in the eyes of Byzantium* in *Nascita dell'Europa ed Europa Carolingia: un'equazione da verificare* SSCI 27 (1981) vol. 2 p.885-916 on p.886.
6. Mayr-Harting, H., *Charlemagne, the Saxons & the imperial coronation of 800* EHR 111 (1996) 1113-1133.
7. See Ganshof, F. L., *The Carolingians & the Frankish monarchy* (London, 1971), chapter four *The imperial coronation of Charlemagne: theories and facts*.
8. Scheibe, F. C., *Alcuin und die Briefe Karls des Grossen* DA 15 (1959) 181-193.
9. ALC 45.92.
10. ALC 45.93.
11. ALC 45.94.
12. C.f. ALC 45.100 - EHD 197 – Odbert was probably the exiled pretender to the Kentish throne who had led the rebellion against Mercian rule.
13. ALC 45.125; the matter of the *pallium* may also be an oblique reference to the vexed issue about the archbishopric of Lichfield, which Leo would resolve in favour of Canterbury before Alcuin died: c.f. ALC 45.255. (n.b. ALC 45.127 is a stray letter from Leo III to the new king of Mercia and his bishops written at the same time as ALC 45.125.)
14. ALC 45.149.
15. ALC 45.173.
16. ALC 45.157.
17. ALC 45.156.
18. ALC 45.159.
19. ALC 45.174.
20. ALC 45.177.
21. ALC 45.178.
22. These words directly echoe those of the *Magnificat*.
23. Proverbs 21.9.
24. ALC 45.179; in Migne this is a composite letter: probably only the first two parts were contiguous. Similar concern is expressed in a letter to Adalhard of Corbie from this year – ALC 45.181.
25. In support of this principle Alcuin cited the purported canons of St Sylvester.
26. ALC 45.180 is an anonymous letter, perhaps by Arno, which sheds interesting light on the expectations of the papacy at this time felt by one of Charlemagne's clerical advisers.
27. ALC 45.184.
28. ALC 45.186.

29. ALC 45.212.
30. ALC 45.216 & 218.
31. ALC 45.234.
32. ALC 45.255.
33. See Ganshof op.cit.45f.
34. Ibid 48.

Notes to Chapter 10
Abbot of Tours

1. See Hartmann, M., *Alcuin et la gestation matérielle de Saint-Martin de Tours* AY 91-102; the most comprehensive account of Alcuin's abbacy at Tours remains Chelini, J., *Alcuin, Charlemagne & St Martin de Tours* Revue d'Histoire de l'Église de France 47 (1961) 19-50.
2. Cap 8.xiv. Alcuin also expressed a wish to participate in a more regular monastic life in a letter to the monastery at Murbach written towards the end of his life; ALC 45.271; he had visited the place many years before with his master Aelbert and there remains an earlier letter to them: ALC 45.117.
3. DAB 341-2.
4. Ibid. cap 6.xii; they are mentioned also two of Alcuin's letters of 798: ALC 45.150 & 153. The English connection with Ferrières remained strong throughout the first half of the ninth century: letters remain from its abbot, Lupus, to the church at York as well as to Aethelwulf the King of Wessex: EHD 215-8.
5. Alcuin mentioned St Josse-sur-Mer in ALC 45.25. It was later recovered from the Vikings by Lupus of Ferrières: EHD 215. It was clearly a vital staging-post for those travelling to and from England. The economic importance of Quentavic is revealed in the account of Gervold of St Wandrille administering the tolls and taxes there and intervening in a trade dispute between Charlemagne and Offa of Mercia, to which Alcuin also refers: EHD 20 & 192 [ALC 45.7].
6. Hartmann, M., art.cit.92.n.9.
7. Notker's *Life of Charlemagne* I.2.
8. ALC 45.200 & ALC 5.
9. The plausibility of the scale of this output by Alcuin has been challenged recently, though not convincingly, in Gorman, M. M., *Alcuin before Migne* RB 112 (2002) 101-130.
10. ALC 45.52.
11. ALC 45.131: see DAB 66 & 386.
12. Lebecq, S., *Alcuin sur la route* AY 15-26, on p.19-20, with a useful map of Alcuin's itinerary in 798 on p.24.
13. ALC 45.156.
14. ALC 45.177.
15. Galinie, H., et al., *Tours et la Touraine au temps d'Alcuin* AY 37-54: there is a useful map on p.38. The situation in Tours was very similar to that in the city of Rome at this time with an extensive area of *dishabitato* within the confines of the old Roman city walls and the waterfront of the Loire.
16. Sato, S., *Rémarques sur les exploitations rurales en Touraine au haut Moyen Âge* AY 27-36.
17. His letter to Arno in August 796 was evidently written from Aachen: ALC 45.112.

18. *Life of Alcuin* cap.11.xxi.
19. See Garrison, M., *The English and the Irish and the court of Charlemagne* in Butzer, P., Kerner, M., & Oberschelp,W., (eds.) *Karl der Grosse und sein Nachwirken, 1200 Jahre Kultur und Wissenschaft in Europa / Charlemagne and his heritage: 1200 years of civilization and science in Europe* (Turnhout, 1997) 97-124.
20. 'La messe occupait donc dans la spiritualité alcuinienne une place de choix, unique a son époque; en cela Alcuin est profondement novateur et en avance sur son temps.' In Chelini, J., *Alcuin, Charlemagne & St Martin de Tours Revue d'Histoire de l'Eglise de France* 47 (1961) 19-50, p.38.
21. *Life of Alcuin* cap.8.xiv: *Vita denique eius non monasticae inferior fuit.*
22. ALC 45.172.
23. Mabillon in his *Elogium Alcuini* records Alcuin's foundation of a *xenodochium* at a place called 'Twelve Bridges' that crossed the Loire: PLCI 1432.
24. ALC 46. [10]. 113.
25. ALC 61.93, 96.1 & 2.
26. ALC 61. 97 & 98.1-3.
27. ALC 61.94: translated in Dales, D. J., *A mind intent on God – an Alcuin anthology* (Canterbury Press, Norwich, 2004), 40-1.
28. ALC 61.108.1.
29. ALC 61.108.3: translated in Dales, D. J., ibid. 90-1.
30. ALC 89 & 81: see Deug-Su, I., *L'opera agiografica di Alcuino* (Spoleto, 1983), 167-93.
31. See Stancliffe, C. E., *St Martin and his hagiographer* (Oxford, 1983); also Dales, D. J., *Light to the Isles – missionary theology in Celtic & Anglo-Saxon Britain* (Cambridge, 1997), chapter 1.
32. ALC 61.88.9a; 89.4; 90.3; 90.11; 90.21; 99.11; 109.22; 110.17 – all are four line inscriptions.
33. See Hartmann, M., art.cit.96; also Chelini, J., art.cit. 44-5.
34. *Life of Alcuin* cap 10.xviii; this may account for a document attributed later to Alcuin which discussed the mode of succession appropriate under Frankish law: ALC 45.132. See Kasten, C., *Alkuins erbrechtliche Expertise fur Karl den Grossen* AY 301-318. Its provenance remains unclear. See also Hammer, C. I., *Christmas Day 800: Charles the younger, Alcuin and the Frankish royal succession* EHR 127 (2012) 1-23.
35. ALC 45.197.
36. The documents are edited in MGH Dipl. Karol. I (Hannover, 1906), 173, 192 & 259.
37. Chelini, J., art.cit.46.
38. Chupin, A., *Alcuin et Cormery* AY 103-112.
39. The two most recent studies of this episode are by Meens, R., *Politics, mirrors of princes and the Bible: sins, kings and the well-being of the realm* Early Medieval Europe 7 (1998) 345-57; & Noizet, H., *Alcuin contre Theodulphe: un conflit producteur de norms* AY 113-132. What follows rests on their analysis. The letters are ALC 45. 245-9: one of which [247] was from Charlemagne to Alcuin.
40. There is a full and detailed discussion of this affair in Wallach, L., *Alcuin & Charlemagne: studies in Carolingian history & literature* Cornell Studies in Classical Philology 32 (Ithaca, 1959/1968), 99-140.
41. ALC 45. 245 & 246; Bullough thought that the recipient of the second letter could be Arno of Salzburg.
42. ALC 45.247.
43. ALC 45. 249 & 248: for Meens' discussion of the identity of this younger monk

see art.cit. 291-2.

44. Meens, R., art.cit. 286-7.

45. Numbers 35. 11-5, Deuteronomy 4. 41-3 & 19. 1-13.

46. This argument by comparison was widely used by Alcuin when reasoning with the king and some of the bishops as mode of moral and intellectual persuasion.

47. ALC 45.247 survives in a single manuscript associated with the time of Fredegisus, Alcuin's successor as abbot of Tours.

48. Meens, R., ibid. 288.

49. ALC 45.249.

50. Meens, R., art.cit 292-3; & Noizet, H., art.cit., which examines the legal consequences of this affair in some detail.

51. I.e. 'calf'.

52. *O key of David and sceptre of the house of Israel, who opens and none may shut, and locks so that none may open: come and lead out the captive from the prison-house and the one sitting in darkness and in the shadow of death.*

53. His entry to heaven was described as being escorted to Christ by the two great deacons, St Stephen the first deacon and martyr of the Church, and St Laurence, a martyr of Rome.

54. ALC 46.[2].123. *Alcuine nomen erat sophiam mihi semper amanti.* This was later used as a model for an epitaph in Verona for an archdeacon there. [Note the existence of an epitaph for another Alcuin buried at Hersfeld, probably in 1034: ALC 1.]

Notes to Chapter 11
Alcuin and Monasticism

1. See Garrison, M., *Les corréspondants d'Alcuin* AY 319-332 for an overview of the scope and tenor of his correspondence.

2. To York, Canterbury, Whithorn, Monkwearmouth-Jarrow, Lindisfarne, and Mayo in Ireland; Chelles, Tours, Corbie, St Vaast, Montolieu, Lerins; Murbach, Echternach, Fulda, Salzburg; Septimania, Montamiata, and Farfa in Italy.

3. ALC 45. 1, 6, 7, 45, 54, 62, 63, 68, 70, 109, 223, 275, 278, 297, 299, 300

4. ALC 60.[1].89.26[c] for St Vaast & ALC 60.[3] for St Riquier.

5. Arno was abbot of St Amand from 782 before becoming also Bishop and later Archbishop of Salzburg.

6. ALC 61.88.1-13

7. ALC 61.89-90.13

8. ALC 61.89.9: Alcuin sent it also to Salzburg: ALC 61.109.13.

9. ALC 61.109 – the 24 Salzburg inscriptions.

10. ALC 61.109.20

11. ALC 46.[4].99.17; [5].92.2; [6].88.1;[11].88.15; & [14].89.2

12. See Hartmann, M., *Alcuin et la gestation matérielle de Saint-Martin de Tours* AY, 93f; also Kasten, B., *Adalhard of Corbie; die Biographie eines karolingisches Politikers und Klostervorstehers* Studia Humaniora (Dusseldorf, 1986).

13. ALC 45.19

14. ALC 11.51.6: translated in Dales, D.J., op.cit 25; the prayer appended there, that invokes St Benedict, comes from *De Psalmu Usu Liber* PLCI 473D [ALC 33] and may not necessarily be by Alcuin himself but is of his spirit: *Enable me, your fragile but beloved one, to follow and imitate the footsteps of my father St Benedict.*

15. *Life of Alcuin* cap 9.xvii

16. Cabaniss, A., [tr.] *Benedict of Aniane, the Emperor's Monk*, (Kalamazoo, 1979/2008) cap 24.5, p. 86-7.

17. ALC 45.184

18. ALC 45.56

19. ALC 45.57

20. Benedict's contribution to the theological polemic of this controversy has already been discussed: see Cavadini, J. C., *The last Christology of the West – Adoptionism in Spain & Gaul, 785-820* (Philadelphia, 1993), appendix II, 128-30.

21. ALC 5; Alcuin referred to their mission in a letter, written in the summer of 799, to Arno: ALC 45.207.

22. ALC 64

23. ALC 6

23. ALC 45.205

24. ALC 45.206

25. ALC 45.303

26. A good overview of Benedict's significance is in Knowles, D., *The Monastic Order in England* (Cambridge, 1966), 25-8; see also the introductions in Cabaniss, A., op.cit.

27. See the most recent study by Cholij, R., *Theodore the Stoudite: the ordering of holiness* (Oxford, 2002).

28. It is interesting to compare the relationship between Alcuin and Benedict with that of Dunstan and Ethelwold in tenth century England: Alcuin and Dunstan both presided over ancient royal foundations and had multiple roles with regard to both church and state, Dunstan becoming Archbishop of Canterbury. Benedict and Ethelwold spear-headed the actual renewal and reform of monasticism along Benedictine lines, creating model monasteries first as foundations of influence, then networks of new monasteries, culminating in the promulgation of a national framework for monastic life. The *Regularis Concordia*, drawn up at Winchester in 973 was closely modelled on that of Benedict at Aachen almost 150 years earlier. Both developments were underpinned, however, by the strength of friendship and common vision shared by the initiators and executors of each reform movement, even though in the case of Alcuin others were involved as well, as Benedict was already underway when Alcuin arrived at the court of Charlemagne. The connection in the tenth century between Oswald and Fleury, which claimed the body of St Benedict, needs to be seen within the continuing tradition of Benedictine reform and renewal that sprang from the Carolingian initiatives.

29. *Life of Alcuin* cap 3.viii. This phrase caused great consternation to subsequent Benedictine historians: could Alcuin really be claimed as a true Benedictine monk? But for the period of his life this was an anachronistic question, although the by death of Benedict of Aniane it was not. See Mabillon's detailed discussion in PLCI 1419-20 and also DAB 166. It is arguable that Alcuin should be regarded as the 'godfather' of Benedictinism as promoted by Benedict of Aniane.

30. His role foreshadowed the great Cluniac reforms and its resulting monastic network.

31. This in turn influenced the formation of the *Concordia regularum*, founded on the work of Benedict of Aniane and completed towards the end of the ninth century.

32. Ardo's *Life of Benedict* cap 17, p.77-9. There is an interesting comparison to be made with the visionary description of a monastic church in Campbell, A., (tr.) *Aethelwulf's 'De Abbatibus'* (Oxford, 1967), cap 22, p.56, which was probably written in Northumbria at the same time as these developments at Aniane and which reflects some cognizance of Alcuin's poetry.

33. ALC 90: the most significant and interesting recent study of Angilbert at St Riquier is Rabe, S. A., *Faith, art and politics at Saint-Riquier: the symbolic vision of Angilbert* (Philadelphia, 1995), which underpins the discussion here.

34. ALC 45. 11, 97, 162, 221; & ALC 11.16, 37[a & b?] & 60

35. Alcuin wrote to him there as such: ALC 45.11.

36. Rabe, S. A., op.cit.81; there were many other three-fold aspects in the structure and ordering of St Riquier. See the interesting discussion & diagram of the elaborate liturgical processions conducted within this complex in Carruthers, M., *The craft of thought: meditation, rhetoric and the making of images, 400-1200* (Cambridge, 1998), 266-9.

37. I. e. 'Mother of God' translating into Latin the Greek title *Theotokos* – 'God-bearer'.

38. Rabe, S. A., ibid. 126-8

39. Ibid.131. See also Rabe's important conclusion with reference to the significance of Benedict's comparable liturgical reordering at Aniane: this too was intended as a bulwark against heresy as well as an assertion of Charlemagne's patronage and power. 138f.

40. Ibid. 144

41. Benedict changed his church dedication from Christ to the Trinity; but elsewhere Frankish dedications to Christ were common: Fulda, Paderborn, & Theodulf's church at St Germigny-des-Pres, as well as the royal chapel at Aachen and the cathedral at Rheims.

42. Ibid.147. It is interesting to note that several of the reformed monasteries with which Alcuin had close connections also had three churches: Aniane, St Bertin, St Vaast; & Corbie.

43. See Diem, A., *The emergence of the monastic schools: the role of Alcuin* in GL3 27-44 on p.30-1.

44. The best introduction to this remains Leclercq, J., *The Love of Learning and the Desire for God: a study of monastic culture* (London, 1978).

45. Jong, M. de., *From scolastici to scioli: Alcuin and the formation of an intellectual elite* in GL3 45-58, on p.55.

46. ALC 4

47. King, P. D., (ed.) *Charlemagne – translated sources* (Lancaster, 1987), 232-3

48. *Admonitio Generalis* cap 72

49. Diem, A., art.cit.38

50. ALC 40. See Alberi, M., *'The better paths of Wisdom': Alcuin's monastic 'true philosophy' and the worldly court* Speculum 76 (2001/4) 896-910; & Alberi, M., *The 'Mystery of the Incarnation' and Wisdom's house (Prov.9.1) in Alcuin's 'Disputatio de Vera Philosophia'* JTS NS 48/2 (1997) 505-516, whose analysis in both important articles is followed here.

51. ALC 9

52. See Courcelle, P., *Les sources antiques du prologue d'Alcuin* Philologus 110 (1966) 293-305; & Courcelle, P., *La 'Consolation de Philosophie dans la tradition littéraire, antécedents et posterité de Boece* (Paris, 1967).

53. See Alberi, M., *'The better paths of Wisdom': Alcuin's monastic 'true philosophy' and the worldly court* Speculum 76 (2001/4) p.900 n.19.

54. The principle of *ne quid nimis.*

55. See Alberi, M., *The 'Mystery of the Incarnation' and Wisdom's house (Prov.9.1) in Alcuin's 'Disputatio de Vera Philosophia'* JTS NS 48/2 (1997) 505-516

56. Ibid. 511

57. Ibid. 515

58. ALC 28

59. ALC 45. 34; 74; 88; 168; 209; 280

60. Alberi, M., *'The better paths of Wisdom': Alcuin's monastic 'true philosophy' and the worldly court* Speculum 76 (2001/4), 898

61. Matthew 13.52

62. ALC 11.62: its provenance was examined in the edition by Boas, M., *Alcuin & Cato* (Leiden, 1937); Alcuin's authorship was challenged in Lapidge, M., *The Adonic verses attributed to Columbanus* Studi Medievali (1977/2) 249-314, who attributed it to Columbanus, Abbot of St Trond, who died in 815 and who was a poet in touch with the court poets surrounding Alcuin; a view not shared however by Herren M., *A ninth century poem for St Gall's feast day and the 'Ad Sethum' of Columbanus* Studi Medievali (1983) 508-9.

63. Perhaps also the view of Notker the Stammerer.

64. One of them, for example, found its way into the *capitula* of the synod of Frankfurt in 794.

65. The most comprehensive treatment of the cultivation of memory in early monasticism is Carruthers, M., *The craft of thought: meditation, rhetoric and the making of images, 400-1200* (Cambridge, 1998).

66. See Alberi, M., *'The better paths of Wisdom': Alcuin's monastic 'true philosophy' and the worldly court* Speculum 76 (2001/4) 888-910

Notes to Chapter 12
Letters, Friends, and Manuscripts

1. Bullough's analysis of the way in which Alcuin's letters were probably collected is in part one of Bullough, D. A., *Alcuin – achievement & reputation* (Brill-Leiden & Boston, 2004): it is masterly and followed here [DAB]. See also Bullough, D. A., *Reminiscence and reality: text, transmission and testimony of an Alcuin letter* JML 5 (1995) 174-201; Cristiani. M., *Le vocabulaire de l'enseignement dans la correspondence d'Alcuin* in Weijers, O., (ed.) *Vocabulaire des écoles et des méthods d'enseignement au moyen âge* (Turnhout, 1992) 13-32; Ganz, D., *An Anglo-Saxon fragment of Alcuin's letters in the Newberry library, Chicago,* ASE 22 (1993) 167-177; Garrison, M., *Alcuin's world through his letters and verse* (Cambridge, PhD thesis, 1995); Mann, G., *The development of Wulfstan's Alcuin manuscript* in M. Townend (ed.) *Wulfstan of York – the proceedings of the second Alcuin conference* (York, 2004) 235-267; Rivas Pereto, R. A., *Alcuino de York y su epistolario* Patristica et Medievalia 22 (2001) 58-75; Thomson, R. M., *William of Malmesbury & the letters of Alcuin,* in ibid. *William of Malmesbury* (Ipswich, 1987); Veyrard-Cosme, C., *Les motifs épistolaires dans la correspondence d'Alcuin* AY 193-208; Veyrard-Cosme, C., *Saint Jerome dans les lettres d'Alcuin* Revue des Études Augustiniennes 49 (2003) 323-351; Viarre, S., *Enjeux épistolaires et présence de la correspondence d'Alcuin* Epistulae Antiquae IV (Louvain, 2006) 285-98.

2. DAB 38-9.

3. Ibid.43.

4. Ibid.44.n.99: for Vienna Nationalbibliothek lat. 795 & Ser. Nov. 3755: see the facsimile of this manuscript in Unterkirchen, F., (ed.) *Alkuin Briefe und andere tractate im Auftrage des Salzburger Erzbischofs Arn um 799 zu einem Sammelband vereinigt [Codex Vindobonensis 795 –Osterreichischen National Bibliothek Faksimileausgab]* (Graz, 1969); and also the discussion in Bischoff, B., *Die südostdeutschen Schreibschulen und Bibliotheken in der Karolingerzeit*, 2 vols (Wiesbaden, 1960-80), vol 2 115-120. There is a detailed discussion of its contents in DAB 44-51.

5. DAB 52: the manuscript is in the Vienna Nationalbibliothek cod. Lat. 808

6. Ibid.55.

7. MS Troyes, BM 1165 pt.i: discussed in detail in DAB 57f; referred to by Dümmler in his edition as T.

8. MS Vatican, BAV Reg. lat. 272: referred to by Dümmler in his edition as T. This was apparently annotated for public reading and reference.

9. DAB 60-1.

10. St Gallen, Stiftsbibliothek cod. 271 (Dümmler's K2); mentioned in the contemporary catalogue of that library.

11. BL Royal 8.E xv (Dümmler's K1).

12. London, BL Cotton Tiberius A.xv; the lost exemplar may be the manuscripts recorded in the first catalogue of the monastery at Lorsch, now MS Vatican Palatinus lat. 1877: see DAB 63.

13. DAB 65.

14. ALC 45.131.

15. MS Rheims, Bibl. Municipale 385; an earlier witness to this tradition is found in MS Munich clm 14468: see DAB 67. A notable example of an isolated Adoptionist letter is the one written by Alcuin to Beatus of Liebana, which is printed from a single manuscript - Madrid, Arch. Hist. Nat c. 1279 (1007B) of the tenth century, in Levison, W., *England & the Continent in the eighth century* (Oxford, 1946), Appendix xi: 314-23: ALC 45.[312].

16. MS Vatican, BAV, Reg. lat 226: see DAB 68 n.164.

17. MS Munich clm. 13581: see discussion in DAB 71f.

18. MS London, BL Harley 208 & Paris, BNF n.a.lat.1096: see DAB 75f.

19. The use made by Paulinus of Aquilea of one of Alcuin's letters in his *Libellus exhortationis*, written in 797-8, is adduced as possible evidence of this in DAB 78-9. Its contents reached England early in the eleventh century, now MS London, BL Harley 208, where it came to rest at York; it may be compared with London BL Royal 6. B. viii containing five Alcuin letters and probably copied early in the eleventh century at Christ Church, Canterbury: see Ganz. D., art.cit.169.

20. Wallach, L., *Charlemagne and Alcuin - Diplomatic studies in Carolingian epistolography* Traditio 9 (1953) 151-4, with examples: p.153 - 'The evidence points clearly to the fact that Alcuin, or his notaries, retained copies of his own letters.'

21. MS London, Lambeth 218 pt. iii; discussed in DAB 68-70.

22. For the general context, see Dales, D. J., *Dunstan – saint & statesman* (Cambridge, 1988).

23. See Ganz, D., art.cit.

24. Bullough, D. A., *The educational tradition in England from Alfred to Aelfric: teaching 'utriusque linguae'* (SSCI 19, 1972).

25. Ibid.174-5: MS London, BL Cotton Vespasian D vi, & Cambridge, Corpus Christi College 206 & 221 respectively. See also Morrish, J., *Dated and datable manuscripts copied in England during the ninth century: a preliminary list* Medieval Studies 50 (1988) 512-38.

26. Wallace-Hadrill, J. M., *Early Germanic kingship in England & on the Continent* (Oxford, 1971), 141f.

27. DAB 81f: significant parts of it are printed in Stubbs, W., *The Memorials of St Dunstan* Rolls Series 63 (London, 1857) [Kraus reprint 1965]; it is most fully described in Brett, C., *A Breton pilgrim in England in the reign of king Athelstan* in G. Jondorf & D. N. Dumville (eds.) *France & the British Isles in the Middle Ages & Renaissance* (Ipswich, 1991) 43-70.

28. Stubbs, W., op.cit.400-3.

29. Ibid.370-1: see DAB 84-5. Abbo of Fleury dedicated some acrostic poems to Dunstan, [printed in Stubbs, W., op.cit. on p.410-1] who himself was an acrostic poet: see Lapidge, M., *St Dunstan's Latin poetry* Anglia xcviii (1980) 101-6; & Gwara, S., *Three acrostic poems by Abbo of Fleury* JML (1992) 203-225, where these poems are translated.

30. DAB 88 & 93: some of the continental correspondence may have come from Tours or even Salzburg at that time.

31. Stubbs, W., op.cit.406-8; see DAB 94 for consideration of whether Alcuin's reformed pupil, Cuculus Dodo should be credited with this collection, which was complete by around 800. There is a very good summary of the likely early development of the letter collections: ibid.101-2.

32. DAB 94 n.232.

33. DAB 97f: see also Whitelock, D., *Gildas, Alcuin and Wulfstan* MLR 38 (1943) 125f; & Whitelock, D., *Archbishop Wulfstan, homilist and statesman* TRHS fourth series xxxi (1949) 75-94;also Bethurum, D., *The homilies of Wulfstan* (Oxford) 1957; & Mann, G., *The development of Wulfstan's Alcuin manuscript* in M. Townend (ed.) *Wulfstan of York – the proceedings of the second Alcuin conference* (York, 2004) 235-267.

34. See the detailed discussion in Levison, W., *England & the Continent in the eighth century* (Oxford, 1946), appendix iii, 241-8; it includes the text of Alcuin's letter to Offa: ALC 45.[314].

35. See Whitelock, D., *Gildas, Alcuin and Wulfstan* MLR 38 (1943) 125f.

36. Mann, G., art.cit.245-6: his analysis is very full and acute and gives a full picture of this fascinating text.

37. Ibid.265.

38. See Thomson, R. M., *William of Malmesbury & the letters of Alcuin,* in Thomson, R. M., *William of Malmesbury* (Ipswich, 1987) 154-67.

39. From Leland's annotations, this may in fact have been the Tiberius manuscript: ibid.167.

40. See Preest, D., (tr.) *William of Malmesbury's 'Gesta Pontificum'* (Ipswich, 2002); & Scott, J., (ed.) *The early history of Glastonbury [De antiquitate Glastonie Ecclesiae]* (Ipswich, 1981).

41. The manuscripts that still remain from the period of the tenth century reformation in England are hardly a complete record of what was then available in the life of the Church and its monasteries.

42. ALC 45.74; see Wallach, L., *Charlemagne and Alcuin - Diplomatic studies in Carolingian epistolography* Traditio 9 (1953) 149-151; also Napier, A. S., (ed.) *The Old English version of the enlarged rule of Chrodegang along with the Latin original* (EETS, 1916; Kraus reprint, New York, 1971) 90-4.

43. See Garmonsway, G. N., (ed.) *Aelfric's Colloquy* (London, 1939/1967): like Alcuin, Aelfric gave his pupils their head; the text is bi-lingual in Latin and Anglo-Saxon.

44. ALC 37: see Szarmach, P., *The Latin tradition of Alcuin's 'Liber de virtutibus et vitiis', cap xxvii-xxv, with special reference to Vercelli homily* XX Mediaevalia 12 (1986) 13-41; & Szarmach, P. E., *Cotton Tiberius A. iii, Arts. 26 & 27* in Korhammer, M., (ed.) *Words, texts & manuscripts: studies in Anglo-Saxon culture presented to Helmut Gneuss* (Cambridge, 1992) 29-42.

45. Marenbon, J., *From the circle of Alcuin to the school of Auxerre: logic, theology and philosophy in the early Middle Ages* (Cambridge, 1981); & Marenbon, J., *Alcuin, the council of Frankfort and the beginnings of medieval philosophy* FK 603-616; see also Ineichen-Eder, C. E., *The authenticity of the 'Dicta Candidi', 'Dicta Albini', and some related texts,* in *Insular Latin Studies: papers on Latin texts and manuscripts of the British Isles, 550-1066,* ed. M. W. Herren, (Toronto, 1981) 179-193; & Lebech, M., et al. (eds.) *'De dignitate conditionis humanae': translation, commentary & reception history of the 'Dicta Albini' & the 'Dicta Candidi'* Viator 40[2] (2009) 1-34.

46. Jones, C. A., *The sermons attributed to Candidus Wizo* in O'Keefe, K. O'Brien & A. Orchard (eds.) *Latin learning and English lore: studies in Anglo-Saxon literature for Michael Lapidge* (Toronto, 2005) 260-279; [see ALC 45.165].

47. ALC 11.44.

48. ALC 50.

49. Candidus seems to have died shortly after Alcuin, unless he is to be identified as the bishop of Trier from 805-9. There has been some confusion with another Candidus Braun, a monk of Fulda.

50. See Howlett, D., *Fredegisus 'De substantia nihili et tenebrarum* Bulletin du Cange 64 (2006) 123-143. There remain nine letters from Alcuin to Fredegisus or referring to him.

51. See Kelly, J. F., *The originality of Josephus Scottus' 'Commentary on Isaiah'* Manuscripta 24 (1980) 176-80; also Garrison, M., *The English and the Irish and the court of Charlemagne* in Butzer, P., Kerner, M., & Oberschelp,W., (eds.) *Karl der Grosse und sein Nachwirken, 1200 Jahre Kultur und Wissenschaft in Europa / Charlemagne and his heritage: 1200 years of civilization and science in Europe* (Turnhout, 1997) 97-124.

52. ALC 45.8; ALC 45.14 may also be to Joseph.

53. Alcuin wrote a letter to Colcu, an Irish master, early in 790: ALC 45.7; this is probably contemporary with a more general letter to monks in Ireland: ALC 45.280.

54. ALC 11.51.2.

55. Dreyer, M., *Alkuin und Hrabanus Maur: wozu wissen?* in Felten, F. J., & Nichtweiss, B., (eds.) *Hrabanus Maur: Gelehrter, Abt. von Fulda und Erzbischof von Mainz* (Mainz, 2006) 35-49; Ferrari, M. C., *Alcuin und Hraban: Freundschaft und auctoritas im 9 Jahrhundert* (Melanges Duchting, Heidelberg, 2001); & Davis, L. D., *Hincmar of Rheims as a theologian of the Trinity* Traditio 27 (1971) 455-468.

56. ALC 45.88.

57. See Song of Songs 3.4 – an interesting and revealing allusion.

58. For an example of Bede's influence upon Hrabanus Maur see Veyrard-Cosme, C., *Bede dans les 'lettres' d'Alcuin: de la source a l'exemplum* in Lebecq, S., Perrin, M., Szerwiniack, O., (eds.) *Bede le vénérable entre tradition et posterité* Villeneuve d'Ascq: Université Charles de Gaulle (Paris, 2005) 223-30.

59. ALC 76.

60. *Epistola* as has been noted already had nothing do to with something concealed

beneath a stole; it came into Latin from the Greek verb 'to send out', reflecting the dominance of *Koine* Greek as the *lingua franca* of the Roman empire, even in Rome itself until well into the fourth century AD.

61. ALC 45.142.

62. ALC 52: see Fransen, I., *Fragments épars du commentaire perdu d'Alcuin sur l'Épître aux Ephésiens* RB 81 (1971) 30-59.

63. I.e. ALC 11.62.

64. For example by using the first six lines of ALC 11.11.

65. Garrison, M., *Alcuin, 'Carmen IX' and Hrabanus, 'Ad Bosonum': a teacher and his pupil write consolation* in Marenbon, J., (ed.) *Poetry and philosophy in the middle ages* (Leiden, 2001) 70-1.

66. Vatican Reg 124.f3r: see Perrin, M. J-L., *La poésie de cour carolingienne, les contacts entre Alcuin et Hraban Maur et les indices de l'influence d'Alcuin sur l' 'In honorem sanctae crucis'* AY 333-352.

67. I.e.ALC 11.9.

68. The relationship between these two poems, and the way in which Hrabanus adopted and adapted elements from Alcuin's poem, is the substance of Garrison's article.

69. See Blumenkranz, B., *Raban Maur et Saint Augustin – compilation ou adaptation?* Revue du Moyen Âge Latin 7 (1951) 97-110, for an example of this process.

70. Ibid.109

71. See Gorman, M. M., *From the classroom at Fulda under Hrabanus: the commentary on the gospel of John prepared by Ercanbertus for his 'praeceptor' Ruodulfus* Augustinianum 44 (2004) 439-490, especially 482-3 for examples of the use of material drawn from Alcuin's commentary. But note the caveats of Tax, P. W., *Der Kommentar des 'Erkanbert' zum Johannes evangelium: ein Beitrag zur Verfasserschaft, Quellenfrage und Textkritik* Sacris Erudiri 48 (2009) 169-90.

72. Bullough, D. A., *Alcuin's cultural influence: the evidence of the manuscripts* GL3 1-26, p.6 n.14: the manuscript is Rheims, Bibliothèque municipale MS 1395.

73. For an overall view see Bullough, D. A., *Alcuin's cultural influence: the evidence of the manuscripts* GL3 1-26; for a comprehensive analysis and list of the ninth century manuscripts remaining, see Ganz, D., *Handschriften der Werke Alkuins aus dem 9. Jarhrhundert* AGG 185-194.

74. Bullough, D. A., art.cit.25.

75. See www.e-codices.ch: *Swiss monastic libraries on-line [St Gallen];* also Tremp, E., *Alkuin und das Kloster St. Gallen* AGG 229-250, whose table of these manuscripts is on p.236-8.

76. St Gallen Stiftsbibliothek cod.75.

77. See Nees, L., *Alcuin and manuscript illumination* AGG 195-228.

Notes to the Conclusion
Memory

1. For what follows, see DAB 1-12; Schmucki, K., *Fruhzeitliche Editionen von Texten Alkuins aus Handschriften der Klosterbibliothek St Gallen* AGG 263-87; & Gorman, M. M., *Alcuin before Migne* RB 112 (2002) 101-130, which examines the early printed editions of *De Fide* in particular.

2. Gorman, M. M., art.cit.107 n.13.

3. DAB 10-1 n.18; Gorman is wrong about this date in his article on p.107.

4. *Antiquae lectionis* tomus I, 1-123; & tomus V 988-1050, containing Alcuin's *De Grammatica*.

5. Note also the preliminary volume collated by Forster and mentioned by Bullough ibid. n.20, being a conspectus of sources pertaining to the study of Alcuin and published at Regensburg somewhat earlier in 1760: *Conspectus omnium, quae hucusque inveniri potuerunt, operum beati Flacci Alcuini quorum novum edition paratur.*

6. Gorman's caveat art.cit.106 about the general reliability and purpose of Migne' texts should be noted; but his reservations about Alcuin's corpus of writings need to be treated with caution, resting as they do upon questionable assumptions. His observation that critical editions are urgently needed of all the main Alcuin texts is undoubtedly true.

7. The story of the collation and publication of Alcuin's works in southern Germany in the period between Canisius and Forster is examined in detail by Karl Schmucki in art.cit., with fine reproductions of some of the title pages of these early printed editions.

8. Ibid. 272f.

9. Ibid. 279f.

10. Gorman, M. M., art.cit.106.

11. Dümmler, E., (ed.) *Carmina* MGH Poetae lat. 1. (Berlin, 1880) 160-351; *Monumenta Alcuina* (Bibliotheca rerum Germanicarum vi, Berlin, 1873) ed. E. Dümmler & W. Wattenbach; Dümmler, E., *Alchvinstudien* (SB Berlin, 1891) 499f; Dümmler, E., *Zur Lebensgeschichte Alchvins,* Neues Archiv der Gesellschaft der deutchser Geschichte des Mittelalters XVIII (Hanover, 1893) 53-70.

12. Arndt, W., (ed.) *Vita Alcuini* MGH Script.XV.1 (Hanover, 1887) 182-97.

13. Lorentz, F., *Alcuins* Leben (Halle, 1829); & Lorentz, F., *The Life of Alcuin* (tr. J. M. Slee) (London, 1837).

14. Sickel, T., *Alcuinstudien,* Journal of the Vienna Academy of Sciences, LXXIX, 461-550 (Vienna 1875).

15. The Alcuin Club has produced a steady stream of valuable liturgical studies ever since.

16. West, A.F., *Alcuin and the Rise of the Christian Schools* (London, 1892).

17. Gaskoin, C.J.B., *Alcuin, his Life and Work,* (London, 1904).

18. Brown, G. F., *Alcuin of York,* (London, 1908).

19. Kleinclausz, A., *Alcuin,* Annales de l'Université de Lyons III/15 (Paris, 1948).

20. ALC 28.

21. ALC 37.

Bibliography

Editions of Alcuin's Writings

Alcuin's works (ALC) are numerated according to Jullien, M-H., & Perelman, F., (ed.) *Clavis Scriptorum Latinorum Medii Aevi – Auctores Galliae 735-987: tomus II – ALCUINUS* (Brepols/Turnhout, 1999). Those included in italics are letters by other people that are closely associated with Alcuin's letters.

Vita Alcuini

Arndt, W., (ed.) *Vita Alcuini* MGH Script.XV.1 (Hanover, 1887) 182-97
PLC 89-106 to which reference is made by chapter and section

Opera Alcuini

Duchesne, A., (ed.) *B. Flacci Albini, sive Alchuuini . . . opera* (Paris, 1617)
Froben, F., (ed.) *B. Flacci Albini se Alcuini abbatis . . . opera omnia* (Tomes I & II, Regensburg, 1777)
Migne, (ed.)PL C & CI (Paris, 1851 & 1863)
Dümmler, E., (ed.)*Carmina* MGH Poetae lat. 1. (Berlin, 1880) 160-351

Epistola Alcuini

Dümmler, E., (ed.) *Alcuini sive Albini Epistolae* MGH Ep.iv (Berlin, 1895) 1-493, 614-6; & v (1899) 643-5
Jaffe, W., (ed.) *Monumenta Alcuina* (Bibliotheca rerum Germanicarum vi, Berlin, 1873) ed. E. Dümmler & W. Wattenbach

Editions and translations

Allott, S., (tr) *Alcuin of York: his life and letters* (York, 1974)
Blumenshine, G. B., *Liber Alcuini contra haeresim Felicis: edition with an introduction* (Studi e Testi 285, Rome, 1980)
Bruni, S., *Alcuino 'De orthographia'* (Florence, Millennio Medievale 2, 1997)
Chase, C., (tr.) *Two Alcuin letter-books* (Toronto, 1975)
Driscoll, M. S., *'Ad pueros sancti Martini': a critical edition, English translation & study of the manuscript transmission* Traditio 53 (1998) 37-59

Folkerts, M., *Die älteste mathematische Aufgabensammlung in lateinischer Sprache: Die Alkuin zugeschriebenen 'Propositiones ad acuendos iuvenes'* Denkschrift der Österreichischen Akademie der Wissenschaft Kl.116.6 (Vienna, 1978) 15-78

Folkerts, M., & Gericke, H., *Die Alcuin zugeschriebenen 'Propositiones ad acuendos iuvenes': Lateinischer Text und deutsche Ubersetzung* in Butzer, P., & D. Lohrmann, (eds.) *Science in Western and Eastern civilization in Carolingian times* (Basel, 1993) 273-362

Folkerts, M., The *'Propositiones ad acuendos iuvenes'* ascribed to *Alcuin* in Folkerts, M., *Essays on early medieval mathematics* (Ashgate 2003) Chapter IV

Godman, P., *Alcuin – the bishops, kings & saints of York* (Oxford, 1982)

Gugielmetti, R. E., (ed.) *Alcuino – Commentato dei Cantici: con I commenti anonimi 'vox ecclesie', 'vox antique ecclesie': edizione critica* (Florence, Millenio Medievale 53, 2004)

Knibbs, E., & Matter, E. A., (eds.) *De Fide Sanctae Trinitate et de Incarnatio Christi. Quaestiones de Sanctae Trinitatis* CCCM 249 (Brepols, 2012)

D'Imperio, F. S., (ed.) *Explanatio super Ecclesiasten: un epitome carolingie del commentario all'Ecclesiaste di Alcuino di York* (Florence, 2008)

Talbot, C.H., (tr.) *Life of St Willibrord* in *The Anglo-Saxon missionaries in Germany* (London, 1954) 3-22

Websites

www.pase.ac.uk (*The prosopography of Anglo-Saxon England*)
www.e-codices.ch (*Swiss monastic libraries on-line for St Gallen*)

Secondary Literature

Alberi, M., *The patristic and Anglo-Latin origins of Alcuin's concept of urbanity* JML (1993) 95-112 Alberi, M., The *'Mystery of the Incarnation' and Wisdom's house (Prov.9.1)* in *Alcuin's 'Disputatio de Vera Philosophia'* JTS NS 48/2 (1997)

Alberi, M., *'The better paths of Wisdom': Alcuin's monastic 'true philosophy' and the worldly court* Speculum 76 (2001/4) 896-910

Alberi, M., *'Like the army of God's camp': political theology and apocalyptic warfare at Charlemagne's court* Viator 41[2] 2010, 1-20

Allott, S., (tr.) *Alcuin of York* (York, 1974)

Angenendt, A., *Karl der Grosse als 'rex et sacerdos'* in FK 255-278

Anton, H. H., *Fürstenspiegel und Herrscherethos in der Karolingerzeit* (Bonn, 1968)

Auzepy, M-F., *Francfort et Nicée II* in FK 279-300

Aylmer G.E. & Cant, R., (eds.) *History of York Minster* (Oxford, 1977)

Bachrach, D., *Religion & the conduct of war, c.300-1215* (Ipswich, 2003)

Barbero, A., *Charlemagne – father of a continent* (tr. A. Cameron) (University of California Press, 2004)

Becher, M., *Charlemagne* (Yale, 2003)

Berndt, R., (ed.) *Das Frankfurter Konzil von 794: Kristallisationspunkt karolingischer Kultur* (2 vol. – Mainz, 1997)

Bethurum, D., *The homilies of Wulfstan* (Oxford, 1957)

Binchy, D. A., *Celtic and Anglo-Saxon kingship* (Oxford, 1970)

Birch, W de G., *An ancient manuscript of the eighth or ninth century formerly belonging to St Mary's abbey* [The Nunnaminster Codex] (London/Winchester, 1889)

Bischoff, B., *Die südostdeutschen Schreibschulen und Bibliotheken in der Karolingerzeit*, 2 vols (Wiesbaden, 1960-80), vol 2 115-120

Blair, J., & Sharpe, R., (eds.) *Pastoral care before the parish* (Leicester, 1992)

Blair, J., *The Anglo-Saxon Church* (Oxford, 2006)

Blair, P.H., *From Bede to Alcuin*, in G. Bonner (ed.), *Famulus Christi* (London, 1976) 239-260

Blumenkranz, B., *Raban Maur et Saint Augustin – compilation ou adaptation?* Revue du Moyen Âge Latin 7 (1951) 97-110

Boas, M., *Alcuin & Cato* (Leiden, 1937)

Bonner, G., *Famulus Christi* (London, 1976)

Bonner, G., Rollason, D., Stancliffe, C., (eds.) *St Cuthbert, his cult and his community to 1200* (Ipswich, 1989)

Bouhot, J-P., *Alcuin et le 'De catechizandis rudibus' de St Augustine* Recherches Augustiniennes 15 (1980) 176-240

Brandes, W., *'Tempora periculosa sunt.' Eschatologisches im Vorfeld der Kaiserkronung Karls des Grossen* in Berndt, R., (ed.) *Das Frankfurter Konzil von 794: Kristallisationspunkt karolingischer Kultur* (2 vol. – Mainz, 1997), vol I. 49-79.

Braunfels. W., et al. (eds.) *Karl der Grosse – Lebenswerk und Nachlegen* (4 vols, Dusseldorf, 1965)

Brett, C., *A Breton pilgrim in England in the reign of king Athelstan* in G. Jondorf & D. N. Dumville (eds.) *France & the British Isles in the Middle Ages & Renaissance* (Ipswich, 1991) 43-70

Brooks, N., *The early history of the Church of Canterbury* (Leicester, 1984)

Brooks, N., *Bede and the English* (Jarrow, 1999)

Brooks, N., *English identity from Bede to the Millennium* Haskins Society Journal 14 (2003) 33-51

Brown, M., *The Lindisfarne Gospels – society, spirituality & the scribe* (British Library, London, 2003) Brown, P. A., *St Augustine's attitude to religious coercion* Journal of Roman Studies 54 (1964) 107-116

Brown, P. A., *Religion & society in the age of Augustine* (London, 1972)

Brown, P. A., *A Dark Age crisis – aspects of the iconoclastic controversy* EHR 78 (1973) 1-34

Brown, P. A., *The Rise of Western Christendom* (2nd ed. Blackwell/Oxford, 2003)

Buck, T. M., *Admonitio und praedicatio: zur religios-pastoralen Dimension von Kapitularien und kapitulariennahen Texten 507-814* (Freiburger Beitrage zur mittelalterliche Geschichte: Studien und Texte 9 - Frankfurt am Main, 1997)

Bullough, D. A., *The educational tradition in England from Alfred to Aelfric: teaching 'utriusque linguae'* (SSCI 19, 1972)

Bullough, D. A., *The Age of Charlemagne* (London, 1973)

Bullough, D. A., *Alcuino el la tradizione culturale insulare* in *I problemi dell'Occidente nel secolo VIII* (SSCI 20, 1973) 571-600

Bullough, D. A., *Hagiography as patriotism: Alcuin's 'York poem' and the early Northumbrian Vitae sanctorum* in Patalagean & Riche, P., (eds.) *Hagiographie, cultures et sociétés VIe-XIIe siècles* (Paris, 1981) 339-359

Bullough, D. A., *Alcuin and the kingdom of heaven: liturgy, theology and the Carolingian age* in U-R. Blumenthal (ed.) *Carolingian Essays* (Washington, 1983) 22-31

Bullough, D. A., *'Albuinus deliciosus Karoli regis': Alcuin of York & the shaping of the early Carolingian court* in (Fenske, L., et al., eds) *Institutionen, Kulture unde Gesellschaft; Festschrift fur Josef Fleckenstein*, (Sigmaringen, 1984) 73-92

Bullough. D. A., *Carolingian renewal: sources & heritage* (Manchester, 1991)

Bullough, D. A., *What has Ingeld to do with Lindisfarne?* ASE 22 (1993) 93-125

Bullough, D. A., *Reminiscence and reality: text, transmission and testimony of an Alcuin letter* JML 5 (1995) 174-201

Bullough, D. A., *Alcuin before Frankfurt* in FK 571-85

Bullough, D. A., *Alcuin's cultural influence: the evidence of the manuscripts* GL3 1-26

Bullough, D. A., *York, Bede's calendar and a pre-Bedan English martyrology* Analecta Bollandia 121 (2003) 329-353

Bullough, D. A., *Empire and emperordom* EME 12 (2003) 377-387

Bullough, D. A., *Was there a Carolingian anti-war movement?* EME 12 (2003) 365-76

Bullough, D. A., *Alcuin – achievement & reputation* (Brill-Leiden & Boston, 2004)

Cabaniss, A., [tr.] *Benedict of Aniane, the Emperor's Monk*, Kalamazoo, 1979/2008

Cameron, A., *Continuity and change* (London, 1981)

Campbell, A., (tr.) *Aethelwulf's 'De Abbatibus'* (Oxford, 1967)

Campbell, J., *Essays in Anglo-Saxon history* (London, 1986)

Carragain, E. O., *The City of Rome & the world of Bede* (Jarrow, 1994)

Carruthers, M., *The craft of thought: meditation, rhetoric and the making of images, 400-1200* (Cambridge, 1998)

Cavadini, J. C., *The last Christology of the West – Adoptionism in Spain & Gaul, 785-820* (Philadelphia, 1993)

Cavadini, J. C., *Elipandus and his critics at the council of Frankfort* in GL3 787-808

Cavill, P., (ed.) *The Christian tradition in Anglo-Saxon England* (Cambridge, 2004)

Chandler, C. J., *Heresy & empire: the role of the Adoptionist controversy in Charlemagne's conquest of the Spanish March* The International History Review 24 (2002) 505-27

Chaney, W. A., *The cult of kingship in Anglo-Saxon England – the transition from paganism to Christianity* (Manchester, 1970)

Chazelle, C. M., *To whom did Christ pay the price? The soteriology of Alcuin's epistola 307* PMR 14 (1989) 53-62

Chazelle, C. M., *The Crucified God in the Carolingian Era* (Cambridge, 2001)

Chelini, J., *Le vocabulaire politique et social dans la correspondence d'Alcuin* Faculté des lettres (Aix en Provence, 1959)

Chelini, J., *Alcuin, Charlemagne et St Martin de Tours* Revue d'Histoire de l'Église de France 47 (1961) 19-50

Cheney, C. R., (ed.) *A handbook of dates for students of British history* – revised edition by M. Jones (Cambridge, 2000)

Cholij, R., *Theodore the Stoudite: the ordering of holiness* (Oxford, 2002)

Christiansen, E., *The Northern Crusades* (London, 1997)

Chupin, A., *Alcuin et Cormery* AY 103-112

Claussen, M., *The reform of the Frankish church: Chrodegang of Metz and the 'regula canonicorum' in the eighth century,* (Cambridge, 2004)

Clemoes, P., *The cult of St Oswald on the continent* (Jarrow, 1983)

Coates, S., *The bishop as benefactor & civic patron: Alcuin, York & episcopal authority in Anglo-Saxon England* Speculum (1996) 529-558

Colgrave, B., (tr.) *The Life of Bishop Wilfrid by Eddius Stephanus* (Cambridge, 1927/1985)

Colgrave, B., (tr.) *The earliest life of Gregory the Great* (Cambridge, 1985)

Colgrave, B., *Two lives of St Cuthbert* (Cambridge, 1940/1985)

Colgrave, B., *Felix's Life of St Guthlac* (Cambridge, 1956/1985)

Colgrave, B. & Mynors, R. A. B., (tr.) *Bede's Ecclesiastical History of the English people,* (Oxford, 1969)

Conant, K.J., *Carolingian & Romanesque architecture* (London, 1978)

Costambleys, M., Innes, M., & MacLean, S., *The Carolingian World* (Cambridge, 2011)

Courcelle, P., *Les sources antiques du prologue d'Alcuin* Philologus 110 (1966) 293-305

Courcelle, P., *La 'Consolation de Philosophie dans la tradition littéraire, antécedents et posterité de Boece* (Paris, 1967)

Cramp, R., *Anglian & Viking York* (York, 1967)

Crawford, S. J., *The Old English Version of the Heptateuch: Aelfric's treatise on the Old and New Testament and his preface to Genesis* (EETS, 1922/1969 reprint)

Crick, J., *An Anglo-Saxon fragment of Justinus's 'Epitome'* ASE 16 (1987) 181-196

Cristiani, M., *"Ars artium" La psicologia di Gregorio Magno* in M. Mazza & C. Giuffrida (eds.) *Le transformazioni della culturà nella tarda Antichità* (Vol 1, Rome, 1985) 309-331

Cristiani. M., *Le vocabulaire de l'enseignement dans la correspondence d'Alcuin* in Weijers, O., (ed.) *Vocabulaire des écoles et des méthods d'enseignement au moyen âge* (Turnhout, 1992) 13-32

Cross, J. E., *Cambridge, Pembroke College MS 25: a Carolingian sermonary used by Anglo-Saxon preachers* King's College London Medieval Studies 1 (1987)

Cubitt, C., *Anglo-Saxon church councils, c.650-850* (Leicester, 1995)

Cubitt, C. (ed.) *Court culture in the early middle ages: proceedings of the first Alcuin conference,* Studies in the early Middle Ages (Turnhout, 2003)

Dales, D. J., *Dunstan – saint & statesman* (Cambridge, 1988)

Dales, D. J., *Light to the Isles – mission & theology in Celtic & Anglo-Saxon Britain,* (Cambridge, 1997)

Dales, D. J., *Alcuin – Theology and Thought* (Cambridge, 2013)

Dales, D. J., *A mind intent on God – an Alcuin anthology* (Norwich, 2004)

Davis, L. D., *Hincmar of Rheims as a theologian of the Trinity* Traditio 27 (1971) 455-468

Davis, R., (tr.) *The Lives of the eighth century Popes [Liber Pontificalis]* (Liverpool, 1992/2007)

Davis, R., (tr.) *The lives of the ninth-century Popes [Liber Pontificalis]* (Liverpool, 1995)

Depreux, P. & Judic, B., (eds.) *Alcuin de York à Tours: écriture, pouvoir et réseaux dans l'Europe du haut moyen âge* (Rennes, 2005)

Deshusses, J., *Les Messes d'Alcuin,* AL 14 (1972) 1-41

Deug-Su I., *Cultura e ideologia nella prima eta Carolingia* (Rome, 1983)

Deug-Su, I., *L'opera agiografica di Alcuino* (Spoleto, 1983)

Diem, A., *The emergence of the monastic schools: the role of Alcuin* in GL3 27-44

Dreyer, M., *Alkuin und Hrabanus Maur: wozu wissen?* in Felten, F. J., & Nichtweiss, B., (eds.) *Hrabanus Maur: Gelehrter, Abt. von Fulda und Erzbischof von Mainz* (Mainz, 2006) 35-49

Driscoll, M. S., *'Ad pueros sancti Martini': a critical edition, English translation & study of the manuscript transmission* Traditio 53 (1998) 37-59

Driscoll, M.S., *Alcuin et la pénitence à l'époque Carolingienne* Liturgiewissenschaftliche Quellen und Forschungen 81 (Munster, 1999)

Dubreucq, A., *Autour du 'De virtutibus et vitiis' d'Alcuin* AY 269-288

Duckett, E., *Alcuin, friend of Charlemagne: his world and his work* (New York, 1951)

Dumont, B., *Alcuin et les missions* AY 417-430

Dutton, P. E., (ed.) *Carolingian Civilization – a reader* (Toronto, 1993)

Dutton, P. E., *The politics of dreaming in the Carolingian empire* (University of Nebraska Press, Lincoln & London, 1994)

Dutton, P. E., (tr.) *Charlemagne's Courtier – the complete Einhard* (Toronto, 1998)

Falkowski, W., *'Barbaricum' comme devoir et défi du souverain chrétien* AY 407-416
Falkowski, W., & Sassier, Y., *Le monde carolingien : bilan, perspectives, champs de recherches* (Brepols, 2010)
Fanning, S., *Bede, Imperium and the Bretwaldas* Speculum 66 (1991) 1-26
Farmer, D. H., *The Oxford Dictionary of Saints* (Oxford, 1978)
Farmer, D. H., *The Age of Bede* (London, 1983)
Felten, F. J., & Nichtweiss, B., (eds.) *Hrabanus Maur: Gelehrter, Abt. von Fulda und Erzbischoff von Mainz* (Mainz, 2006)
Ferrari, M. C., Schroeder, J., Trauffler, H., & Krier, J., (eds.) *Die Abtei Echternach: 698-1998* (Luxembourg, 1999)
Ferrari, M. C., *Alcuin und Hraban: Freundschaft und auctoritas im 9 Jahrhundert* (Melanges Duchting, Heidelberg, 2001)
Fichtenau, H., *The Carolingian Empire* (tr. P. Munz) (New York, 1962)
Firchow, E. S. (tr.) *Einhard – Vita Karoli Magni* (Stuttgart, 1981)
Fleckenstein, J., *Alcuin im Kreis der Hofgelerhten Karls des Grossen* in Butzer, P., & D. Lohrmann, (eds.) *Science in Western and Eastern civilization in Carolingian times* (Basel, 1993) 3-22
Fletcher, R., *The Conversion of Europe* (London, 1997)
Foot, S., *Monastic life in Anglo-Saxon England c.600-900* (Cambridge, 2006)
Foulke, W. D., (tr.) *Paul the Deacon's History of the Lombards* (Philadelphia, 2003)
Fransen, I., *Fragments épars du commentaire perdu d'Alcuin sur l'Épître aux Ephésiens* RB 81 (1971) 30-59

Galinie, H., et al. *Tours et la Touraine au temps d'Alcuin* AY 37-54
Gandino, G., *Il 'palatium' e l'immagine della casà del padre: l'evoluzione di un modello nel mondo franco* Studi Medievali 50 (2009) 75-104
Ganshof, F. L., *The Carolingians & the Frankish monarchy* (London, 1971)
Ganz, D., *Corbie in the Carolingian renaissance* Beiheft der Francia 20 (Sigmaringen 1990)
Ganz, D., *An Anglo-Saxon fragment of Alcuin's letters in the Newberry library, Chicago,* ASE 22 (1993) 167-177
Ganz, D., *Le 'De laude Dei' d'Alcuin* AY 387-392
Ganz, D., *Handschriften der Werke Alkuins aus dem 9. Jarhrhundert* AGG 185-194
Garmonsway, G. N., (ed.) *Aelfric's Colloquy* (London, 1939/1967)
Garrison, M., *Alcuin's world through his letters and verse* (Cambridge, PhD thesis, 1995)
Garrison, M., *The English and the Irish and the court of Charlemagne* in Butzer, P., Kerner, M., & Oberschelp,W., (eds.) *Karl der Grosse und sein Nachwirken, 1200 Jahre Kultur und Wissenschaft in Europa / Charlemagne and his heritage: 1200 years of civilization and science in Europe* (Turnhout, 1997) 97-124
Garrison, M., *The social world of Alcuin: nicknames at York and at the Carolingian court* in GL p.59-80
Garrison, M., *The Franks as the New Israel? Education for an identity from Pippin to Charlemagne* in Hen, Y., & Innes, M., (eds.) *The uses of the past in early medieval Europe* (Cambridge, 2000) 114-161
Garrison, M., *Letters to a king and biblical exegesis: the examples of Cathulf and Clemens Peregrinus* EME 7 (1998) 305-328
Garrison, M., et al., *Alcuin & Charlemagne – the Golden Age of York* (York, 2001)

Garrison, M., *Alcuin, 'Carmen IX' and Hrabanus, 'Ad Bosonum': a teacher and his pupil write consolation* in Marenbon, J., (ed.) *Poetry and philosophy in the middle ages* (Leiden, 2001) 63-78

Garrison, M., *The Bible and Alcuin's interpretation of current events* Peritia 16 (2002) 68-84

des Instituts fur Österreichische Geschichtsforschung 40 (Vienna & Munich, 2004) 107-127

Garrison, M., *Les corréspondants d'Alcuin* AY 319-332

Garrison, M., *An aspect of Alcuin: 'tuus Albinus': a peevish egotist or parrhesiast?* in Corradini, R., (ed.) *Ego trouble: authors and their identities in the early middle ages* (Vienna, 2010) 137-51

Garrison, M., *The library of Alcuin's York* in Gameson, R., (ed.) *The Book in Britain, c.400-1100* (Cambridge, 2012), 633-664

Gautier, A., *Alcuin, la bière et le vin: comportements alimentaires et choix identitaires dans la correspondance d'Alcuin* AY 431-442

Glatthaar, M., *Zur datierung der Epistola Generalis Karls des Grossen* DA 66[2] (2010) 455-78

Godden, M. R., *Aelfric's Catholic homilies: the second series text* (EETS SS 5, London, 1979) Godman, P., *Alcuin's poetic style & the authenticity of 'O mea cella'* Studi Medievali. iii. 20 (1979) 555-583

Godman, P., *The Anglo-Latin 'opus geminatum' from Aldhelm to Alcuin* Medium Aevum 50/2 (1981) 215-29

Godman, P., *Alcuin – the bishops, kings & saints of York* (Oxford, 1982)

Godman, P., (tr.) *Poetry of the Carolingian Renaissance* (London, 1985)

Godman, P., *Poets & Emperors* (Oxford, 1987)

Goffart, W., *The narrators of barbarian history – Jordanes, Gregory of Tours, Bede and Paul the Deacon* (Princeton, 1988)

Goodson, C. J., *The Rome of Pope Paschal I: papal power, urban renovation, church rebuilding and relic translation: 817-824* (Cambridge, 2012)

Gorman, M. M., *Alcuin before Migne* RB 112 (2002) 101-130

Gorman, M. M., *From the classroom at Fulda under Hrabanus: the commentary on the gospel of John prepared by Ercanbertus for his 'praeceptor' Ruodulfus* Augustinianum 44 (2004) 439-490

Gottschalk, D., (ed) *Testi cosmografici, geografici ed odeoporici del medioevo germanico* (Louvain, 2005)

Grierson, P., *The Carolingian empire in the eyes of Byzantium* in *Nascita dell'Europa ed Europa Carolingia: un'equazione da verificare* SSCI 27 vol. 2 (1981) 885-916

Grosjean, P., *Le 'De Excidio' chez Bede et chez Alcuin* Analecta Bollandia 75 (1957) 222-6

Gwara, S., *Three acrostic poems of Abbo of Fleury* JML (1992) 203-25

Haddan, A., & Stubbs, W., (ed.) *Councils & Ecclesiastical Documents* (Oxford, 1869)

Hammer, C. I., *Christmas Day 800: Charles the younger, Alcuin and the Frankish royal succession* EHR 127 (2012) 1-23

Hartmann, F., *Hadrian I (772-795)* Papste und Papsttum 34 (Stuttgart, 2006)

Hartmann, L. M., *The early medieval state; Byzantium, Italy and the West* (Historical Association, London, 1949)

Hartmann, M., *Alcuin et la gestation matérielle de Saint-Martin de Tours* AY 91-102

Hartmann, W., *Die Synoden der Karolingerzeit im Frankenreich und in Italien* (Paderborn, Munich & Vienna, 1989)

Hartmann, W., *Alkuin und die Gesetzgebung Karls des Grossen* AGG 33-50

Haussling, A. A., *Alkuin und der Gottesdienst der Hofkapelle* DA 25 (1969) 223-9

Heil, W., *Alkuinstudien 1 – zur Chronologie und Bedeutung des Adoptianismusstreites* (Dusseldorf, 1970)

Hein, W., *Die Mathematik im Mitterlalter: von Abakus bis Zahlenspiel* (Darmstadt, 2010)

Hen, Y., & Innes, M., (eds.) *The uses of the past in early medieval Europe* (Cambridge, 2000)

Hen, Y., *The royal patronage of liturgy in Frankish Gaul – to the death of Charles the Bald (877)* HBS (2001)

Hen, Y., *Rome, Anglo-Saxon England the formation of the Frankish liturgy* RB 112 (2002) 301-322

Hen, Y., *Charlemagne's Jihad* Viator 37 (2006) 33-51

Henel, H., (ed.) *Aelfric's De Temporibus Anni* EETS (1942/1970)

Herbers, K., *Der Beitrag der Papste zur geistigen Grundlegung Europas im Zeitalter Alkuins* AGG 51-72

Herren, M. (ed.) *Insular Latin Studies* (Toronto, 1981)

Herren M., *A ninth century poem for St Gall's feast day and the 'Ad Sethum' of Columbanus* Studi Medievali (1983) 508-9

Herren M., *A ninth century poem for St Gall's feast day and the 'Ad Sethum' of Columbanus* Studi Medievali (1983) 508-9

Herrin, J., *The formation of Christendom*, (Oxford, 1987)

Hildebrandt, M. M., *The external school in Carolingian society* (Leiden, 1992)

Hiscox, N., *The Aachen chapel: a model of salvation* in *Science and western and eastern civilisation in Carolingian times*, in Butzer, P., & D. Lohrmann, (eds.) *Science in Western and Eastern civilization in Carolingian times* (Basel, 1993) 115-126

Hocquard, G., *Quelques réflexions sur les idées politico-réligieuses d'Alcuin* Bulletin des Facultés Catholiques de Lyon 12 (1952) 13-30

Hohler, C., *Some service books of the later Saxon church* in *Tenth Century Studies* (ed.) D. Parsons (London/Chichester, 1975) 60-83

Holder, A. G., (tr.) *Bede – on the Tabernacle* (Liverpool, 1994)

Holtz, L., *Le Parisinus Latinus 7530, synthèse cassinienne des artes liberaux* Studi Medievali 3/16 (1975) 97-152

Holtz, L., *Alcuin et la réception de Virgile au temps de Charlemagne* in *Einhard: Studien zu Leben und Werk* (ed.) H Scheffers (Darmstadt, 1997) 67-80

Houwen L. & Mac Donald, A., (eds.) *Alcuin of York: scholar at the Carolingian court* - Proceedings of the Third Germania Latina Conference held at the University of Groningen, Germania Latina 3, (Groningen, 1998)

Howell, W. S., *The rhetoric of Alcuin & Charlemagne. Latin text, translation & notes* (Princeton, 1941/1965)

Howlett, D., *Fredegisus 'De substantia nihili et tenebrarum* Bulletin du Cange 64 (2006) 123-143

Hurst, D., (tr.) *Bede the Venerable – Commentary on the seven Catholic Epistles* (Kalamazoo, 1985)

Imhoff, M., & Stasch, G. F., (eds.) *Bonifatius: vom angelsächsischen Missionar zum Apostel der Deutschen* (Petersberg, 2004)

Ineichen-Eder C. E., *Theologisches und philosophisches Lehrmaterial aus dem Alkuin-Kreis* DA 34 (1978) 192-201

Ineichen-Eder, C. E., *The authenticity of the 'Dicta Candidi', 'Dicta Albini', and some related texts*, in *Insular Latin Studies: papers on Latin texts and manuscripts of the British Isles, 550-1066*, ed. M. W. Herren, (Toronto, 1981) 179-193

Innes, M., *"He never even allowed his white teeth to be bared in laughter"*: *the politics of humour in the Carolingian renaissance* in Halsall, G., *Humour, history and politics in late antiquity and the early middle ages* (Cambridge, 2002) 131 -156

James, E., *Alcuin and York in the eighth century* in P. L. Butzer & D. Lohrmann (eds.) *Science in western and eastern civilisation in Carolingian times* (Basel, 1993) 23-39

Jones, C. A., *The sermons attributed to Candidus Wizo* in O'Keefe, K. O'Brien & A. Orchard (eds.) *Latin learning and English lore: studies in Anglo-Saxon literature for Michael Lapidge* (Toronto, 2005) 260-279

Jong, M. de., (ed.) *The power of the word: the influence of the Bible on early medieval politics* EME 7 (1998)

Jong, M. de., *From scolastici to scioli: Alcuin and the formation of an intellectual elite* in GL3 45-58

Jong, M. de., *The Empire as 'Ecclesia': Hrabanus Maurus and biblical 'historia' for rulers* in Hen, Y., & Innes, M., (eds.) *The uses of the past in early medieval Europe* (Cambridge, 2000), 191-226

Judic, B., *Grégoire le Grand, Alcuin et l'ideologie carolingienne* in Falkowski, W., & Sassier, Y., *Le monde carolingien : bilan, perspectives, champs de recherches* (Brepols, 2010)

Jullien, M-H., & Perelman, F., (ed.) *Clavis Scriptorum Latinorum Medii Aevi – Auctores Galliae 735-987: tomus II – ALCUINUS* (Brepols/Turnhout, 1999)

Jullien, M-H., *Alcuin et l'Italie* AY 393-406

Kantorowicz, E. H., *The King's two bodies: a study in medieval political theory* (Princeton, 1957) Kasten, B., *Adalhard of Corbie; die Biographie eines karolingisches Politikers und Klostervorstehers* Studia Humaniora (Dusseldorf, 1986).

Kasten, B., *Alkuins erbrechtliche Expertise fur Karl den Grossen* AY 301-318

Kelly, J. F., *The originality of Josephus Scottus' 'Commentary on Isaiah'* Manuscripta 24 (1980) 176-80

Kelly, J. N. D., *The Athanasian Creed* (London, 1964)

Kelly, J. N. D., *The Oxford Dictionary of Popes* (Oxford, 1986)

Kempshall, M. S., *The virtues of rhetoric: Alcuin's 'Disputatio de rhetorica et de virtutibus'* ASE 35 (2006) 7-30

Ker, N. R., (ed.) *Medieval libraries of Great Britain: a list of surviving books* (2nded. R.Hist. Soc, 1964)

King, P. D., *Charlemagne* (London, 1986)

King, P. D., (ed.) *Charlemagne – translated sources* (Lancaster, 1987)

Kleinclausz, A., *Alcuin*, Annales de l'Université de Lyons III/15 (Paris, 1948)

Knowles, D., *The Monastic Order in England* (Cambridge, 1966)

Kottje, R., *Hrabanus Maurus: 'Praeceptor Germaniae'?* DA 31 (1975) 534-545

Krautheimer, R., *Studies in early Christian, medieval & renaissance architecture* (New York, 1969)

Krautheimer, R, *Rome: profile of a city* (Princeton, 1980)

Lapidge, M., *The Adonic verses attributed to Columbanus* Studi Medievali (1977/2) 249-314

Lapidge, M., & Herren, M., *Aldhelm – the prose works* (Ipswich, 1979)

Lapidge, M., *Knowledge of the poems [of Venantius Fortunatus] in the earlier [Anglo-Saxon] period* – appendix to R. W. Hunt, *Manuscript evidence for knowledge of the poems of Venantius Fortunatus in late Anglo-Saxon England* ASE 8 (1979) 287-295

Lapidge, M., *St Dunstan's Latin poetry* Anglia xcviii (1980) 101-6

Lapidge, M., *Anglo-Latin literature* (London, 1996)

Lapidge, M., *The Anglo-Saxon Library* (Oxford, 2006)

Lauwers, M., *Le glaive et la parole. Charlemagne, Alcuin et le modèle du 'rex praedicator': notes d'écclesiologie carolingienne* AY 221-244

Lebech, M., et al. (eds.) *'De dignitate conditionis humanae': translation, commentary & reception history of the 'Dicta Albini' & the 'Dicta Candidi'* Viator 40[2] (2009) 1-34

Lebecq, S., *Alcuin sur la route* AY 15-26

Leclercq, J., *The Love of Learning and the Desire for God: a study of monastic culture* (London, 1978)

Lees, C. A., *The dissemination of Alcuin's 'De virtutibus et vitiis' in Old English: a preliminary survey* Leeds Studies in English 16 (1985) 174-189

Leonardi, C., *Alcuino e la scuola palatina: le ambizioni di una cultura unitaria* SSCI 27 (1981) 459-96; also in Leonardi, C., *Medioevo Latino – la cultura dell'Europa Cristiana* (Florence, 2004), 191-218

Leonardi, C., *I racconti di Eginardo* in Leonardi, C., *Medioevo Latino – la cultura dell'Europa Cristiana* (Florence, 2004), 249-274

Leonardi, C., *Medioevo Latino – la cultura dell'Europa Cristiana* (Florence, 2004)

Levison, W., *England & the Continent in the eighth century* (Oxford, 1946)

Llewellyn, P., *Dark Age Rome* (London, 1971)

Lohrmann, D., *Alcuins Korrespondenz mit Karl dem Grossen uber Kalender und Astronomie* in P. L. Butzer & D. Lohrmann (eds.) *Science in Western & Eastern Civilisation in Carolingian times* (Basel/Boston/Berlin, 1993)

Louth, A., *Greek East and Latin West – the Church AD 681-1071* (New York, 2007)

Lowe, H., *Pirmin, Willibrord und Bonifatius: Ihre Bedeutung fur die Missiongeschichte ihrer Zeit* SSCI 14 (1967)

Lubke, H., (ed.) *Charlemagne – oeuvre, rayonnement et survivances* (Aachen, 1965)

Mann, G., *The development of Wulfstan's Alcuin manuscript* in M. Townend (ed.) *Wulfstan of York – the proceedings of the second Alcuin conference* (York, 2004) 235-267

Marenbon, J., *From the circle of Alcuin to the school of Auxerre: logic, theology and philosophy in the early Middle Ages* (Cambridge, 1981)

Marenbon, J., *Alcuin, the council of Frankfort and the beginnings of medieval philosophy* FK 603-616 Markus, R.A., *Gregory the Great & his world* (Cambridge, 1997)

Martin, T., *Bemerkungen zur 'Epistola de litteris colendis'* Archiv fur Diplomatik 31 (Cologne/Vienna, 1985) 227-272

Mattei-Cerasoli, D. L., *Una letterà inedita di Alcuno* Benedictina 1:2 (1947-8) 227-230

Mayr-Harting, H., *The coming of Christianity to Anglo-Saxon England* (3rd edition – London, 1991)

Mayr-Harting, H., *Charlemagne, the Saxons & the imperial coronation of 800* EHR 111 (1996) 1113-1133

Mayr-Harting, H., *Alcuin, Charlemagne and the problem of sanctions* in Baxter, S., Karkov, C., Nelson, J. L., & Pelteret, D., (eds.) *Early medieval studies in memory of Patrick Wormald* (Ashgate, 2009) 207-218

McCormick, M., *The liturgy of war in the early middle ages: crises, litanies & the Carolingian monarchy* Viator 15 (1984) 1-23

McCormick, M., *Eternal victory: triumphal rulership in late antiquity, Byzantium and the early medieval West* (Cambridge, 1986)

McCune, J. C., *Four pseudo-Augustinian sermons 'De concupiscentia fugienda' from the Carolingian sermonary of Wurzburg* Revue des Etudes Augustiniennes et Patristiques 52 (2006) 391-431

McCune, J. C., *The sermons on the virtues and vices for lay potentates in the Carolingian sermonary of Salzburg* Journal of Medieval Latin 19 (2009) 250f

McKitterick, R., *The Frankish Kingdoms under the Carolingians* (London, 1983)

McKitterick, R., (ed.) *The New Cambridge Medieval History, c.700-c.900* (Cambridge, 1995)

McKitterick, R., *Das Konzil [von Frankfort] im Kontext der karolingischen Renaissance* in GL3 617-634

McKitterick, R., *Political ideology in Carolingian historiography* in Hen, Y., & Innes, M., (eds.) *The uses of the past in early medieval Europe* (Cambridge, 2000), 162-74

McKitterick, R., *History & Memory in the Carolingian world* (Cambridge, 2004)

McKitterick, R., (ed.) *Carolingian culture: emulation & innovation* (Cambridge, 2004)

McKitterick, R., *Perceptions of the past in the early middle ages* (Notre Dame, 2006)

McKitterick, R., *Charlemagne – the formation of a European identity* (Cambridge, 2008)

Meens, R., *Politics, mirrors of princes and the Bible: sins, kings and the well-being of the realm* EME 7 (1998) 345-57

Meens, R., *Sanctuary, penance and dispute settlement under Charlemagne: the conflict between Alcuin and Theodulf of Orleans over a sinful cleric* Speculum 82:2 (2007) 277-300

Meyer, H.-B., *Alkuin zwischen Antike und Mittelalter* Zeitschrift fur Katholische Theologie 81 (1959) 405-60

Meyer, H.-B., *Zur Stellung Alkuins auf dem Frankfurter Konzil (794)* Zeitschrift fur Katholische Theologie 81 (1959) 455-460

Meyer, H.-B., *'Crux, decus es mundi' - Alkuins Kreuz- und Osterfrommigkeit*, in B. Fischer & J. Wagner (ed.) *Paschatis sollemnia: Studien zu Osterfeier und Osterfrommigkeit*, (Basel, 1959) 96-107

Meyvaert, P., *Medieval notions of publication: the "unpublished" 'Opus Caroli Regis contra synodum' and the council of Frankfort (794)* JML 12 (2002) 78-89

Morris, R. K., *Alcuin, York and the 'Alma Sophia'* in L. A. S. Butler & R. K. Morris (eds.) *The Anglo-Saxon Church* CBA 60 (London, 1986) 80-89

Morrish, J., *Dated and datable manuscripts copied in England during the ninth century: a preliminary list* Medieval Studies 50 (1988) 512-38

Morrison, K. F., *The two Kingdoms: ecclesiology in Carolingian political thought* (Princeton, 1964)

Morison, S., *Politics & Script* (Oxford, 1972)

Napier, A. S., (ed.) *The Old English version of the enlarged rule of Chrodegang along with the Latin original* (EETS, 1916; Kraus reprint, New York, 1971)

Nees, L., *Alcuin and manuscript illumination* AGG 195-228

Nelson, J. L., *Politics & ritual in early medieval Europe* (Hambledon/London, 1986)

Nelson, J. L., *The Frankish world* (Hambledon/London, 1996)

Netzer, N., *Willibrord's scriptorium at Echternach & its relationship to Ireland & Lindisfarne*, in G., Bonner et al., (ed.) *St Cuthbert, his cult and his community to 1200* (Ipswich, 1989) 203-212

Newhauser, R. G., *The treatise on vices and virtues in Latin and the vernacular* (Turnhout, 1993)

Newhauser, R. G., (ed.) *In the Garden of Eden: the vices and culture in the Middle Ages* (Toronto, 2005)

Newlands, C., *Alcuin's poem of exile 'O mea cella'* Mediaevalia II (1985) 19-45

Noble, T. F. X., *The Republic of St Peter: the birth of the papal state, 680-825* (Philadelphia, 1984)

Noble, T. F. X., *Kings, clergy and dogma: the settlement of doctrinal disputes in the Carolingian world* in Baxter, S., Karkov, C., Nelson, J. L., & Pelteret, D., (eds.) *Early medieval studies in memory of Patrick Wormald* (Ashgate, 2009) 237-252

Noizet, H., *Alcuin contre Theodulphe: un conflit producteur de norms* AY 113-132

Norton, C., *The Anglo-Saxon cathedral at York and the topography of the Anglian city* Journal of the British Archaeological Association 151 (1998) 1-42

Orchard, N., *The English and German masses in honour of St Oswald of Northumbria* AL 37 (1995) 347-358

Orchard, A., *Wish you were here: Alcuin's courtly poetry & the boys back home*, in *Courts & regions in medieval Europe*, S. Rees-Jones et al. (ed.) (York, 2000) 21-44

Palmer, J. T., *Anglo-Saxons in a Frankish world: 690-900* (Brepols, 2009)

Palmer, J. T., *Calculating time and the end of time in the Carolingian world* EHR 126 (2011) 1307-1331

Panofsky, E., *Renaissance and renascences in Western art* (London, 1965)

Parsons, D., (ed.) *Tenth century studies* (London & Chichester, 1975)

Petts, D., et al., (eds.) *Early medieval Northumbria: kingdoms and communities, AD 450-1100* (Brepols, 2011)

Phelan, O. M., *The Carolingian renewal and Christian formation in ninth century Bavaria* in Corradini, R., et al. (eds.) *Texts and identities in the early middle ages* (Vienna, 2006) 389-400

Phelan, O. M., *Textual transmission and authorship in Carolingian Europe: 'Primo paganus', baptism and Alcuin of York* RB 118 (2008) 262-285

Phelan, O. M., *Catechising the wild: the continuity & innovation of missionary catechesis under the Carolingians* JEH 61 (2010) 455-474

Pirenne, H., *Mohammed & Charlemagne* (New York, 1954)

Plummer, C., *Baedae Opera Historica* (Oxford, 1896)

Plummer, C., *Two of the Saxon Chronicles* (Oxford, 1899)

Preest, D., (tr.) *William of Malmesbury's 'Gesta Pontificum'* (Ipswich, 2002)

Pucci, J., *Alcuin's cell poem: a Virgilian reappraisal* Latomus 49 (1990) 839-49

Rabe, S. A., *Faith, art and politics at Saint-Riquier: the symbolic vision of Angilbert* (Philadelphia, 1995)

Rambridge, K., *Alcuin, Willibrord & the cultivation of faith*, Haskins Society Journal 14 (2003) 15-31

Rambridge, K., *Alcuin's narratives of evangelism: the Life of St Willibrord and the Northumbian hagiographical tradition* in M. Carver (ed.) *The Cross goes North – processes of conversion in northern Europe AD 300-1300* (York, 2003) 371-382

Reuter, T.M., *Germany in the early Middle Ages: 800-1056* (London, 1991)

Reuter, T., *Charlemagne and the world beyond the Rhine*, in Story, J., (ed.) *Charlemagne – empire & society* (Manchester, 2005) 183-94.

Reynolds, R. E., *The Visigothic liturgy in the realm of Charlemagne* in FK 919-946

Ricciardi, A., *Dal 'palatium' di Aquisgrana al cenobio di Saint Martin. Le nozione di 'ordo' e 'correctio' in Alcuino di York tra l'esperienza della 'renovatio' carolingia e i primi anni del soggiorno a Tours* Bulletin dell'Istituto storico Italiano per il Medio Evo 100 (Rome, 2008) 3-55

Rivas Pereto, R. A., *Alcuino de York y su epistolario* Patristica et Medievalia 22 (2001) 58-75 Roccaro, C., *Rinnegamento e divieto della 'lectio' virgiliana nella 'Vita Alcuini'* in *Studi di filogia classica in onore di Giusto Monaco 4* (Palermo, 1991) 1519-33

Rochais, H., *Le 'Liber de virtutibus et vitiis' d'Alcuin. Note pour l'étude de ses sources* Revue Mabillon 41 (1951) 77-86

Rollason, D., et al., (eds.) *Sources for York history to AD 1100*, The Archaeology of York 1 (York, 1998)

Rollason, D., *Bede and Germany* (Jarrow, 2001)

Rollason, D., et al., (eds.) *England and the Continent in the tenth century* (Brepols, 2011)

Rushforth, R. J., *Two fragmentary Anglo-Saxon manuscripts at St John's College, Cambridge* Scriptorium 63 (2009) 73-9

Sato, S., *Rémarques sur les exploitations rurales en Touraine au haut Moyen Âge* AY 27-36

Schaller, D., *Poetic rivalries in the court of Charlemagne* in R. R. Bolgar ed. *Classical influences on European culture 500-1500* (Vol.1 - Cambridge, 1973) 151-7

Scharer, A., *Charlemagne's daughters* in Baxter, S., Karkov, C., Nelson, J. L., & Pelteret, D., (eds.) *Early medieval studies in memory of Patrick Wormald* (Ashgate, 2009) 269-282

Schaller, D., *Das Aachener Epos fur Karl den Kaiser* Fruhmittelalterliche Studien 10 (1976) 134-68

Scheck, H., *Reform and resistance: the formation of female subjectivity in early medieval ecclesiastical culture* (New York, 2008)

Scheibe, F. C., *Alcuin und die Admonitio Generalis* DA 14 (1958) 221-9

Scheibe, F. C., *Alcuin und die Briefe Karls des Grossen* DA 15 (1959) 181-193

Scheibe, F.C., *Geschichtsbild, Zeitbewusstsein und Reform will bei Alcuin* Archiv fur Kulturgeschichte 41 (1959) 35-62

Schieffer, R., *Charlemagne and Rome* in Smith, J. H. M., (ed.) *Early medieval Rome & the Christian West: essays in honour of Donald A. Bullough* The Medieval Mediterranean 28 (Leiden, 2000) 279-295

Schieffer, R., *Alkuin und Karl der Grosse* AGG 15-32

Schmitz, G., *Bonifatius und Alkuin: ein Beitrag zur Glaubensverkundigung in der Karolingerzeit* AGG 73-90

Schmucki, K., *Fruhzeitliche Editionen von Texten Alkuins aus Handschriften der Klosterbibliothek St Gallen* AGG 263-87

Schoebe, G., *The chapters of archbishop Oda [942-6] and the canons of the legatine council of 786* Bulletin of the Institute of Historical Research, 35 (1962) 75-83

Scholz, S., *Karl der Grosse und das Epitaphium Hadriani: ein Beitrag zum Gebetsgedenken der Karolinger* in FK 373-394

Schutz, H., *The Carolingians in central Europe, their history, arts & architecture* (Brill/Leiden, 2004)

Scott, J., (ed.) *The early history of Glastonbury [De antiquitate Glastonie Ecclesiae]* (Ipswich, 1981) Scott, P. D., *Alcuin as poet: rhetoric & belief in his Latin verse* University of Toronto Quarterly 33 (1964) 233-257

Simisi, L., *La 'Cartula' di Alcuino, viaggio virtuale attraverso la Frisia e l'Austrasia* in Gottschalk, D., (ed) *Testi cosmografici, geografici ed odeoporici del medioevo germanico* (Louvain, 2005) 239-59

Sims-Williams, P., *Milred of Worcester's collection of Latin epigrams and its continental counterparts* ASE 10 (1982) 21-38

Sims-Williams, P., *Ephrem the Syrian in Anglo-Saxon England* in Lapidge, M., & H. Gneuss (eds.) *Learning and literature in Anglo-Saxon England* (Cambridge, 1985)

Sims-Williams, P., *Religion & literature in western England, 600-800* Cambridge studies in Anglo-Saxon England 3 (Cambridge, 1990)

Smardi, D. M., *Alcuino di York nella tradizione degli 'Specula Principis'* (Milan, 1999)

Smetana, C. L., *Aelfric and the early medieval homiliary* Traditio 15 (1959) 163-204

Smith, J. H. M., (ed.) *Early medieval Rome & the Christian West: essays in honour of Donald A. Bullough* The Medieval Mediterranean 28 (Leiden, 2000)

Smith, J. H. M., *Europe after Rome* (Oxford, 2005)

Sot, M., et al., *Histoire et écriture de l'histoire dans l'oeuvre d'Alcuin* AY 175-192

Springsfeld, K., *Alkuins Einfluss auf die Komputistik zur Zeit Karls des Grossen* (Stuttgart, 2002)

Springsfeld, K., *Karl der Grosse, Alkuin und die Zeitrechnung* in Berichte zur Wissenschaftsgeschichte 27 (Wiesbaden, 2004) 53-66

Stallbaumer, V. R., *The York cathedral school* American Benedictine Review 22 (1971) 286-97

Stancliffe, C. E., *St Martin and his hagiographer* (Oxford, 1983)

Stapleton, P. J., *'Kontrastimitation' and typology in Alcuin's York poem* Viator 43[1] (2012) 67-78

Staubach, N., *'Cultus Divinus'* Fruhmittelalterlischen Studien 18 (1984) 546-581

Steinen, W. von den, *Karl und die Dichter* in Bischoff, B., (ed.) *Karl der Grosse – Lebenswerk und Nachleben: vol II – Das Geistige Leben* (Dusseldorf, 1966) 63-94

Stenton, F. M., *Anglo-Saxon England* (3rd ed. Oxford, 1971)

Sterk, A., *The silver shields of Leo III: a reassessment of the evidence* Comitatus: a Journal of Medieval & Renaissance Studies 19 (1988) 62-79

Stone, R., *Masculinity and morality in the Carolingian empire* (Cambridge, 2012)

Story, J., *Cathwulf, Kingship & the royal abbey of St Denis* Speculum 74 (1999) 3-21

Story, J., *Carolingian connections: Anglo-Saxon England and Carolingian Francia, c.750-870* (Ashgate, 2003)

Story, J., *The Frankish annals of Lindisfarne & Kent* ASE 34 (2005) 59-110

Story, J., (ed.) *Charlemagne – empire & society* (Manchester, 2005)

Story, J., et al., *Charlemagne's black marble: the origins of the epitaph of Pope Hadrian I* Papers of the British School at Rome vol.73 (2005) 157-90

Straw, C., *Gregory the Great – perfection in imperfection* (University of California Press, 1988)

Stubbs, W., *The Memorials of St Dunstan* Rolls Series 63 (London, 1857, Kraus reprint 1965)

Sullivan, R. E., (ed.) *The Coronation of Charlemagne: what did it signify?* (Boston, 1959)

Symons, T., (ed.) *The Regularis Concordia* (London, 1953)

Szarmach, P., *A preliminary handlist of manuscripts containing Alcuin's 'Liber de virtutibus et vitiis'* Manuscripta 25 (1981) 131-40

Szarmach, P., *The Latin tradition of Alcuin's 'Liber de virtutibus et vitiis', cap xxvii-xxv, with special reference to Vercelli homily XX* Mediaevalia 12 (1986) 13-41

Szarmach, P., (ed.) *Sources of Anglo-Saxon Culture* (Kalamazoo, 1986)

Szarmach, P. E., *Cotton Tiberius A. iii, Arts. 26 & 27* in Korhammer, M., (ed.) *Words, texts & manuscripts: studies in Anglo-Saxon culture presented to Helmut Gneuss* (Cambridge, 1992) 29-42

Talbot, C.H., *The Anglo-Saxon missionaries in Germany* (London, 1954)

Tax, P. W., *Der Kommentar des 'Erkanbert' zum Johannes evangelium: ein Beitrag zur Verfasserschaft, Quellenfrage und Textkritik* Sacris Eruditi 48 (2009) 169-90

Thacker, A., *Memorialising Gregory the Great: the origin and transmission of a papal cult in the seventh and eighth centuries* EME 7 (1998) 59-84

Thompson, A. H. (ed.) *Bede: his life, times and writings* (Oxford, 1935)

Thomson, R. M., *William of Malmesbury & the letters of Alcuin,* in Thomson, R. M.,

William of Malmesbury (Ipswich, 1987) 154-67

Thorpe, L., *Two Lives of Charlemagne – Einhard & Notker the Stammerer* (London, 1969)

Thummel, H. G., *Die frankische Reaktion auf das 2 Nicaenum in den 'Libri Carolini'* FK 965-980

Thuno, E., *Materializing the invisible in early medieval art: the mosaic of Santa Maria in Domnica in Rome* in Nie, G. de, et al. (ed.) *Seeing the invisible in late antiquity and the early middle ages* (Brepols, 2005) 239-290

Tischler, M. M., *Alcuin, biographe de Charlemagne. Possibilités et limites de l'historiographie littéraire au Moyen Âge* AY 443-460

Torkar, R., *Eine altenglische Ubersetzung von Alkuins 'De virtutibus et vitiis' kap.21* (Munich, 1977)

Treffort, C., *La place d'Alcuin dans la rédaction épigraphique carolingienne* AY 353-370

Tremp, E., & Schmuki, K., (eds.) *Alkuin von York und die geistige Grundlegung Europas* (St Gallen, 2010)

Tremp, E., *Alkuin und das Kloster St. Gallen* AGG 229-250

Ullmann, W., *The Growth of Papal government in the Middle Ages* (London, 1955)

Ullmann, W., *The Carolingian renaissance & the idea of kingship* (London, 1969)

Ullmann, W., *A short history of the Papacy in the Middle Ages* (London, 1972)

Unterkirchen, F., (ed.) *Alkuin Briefe und andere tractate im Auftrage des Salzburger Erzbischofs Arn um 799 zu einem Sammelband vereinigt [Codex Vindobonensis 795 – Osterreichischen National Bibliothek Faksimileausgab]* (Graz, 1969)

Van de Lisdonk, M. L. Van Poll, *Alcuins de Sanctis Euboricensis Ecclesiae – vers 1-605: de Bronnen van een Carolingisch Epos* (Rotterdam, 1981)

Veyrard-Cosme, C., *Littérature latine du haut Moyen Âge et idéologie politique: l'exemple d'Alcuin* Revue des Études Latines 72 (1994) 192-207

Veyrard-Cosme, C., *Réflexion politique et pratique du pouvoir dans l'oeuvre d'Alcuin* in D. Boutet et al. (eds.) *Pensée et pouvoir au Moyen Âge [viii–xv siècle]. Études offertes à Francoise Autrand* (Paris, 1999) 401-25

Veyrard-Cosme, C., *Les motifs épistolaires dans la correspondence d'Alcuin* AY 193-208

Veyrard-Cosme, C., *Le paganisme dans l'oeuvre d'Alcuin* in L. Mary et M. Sot (eds.) *Impiés et paiens entre Antiquité et Moyen Âge: Textes, images et monuments de l'Antiquité au haut Moyen Âge* (Paris, 2002) 323-51

Veyrard-Cosme, C., *Saint Jerome dans les lettres d'Alcuin* Revue des Études Augustiniennes 49 (2003) 323-351

Veyrard-Cosme, C., *L'image de Charlemagne dans la correspondance d'Alcuin* in Cogitore, I., & Goyet, Fr., (eds) *L'éloge du Prince : de l'Antiquité au temps des lumières* (Grenoble, 2003) 145-50 Veyrard-Cosme, C., *Bede dans les 'lettres' d'Alcuin: de la source a l'exemplum* in Lebecq, S., Perrin, M., Szerwiniack, O., (eds.) *Bede le vénérable entre tradition et posterité* Villeneuve d'Ascq: Université Charles de Gaulle (Paris, 2005) 223-30

Viarre, S., *Enjeux épistolaires et présence de la correspondance d'Alcuin* Epistulae Antiquae IV (Louvain, 2006) 285-98

Vielberg, M., *Der Monchsbischof von Tours in 'Martinellus': zur Form des hagiographischen Dossier und seines spätantiken Leitbilds* (Berlin/New York, 2006

Von Euw, A., *Alkuin als Lehrer de Komputistikik und Rhetorik Karls des Grossen im Spiegel der St. Galler Handschriften* AGG 251-262

Wallace-Hadrill, J. M., *The Via Regia of the Carolingian age* in B. Smalley (ed.) *Trends in medieval political thought* (Oxford, 1965) 22-41 [in *Early medieval history* (Oxford, 1975) 181-200]

Wallace-Hadrill, J. M., *Early Germanic kingship in England & on the Continent* (Oxford, 1971)

Wallace-Hadrill, J. M., *Charlemagne and England* in *Karl der Grosse I – Personlichkeit und Geschichte* (Dusseldorf) 683-698 [also in *Early medieval history* (Oxford, 1975)155-180]

Wallace-Hadrill, J. M., *Early medieval history* (Oxford, 1975)

Wallace-Hadrill, J. M., *The Frankish Church* (Oxford, 1983)

Wallach, L., *Charlemagne's 'De Litteris Colendis' and Alcuin* Speculum 26 (1951) 288-305

Wallach, L., *Alcuin's epitaph of Hadrian I* American Journal of Philology 72 (1951) 128-144

Wallach, L., *Charlemagne and Alcuin - Diplomatic studies in Carolingian epistolography* Traditio 9 (1953) 127-154

Wallach, L., *The genuine and the forged oath of Leo III* Traditio 11 (1955) 39f

Wallach, L., *Alcuin on virtues and vices. A manual for a Carolingian soldier* HTR 46 (1955) 175-195

Wallach, L., *The Roman synod of December 800 and the alleged trial of Leo III* HTR 49 (1956) 123-144

Wallach, L., *Alcuin & Charlemagne: studies in Carolingian history & literature* Cornell Studies in Classical Philology 32 (Ithaca, 1959/1968)

Wallach, L., *Diplomatic studies in Latin and Greek documents from the Carolingian age* (Ithaca & London, 1977)

Wallis, F., *Bede – the reckoning of time* (Liverpool, 1999)

Whitelock, D., *Gildas, Alcuin and Wulfstan* MLR 38 (1943) 125f

Whitelock, D., *Archbishop Wulfstan, homilist and statesman* TRHS fourth series xxxi (1949) 75-94

Whitelock, D., *The audience of Beowulf* (Oxford, 1951)

Whitelock, D., *After Bede* (Jarrow, 1960)

Whitelock, D., (ed.) *English Historical Documents* vol.1 (2nd ed. London, 1979)

Whitelock, D., et al., (ed.) *Councils & Synods AD 871-1204*, vol. 1 (Oxford, 1981)

Wickham, C., *Early Medieval Italy* (London, 1982)

Widding, O., *Alkuin I Norsk-Islandsk Overlevering* (Copenhagen, 1960)

Wilmart, A., *Un témoin Anglo-Saxon du calendrier métrique d'York* RB 46 (1934) 41-69

Wilson, D. M., (ed.) *The Archaeology of Anglo-Saxon England* (Cambridge, 1981)

Wilson, H. A., *The Calendar of St Willibrord* HBS (1918)

Withers, B. C., *The illustrated Old English Hexateuch, Cotton Claudius B.iv – the frontier of seeing & reading in Anglo-Saxon England* (London & Toronto, 2007)

Wood, I., *Missionary hagiography in the eighth and ninth centuries* in Brunner, K. & Merta. B., (eds) *Ethnogenese und Uberlieferung: Angewandte Methoden der Fruhmittelalterforschung* (Vienna, 1994) 189-99

Wood, I., *The missionary life: saints & the evangelisation of Europe 400-1050* (London, 2006)

Wormald, P., *Bede, Beowulf & the conversion of the Anglo-Saxon aristocracy* in R. T Farrell, (Ed.) *Bede and Anglo-Saxon England* (British Archaeological Reports 46, Oxford, BAR, 1978) 32-95

Wormald, P., (ed.) *Ideal & reality in Frankish & Anglo-Saxon society* (Oxford, 1983)

Wormald, P., *In search of king Offa's 'law-code'* in I. N. Wood & N. Lund (eds.) *People and places in northern Europe 500-1600. Essays in honour of Peter Sawyer* (Ipswich, 1991) 25-45

Wormald, P., *The Making of English Law – king Alfred to the twelfth century*, vol 1 (Oxford, 1999)

Wormald P., & Nelson, J. L., (eds.) *Lay intellectuals in the Carolingian world* (Cambridge, 2007)

Yorke, B., *Nunneries and the Anglo-Saxon royal houses* (London / New York, 2003)

Yorke, B., *'Rex doctissimus': Bede and king Aldfrith of Northumbria* (Jarrow,) 2009

Supplementary Bibliography for Chapter 11
Nineteenth-Century Historiography in Chronological Order
From Before 1914

Ceillier, (ed.) *Histoire Générale des Auteurs Sacrés & Écclesiastiques,* Vol XII, (Paris, 1762)

Lorentz, F., *Alcuins Leben* (Halle, 1829)

Lorentz, F., *The Life of Alcuin* (tr. J. M. Slee) (London, 1837)

Laforet, *Alcuin réstaurateur des sciences en Occident sous Charlemagne* (Louvain, 1851)

Barhdt, *Alcuin der Lehrer Karls des Grossen* (Lauenburg, 1861)

Monnier, F., *Alcuin et son influence littéraire, réligieuse, et politique sur les Francs* (Paris, 1853)

Monnier, F., *Alcuin et Charlemagne* (Paris, 1864)

Jaffé, P., (ed. Wattenbach & Dümmler, E.,) *Monumenta Alcuiniana,* Bibliotheca Rerum Germanicarum VI (Berlin, 1873)

Hamelin, F., *Essai sur la Vie et les Ouvrages d'Alcuin* (Rennes, 1873)

Sickel, T., *Alcuinstudien,* Journal of the Vienna Academy of Sciences, LXXIX, 461-550 (Vienna 1875)

Dupuy, *Alcuin et l'École de St Martin de Tours* (Tours, 1876)

Werner, K., *Alcuin und sein Jahrhundert* (Vienna, 1876)

Werner, K., *Der Entwicklungsgang der mittelalterlichen Psychologie von Alcuin bis Albertus Magnus* (Vienna, 1876)

Mullinger, J. B., *The Schools of Charles the Great & the restoration of education in the ninth century* (London, 1877)

Thery, *Alcuin: L'École et l'Académie Palatine* (Amiens, 1878)

Largeault, A., *Inscriptions métriques composées par Alcuin à la fin du VIIIe siècle pour les monastères de Saint-Hilaire de Poitiers et de Nouaille* Mémoires de la Societé des Antiquaires de l'Ouest, ii série, VII (1884) 217-283

Dümmler, E., *Alchvinstudien* (SB Berlin, 1891) 499f

West, A.F., *Alcuin and the Rise of the Christian Schools* (London, 1892)

Dümmler, E., *Zur Lebensgeschichte Alchvins,* Neues Archiv der Gesellschaft der deutchser Geschichte des Mittelalters XVIII (Hanover, 1893) 53-70

Puckert, W., *Aniane und Gellone* (Leipzig, 1899)

Schonbach, A.E., *Uber einige Evangelienkommentare des Mittelalters,* (SB Wien 1903-4)

Gaskoin, C.J.B., *Alcuin, his Life and Work* (London, 1904)

Roger, M., *L'Enseignement des lettres classiques d'Ausone à Alcuin* (Paris, 1905)

Dreves, G.M., *Analecta humanica medii aevi* (Leipzig, 1907)

Brown, G. F., *Alcuin of York* (London, 1908)

Manitius, M., *Geschichte der lateinischen literature des mittelalters,* I (Munich, 1911)

Seydl, E., *Alcuins Psychologie,* Jahrbuch fur Philosophie und spekulative Theologie XXVI, (1910/11)

Moncelle, P., article on Alcuin in *Dictionnaire d'Histoire et de Géographie Ecclésiastiques,* (ed. A. Baudrillart, et.al.) II, (1914) cols 30-40

Index

#0019 - 050718 - C0 - 234/156/12 - PB - 9780227173466